NEVER ON YOUR OWN

A course of study on the

HEIDELBERG CATECHISM

and

COMPENDIUM

Written by

GORDON J. SPYKMAN, Th. D.

Illustrations by

ROBIN JENSEN, M.F.A.

Produced by
Board of Publications of the Christian Reformed Church
Grand Rapids, Michigan

Bible quotations from the Revised Standard Version, copyright 1946 and 1962 by the Division of Christian Education, National Council of Churches, are used by permission.

CONTENTS

PART THREE: SERVICE

NEVER ON MY OWN!

INTRODUCTION

I. INTRODUCING THIS BOOK

Welcome aboard! You're ready now for the next leg in your trip along the Christian way. This book is especially for you, to help you make progress. We are placing it in your hands as a kind of map, laying out the landmarks of the Christian faith and life. Or better still, it's a traveler's guide for young Christians, spelling out the signposts along the way. As you travel onward we hope this book will show signs of wear. And we hope that following its lead will make your journey through the Christian life exciting and worthwhile.

You are no longer a stranger to catechism. By this time in your life you can probably look back on two or four or six years of catechism training. Your earlier studies were designed to pave the way for this book. Now you are ready to learn about the Christian faith and life from one of the best guides ever written by the church, the Heidelberg Catechism, with its shorter version called the Compendium. The Catechism, divided into fifty-two sections called Lord's Days, one for each Sunday in the year, is written in question and answer form as a handy way of leading you into the truths of the Bible. This book is a point by point explanation of the main teachings of the Catechism and the Compendium, written in the light of the Bible and with a view to your life. Your *Study Guide* will tell you how to use it.

II. THINKING ABOUT CATECHISM

Now that you are stepping up to a new phase in your catechism training, it's a good time to think about the meaning of it all. What's the good of

catechism? Why does the church spend so much effort over so many years to instruct you in the Christian faith and life?

Look at it this way. One of the most important parts of the church's work is its teaching program, and the most important part of its teaching program is catechism.

The word *catechism* simply means instruction by the church in the Christian faith and life. This kind of teaching has been going on ever since the times of Jesus and the apostles. During the age of the Reformation both Martin Luther and John Calvin wrote catechism books for younger members of the church, like you. So you see, in going to catechism you are standing in a long line of young Christians reaching back over nineteen hundred years.

In our churches we think of catechism as our official teaching program for younger members of the congregation. In our catechism books we have you in mind—your needs, your problems, your point of view. We want to guide you toward a good profession of faith in Christ as your Savior and Lord, and we want to help you along the way to a life of Christian service. The church has a right to expect from you a profession of faith that is grounded in the Bible and the creeds. And you, in turn, have a right to know what you are doing when you profess your faith, so that you may do it with a clear conscience, sincerely, and with good understanding.

III. LOOKING FOR MEANING

All around us, in many different ways, people are asking desperately, "What is the purpose of life?" We need solid ground under our feet, a clear sense of direction, and great goals to live for. Otherwise we shall lose our way. Without a doubt you too wonder sometimes about the mean-

ing of your life. Sometimes you probably have the feeling that everything is going wrong. To help you chart your way this catechism course will explore with you answers to such basic questions as these: Who am I?

Where am I going? What am I doing here? What's so great about being a Christian?

We hope this course of studies will help you get a better hold of Christ. Big things are at stake—your faith, your future, your life. To help you walk the Christian way, we want you to look at the catechism from three points of view. We want you to see, first, that catechism is rooted in the truths of the Bible; second, that catechism helps us share in the confession of the church; third, that catechism is geared to the practical experiences of everyday Christian living.

Let's take a brief look at each of these three points.

A. CATECHISM IS BIBLICAL: the Word of God is the very basis, standard, and center of all our studies. The Bible is our rule for faith and life. It's the final answer to all our needs. We can't stand above the Bible to judge it. Instead, we must submit ourselves to the Bible as it judges us.

Learning God's will for our lives is not so much a matter of our mastering the Bible as allowing the Christ of the Bible to master our words and thoughts and deeds. This is how the renewing power of God's Word works in our lives. It demands our believing, obedient response to the Master.

In this library of sixty-six books—the Bible—God makes us face up to ourselves, to Him, and to His world. The Bible is the school of the Holy Spirit, and as disciples of Christ we must enroll for life in this course of studies. God's Word, like His grace, is free for all, but it is not cheap or easy. As Christ says, we must "search the scriptures." Catechism seeks to echo God's Word. By the question and answer method it lays out the truths of the Bible in an orderly pattern. In the three parts of the Heidelberg Catechism and the Compendium—namely, sin, salvation, and service; or, guilt, grace, and gratitude—we must seek to relive the central message of the Bible, which revolves around the central themes of creation, fall, and redemption.

B. CATECHISM IS CONFESSIONAL: it introduces us to the confession of faith upon which the church stands, so that we in turn may be confessing Christians in the church and in the world. The confessions of the church, such as the Heidelberg Catechism and the Compendium, bind us together as Christians for our witness in the world. By our Christian confession we say to our fellowmen, "This is what we believe" and "This is the way we want to live."

By means of catechism classes we are trying to help you give shape to your Christian belief. The church cannot make you believe. This is God's work in your life. But we can teach you what you ought to believe and how you ought to put these beliefs into practice. And as we teach you we pray that God will make your faith come alive. More than anything else in the world we want to help you advance toward Christian maturity by a wholehearted declaration of faith in Christ, so that you may share fully in the life and work of the church.

3

C. CATECHISM IS PRACTICAL: it is geared to the everyday needs of every Christian. It was not born in some ivory tower, far removed from life, but amid the religious struggles of real flesh-and-blood Christians. It shows us the practical meaning of the Ten Commandments, the Apostles' Creed, and the Lord's Prayer. It talks about the important questions of life here and now. It meets you right where you are, and tries to lead you to where you ought to be. Time after time it puts you on the spot, asking very important and personal questions: What is happiness to you? What's the good of believing the gospel? Why should you want to be a Christian? It helps you ask the right kinds of questions, and then helps you find the right kinds of answers. What are your problems? A guilty conscience? Temptations? Sex? Forgiveness? Swearing? Revenge? Dating? Cheating? Sickness? Prayer? Money? Poverty? Life? Death? Faith? Creation? Parents?

4

You name it—the Catechism deals with it. "I" and "you" and "we" —that's the language of our confession. The Catechism knows the Bible well. And it knows you well. What could be more important to you?

IV. THE HEIDELBERG STORY

Dateline: Heidelberg, Germany; Easter Sunday, 1945. The bridge spanning the Neckar River had just been blown up to slow down the advance of the Allied troops storming into Germany. Across a newly constructed pontoon bridge American tanks rumbled into the city. But by a dramatic turn of events, there was no fighting. All around, Germany was crumbling under Allied bombardment. But in Heidelberg a bell tolled out for joy to proclaim the saving of this city, the Gem of the Neckar Valley, the oldest university town in Germany, the home of the Heidelberg Catechism. By an agreement between German and American officers, Heidelberg was spared the ravages of World War II and so its rich heritage of the past was kept alive for us today.

In Reformation times Heidelberg was the capital of its province, the Palatinate. It was built into the rocky hillside, between the Neckar River and the Odenwald forest. For the tourist today it is still one of the most charming and picturesque cities in the world. Sprawling along the south bank of the Neckar, ten miles from where it empties into the famous Rhine River, near the edge of the romantic Black Forest—it stands as an unforgettable sight. Its illustrious history centers around the castle, the Holy Ghost Church, and the university.

Here in 1563 the Heidelberg Catechism was born. It was written to serve the needs of the Reformation churches. Yet its message reaches all the way back to the earliest pages of the Bible itself. Some old Dutch Bibles carry a picture of Adam sitting on a log teaching his sons, Cain and Abel. In his lap he holds a book with this title, Heidelberg Catechism. We smile at this. Yet there is a point to it. The truth of the Heidelberg Catechism is about as old as the hills.

As you recall, it was in 1517 that Martin Luther's hammer blows rang out with the call to reformation. In 1536 John Calvin, as a second-generation Reformer, launched his career as the master-mind of Geneva. At the time the Heidelberg Catechism was published, a third generation of Reformers was appearing on the scene. Luther was dead. Calvin's life was nearly over. The Reformation had taken a firm hold in the hearts and lives of Christians all across Western Europe, including Heidelberg. It had come to stay. But it was not easy going. Those were stormy days in Heidelberg. Throughout the Palatinate there were still many Roman Catholics living among the Lutherans, Zwinglians, and Calvinists. Besides native Germans, there were also many refugees from abroad. Religious struggles broke out repeatedly. In this situation Christian leaders sensed a deep need for a better understanding of the Christian religion and for greater unity among the people. The Heidelberg Catechism was written as an answer to this great need.

The Heidelberg story began to take shape around 1560 when three dedicated Christians came to this famous city. The first was a prince who came to reside in the castle. We know him as Elector Frederick III, "Frederick the Good." Through his influence the second and third men came to Heidelberg. The second was a preacher, Caspar Olevianus, who came to serve the church. The third was a professor, Zacharias Ursinus, who came to teach in the university. Brought together by a remarkable providence of God, these were the three leading players in the unfolding drama of the Heidelberg Catechism.

It is a striking thing that in Heidelberg, as in other places, the Reformation spirit was generated largely by young leaders. Luther was only thirty-four when he nailed his Ninety-Five Theses to the cathedral door in Wittenberg. Calvin was only twenty-seven when he wrote the first edition of his classic work, *The Institutes of the Christian Religion*. Olevianus and Ursinus were only twenty-six and twenty-eight, respectively, when they wrote the Heidelberg Catechism.

Often the young preacher and professor would exchange thoughts while strolling together along the "Philosopher's Path" on the north bank of the Neckar River. These walks bore their timely and lasting fruit in our Catechism. In 1562 Elector Frederick, building on the solid Protestant foundations laid by those who preceded him, and surveying the needs of his province, gave his young preacher and his young professor the assignment of writing a new catechism for the purpose of instructing and unifying his people. Ursinus and Olevianus worked together for nearly a year on this important project.

How they divided their task nobody really knows. Did Ursinus draw up the outline and Olevianus fill it in? That is one theory. It is probably as good a guess as any. At any rate, their finished product turned out to be a harmonious blend of two great Christian hearts and minds and pens. Once again, as with Moses and Aaron, and later with Paul and Barnabas, God made use of a team of two devoted men to build His church.

The Heidelberg Catechism was written especially for the youth of the church. After it had been confirmed by a synod meeting in Heidelberg, the good Elector Frederick addressed the pastors with these words: "We have been informed that you have given your unanimous approval. This pleases us very much. It is our wish that you faithfully adhere to it." In his introduction to the first edition Frederick left us these words: "It is essential that our youth be trained early in life, and above all, in the pure and consistent doctrine of the holy gospel. Accordingly, we have secured the preparation of a summary course of instruction in order not only that the youth, in churches and schools, may be thoroughly trained therein, but also that pastors and schoolmasters themselves may be provided with a fixed form and model by which to regulate the instruction of the youth."

You see, the emphasis is on youth. The full gospel for full Christian living —that's the keynote.

These three men who came to Heidelberg—little could they dream that their work would stand the test of time so well. In many lands and languages the Heidelberg Catechism still stands as a witness to the gospel of Christ Jesus. More than one hundred thousand copies of the Catechism are sold each year in about thirty world languages. The Heidelberg Catechism serves today as a creed for more than five million Christians around the world. It is the most ecumenical creed (representing many churches throughout the world) that has come out of the Reformation. In 1963 many Christians joined to celebrate its four-hundredth anniversary. Not a dead document, today it still pulsates with the heartbeat of the living Word of God. You can read it through in one evening. An hour a week studying it will be time well spent. As a guide to Christian faith and practice it will serve you well for a lifetime.

THE CENTRAL THEME

1. CHRISTIAN COMFORT

The Catechism is a little book dedicated to Christian comfort. The opening line drives home the central theme of the whole Catechism with this penetrating question, "What is your only comfort . . . ?" Not what are your likes and dislikes, but what is your *comfort*. Not what are some things that make life comfortable, but what is your *only* comfort. This is the doorway to the whole pattern of biblical truth that lies ahead. Think back to the words of the prophet, "Comfort ye, comfort ye my people . . ." (Isa. 40:1).

But you say, Comfort is the last thing in the world I need. So what's in it for me? Granted that Israel needed comfort, for those were hard times; that the apostles needed the Comforter whom Jesus promised to send, for they were given a tough assignment; that the Reformers who wrote the Catechism needed comfort, for they faced persecution. Even today little children need comfort, for they suffer bumps and bruises; and old people need comfort, for they are near the end of life. But me, I'm young and healthy and strong. I don't need comfort. I need excitement. Give me action. Let me live dangerously.

Well, let's get this straight. Every person needs someone to lean on. All of us need comfort in this kind of world. And you do too. Just look at the word itself—*comfort*. The second part is *fort,* from the Latin word *fortis,* which means strong. From this Latin word we get our word *fortitude,* which means strength. Comfort, therefore, means having someone standing with you to make you strong. It means having the courage to live bravely. It means strength to face troubles. Comfort is happiness. It's not an old-fashioned idea. It's as up-to-date as salvation and service. You need comfort too, for I dare say that even your life seems pretty uneasy at times.

Let's rephrase the question: What is your happiness in life? Fun, you say? But happiness is more than fun. Friends, you say? But friends often let you down. You need a Friend who will stick with you through thick and thin. That's what comfort is—knowing Christ as your Savior and Lord, and knowing that He is always at your side. Comfort is happiness, satisfaction, strength, courage.

Look at it this way. When something bad happens, and then something else takes its place and makes up for it and gives you a lift—that's comfort. When you're lonely, and then the telephone rings and it's your best friend on the line—that's comfort. Or when a soldier in battle gets a love letter from home—that's comfort.

That's the way it is with all of us. Sin is our great trouble. But Christ paid for our sins. He gave us a new lease on life. That's the greatest comfort in the world. And salvation is our greatest happiness. The comfort of salvation covers our whole life—not just when we read the Bible or listen to sermons and sing hymns. It covers us when we go out for a snack, or study, or work around the house, or play basketball, or go camping. Comfort is for dying too, whenever that time comes for us.

Yes, comfort covers everything in our Christian life. Let's try to pinpoint some of its meaning.

A. COMFORT MEANS A SENSE OF BELONGING. It means being at home in God's world. It means knowing "whose we are and whom we serve."

WHAT A
RELIEF

I'M A CHRISTIAN! CHRIST
IS **BOSS** OF MY LIFE ...

I WAS A
TERRIBLE
BOSS

8

Comfort means having a name to carry with us through life—the name "Christian." With body and soul, for time and eternity, with all we are and have and hope to be, we belong to our Master.

You see, every man needs a "master." Every man must belong to "someone." Jesus told certain unbelievers of His day that they belonged to their father, the devil. So it's not a question of whether or not we belong to "another," but who that "other one" is. To Christians Paul said: "You are not your own; you were bought with a price; therefore glorify God in your body" (I Cor. 6:19, 20). And this: "You are Christ's" (I Cor. 3:23).

B. COMFORT MEANS FREEDOM TO LIVE. Christ has freed us from ourselves, from the devil, from the bottomless pit of sin, from the world of evil within us and around us. As Paul says, "If the Son makes you free, you will be free indeed" (John 8:36 RSV). And "where the Spirit of the Lord is, there is freedom" (II Cor. 3:17 RSV). Freedom from fear. Freedom from mere conformity—simply following the crowd. Freedom to serve Christ and our fellowmen. Then we can take Paul's words to heart, "In nothing be anxious" (Phil. 4:6). We are free from now on, as the Catechism says, to live for Christ.

C. COMFORT MEANS DEBTS PAID. Bankrupt—that's how we all got our start in life! But Christ has taken our unpayable bills and written across the face of them all, "Paid in full." Now we don't have to pay our own way through life. What a tremendous load off our mind! Talk about comfort! Forgiven—that's the richest blessing a person can have in this life. Jesus once said of the Pharisees that they had no covering for their sins. How awful! Nothing to cover their sin! Read Psalm 32:1-5. Christian comfort is this, that the cross has covered it all. Peter puts it this way, "You were redeemed . . . with precious blood, . . . even the blood of Christ" (I Pet. 1:18-19).

9

D. Comfort Means Being Cared For. Now I don't have to be afraid of living or dying, of today or tomorrow, of anything or anyone. My life is in good hands. For comfort means being cared for, and being cared for spells confidence. Nothing can ever really hurt me. For nothing happens by accident. It's all under my Lord's control. Therefore I can live with the "bad" happenings as well as with the pleasant. For Christ makes all things work together for my good (Rom. 8:28).

2. TRUE KNOWLEDGE

What must you know to live and die happily? This question takes top priority. It's everybody's question. For knowing is the key that unlocks the meaning of real living. The Bible says, "This is life eternal [now and forever], that they might know thee the only true God, and Jesus Christ, whom thou hast sent" (John 17:3).

The Catechism makes us face up to this basic question in the very first Lord's Day. And this question keeps coming back again and again. It's woven into the entire Catechism. It never lets you go. What must you *know* to live and die happily? How do you *know* your sin? How do you *know* your salvation? How do you *know* how to serve?

Well, what does it mean to know? What is true knowledge?

We live in a highly scientific age that boasts of its almost unlimited store of knowledge. Microscopic knowledge. Telescopic knowledge. Encyclopedic knowledge. Think-tanks. Knowledge explosion. Research. This jargon sticks to our tongues. The volume of knowledge is piling up so fast that textbooks go out of date every few years.

WE SURE LIVE IN A HIGHLY KNOWLEDGEABLE AGE...

BUT WHAT BOTHERS ME ...

I DON'T UNDERSTAND ONE BIT OF IT ?!

Is the Catechism, then, hopelessly out of date? True, it's more than four hundred years old. It was published almost half a century before the early colonists set foot on North American soil. And like every piece of literature, it was conditioned by the time in which it was written. Nevertheless, those who read the Catechism carefully come away with the feeling that it still addresses itself to the basic questions of today.

How can this be?

Well, if the knowledge the Catechism talks about were intellectual knowledge—facts, figures, data that scientists run through computers—then it would never have survived. The reason the Catechism is still so up-to-date is that it deals with knowledge of basic human problems—and God's solutions to them. These basic problems have never really changed from the beginning of human history. And the solutions will remain the same for all time.

When the Catechism speaks about knowledge, it echoes what the Bible says. That is why it never wears out. For the Word of God endures forever (I Pet. 1:25). It speaks to every man in every age—in Old Testament times, in New Testament times, in the time of the Reformation, and today too.

True knowledge, you see, is heart-knowledge, which is much deeper and fuller than mere thinking-knowledge or feeling-knowledge or doing-knowledge. Knowing the truth is more than knowing facts. The Christian religion is more than a how-to-do-it course. It's more than knowing about God; it's knowing God Himself. It's more than knowing the facts of the Bible; it's knowing the God who speaks in the Bible. It's more than memorizing Catechism answers; it's knowing the Christ to whom those answers point. It's from the bottom of his heart that Paul says, "I *know* in whom I have believed and am persuaded . . . ."

This is what the Bible and the Catechism mean by knowledge—heart-knowledge. Deep down inside us, at the very center where all the spokes of life come together, is that rock-bottom point where we stand before God, answering His call. This is what the Bible calls our heart. It's the wellspring, the fountainhead of our lives. As the Bible says, "Out of the heart are the issues of life" (Prov. 4:23).

Without this true knowledge—this heart-knowledge—many a student today is "ever learning, and never able to come to a knowledge of the truth" (II Tim. 3:7). When heart-knowledge is not present, you may have information but without understanding, facts without truth, statistics without wisdom. In his heart the uneducated child of God has more true knowledge than the most learned unbelieving scientist in the world.

Perhaps we can think of true knowledge this way: You are talking to a friend about your mother. She says, "I know your mother; I met her once at a basketball game." What your friend means is: she could recognize your mother in a crowd, or she knows something about her general appearance and manners. However, you might answer your friend by saying, "But you don't really know my mother." Your friend doesn't know her the way you do; for you know her intimately. You've had many heart-to-heart talks. This is what we mean by heart-knowledge.

This is the kind of knowledge we are after in the catechism—intimate, deep, full heart-knowledge of God as He came to us in Jesus Christ. Christ

11

alone is the Way to true knowledge (John 14:6). He Himself is the Truth, and the Key to wisdom. True knowledge, therefore, springs from a heart

that is right with Christ, and such knowledge shapes our whole life. For He who has our *heart* has *us*.

3. MASTER-PLAN

Our Christian faith rests upon the plan of salvation in the Bible. There we learn to see that salvation is from the Lord. He designed it. It's a plan that covers everything: our lives, the course of nature, the history of the world. It's a grand master-plan, aimed at the coming of His kingdom. Every day God moves forward, working out His plan in Jesus Christ through the power of the Holy Spirit. And we all have our place in His plan.

This plan of salvation is spelled out for us in the Bible in the unfolding theme of creation–fall–redemption. It's a historical plan: that is, it takes place in history and it sweeps all the events of history along toward its final goal. The history of the Old and New Testament is crowded with the mighty acts of God in the lives of His people. Christ is the Lord of history, for all of history is His story. He makes God's rich promises come true. Everything serves His purpose. Under God's control the plan of salvation unfolds like a drama, with countless characters making their entrances and exits. But God, as the great Director, governs the lives of all these men—Adam, Noah, Abraham, Moses, David, Isaiah, John the Baptist, Peter, Paul—as they play their roles in carrying out His plan of salvation.

Like the Bible, the Catechism also lays out the plan of salvation. But the Catechism lays it out in a different way. Its order is not historical, but logical. However, its logic is true to the Bible. Its line of thought follows certain basic themes. The Catechism takes the central teachings of the Bible and groups them under three main headings. We must get this threefold picture clearly in mind. We can't understand the Catechism without gaining a view of its plan of salvation unfolding like a three-in-one act. And remember, we are players who have an active role in this drama. So we must learn to see ourselves from three points of view, like a man buying a suit, looking at himself in a three-sided mirror.

Well, what is the Catechism's plan? Take a look at Question and Answer 2. There the three parts of Christian doctrine come through loud and clear. The rest of the Catechism follows through on this lead. Perhaps a little sketch is the best way to get a clear picture of this threefold plan:

Theme: Christian Comfort

Part I:	Sin		Guilt
Part II:	Salvation	or	Grace
Part III:	Service		Gratitude

There you have the ABC's of the Christian faith and life. But don't think that this simplification is something childish, like alphabet blocks. For this triple truth reaches down to the deepest needs and reaches up to the highest hopes of human life.

Sometimes these three truths are called three heads of doctrine. In our studies we shall move through this three-point plan step by step. First, our sin and guilt. Then, our salvation by grace. Finally, our service of gratitude. As a program of Christian instruction, this is a very good order to follow.

But remember, this is not exactly the way it goes in everyday Christian living. These three parts are not like a three-stage rocket that sends its payload into space by firing first stage one, then stage two, and finally stage three. Some people seem to think this way about the Christian life. They give the impression that we must first spend a long time (say, the earlier years of our lives, until about twenty-five years of age) wandering about in the dark valleys of sin and guilt. Then we can climb to the higher plateaus of salvation (say, from age twenty-five to fifty). Finally, when we have attained old age, we may reach the heights of piety, or true religion, where grateful Christian service is possible.

It should be clear to all of us that this is a false picture of the Christian life. Sin and guilt, salvation and grace and freedom, gratitude and obedience and service—these are not three stages that we pass through one after another, like moving from childhood through adolescence to adulthood. No, they go together and must grow together all along the way. The greater our consciousness of sin, the greater our realization of salvation, the greater our obligation to service. Even the holiest Christian still wrestles with sin in his life, right down to his deathbed. Salvation is for every season in our lives. And young Christians, like you, can also experience the joys of true gratitude and service. All three truths accompany us at every step along the way. You cannot have one or two of the three. It's all or nothing.

13

PART ONE: OUR SIN AND MISERY

4. OUR GREAT SINFULNESS

The Catechism doesn't lift a finger to prove our sin. It simply states it. It accepts the testimony of the Bible that "all have sinned, and fall short of the glory of God" (Rom. 3:23). We all stand under this judgment. God our Judge pronounces His verdict over our lives—"Guilty!" That's

what the Bible says of us. The Catechism simply records this judgment. It doesn't try to explain it. In fact, there is something unexplainable about sin. It's hard to pin it down. But we all know it's there. It's the loss of everything good. It's the shadow side of life. It's a hankering after evil. It's always getting into big trouble, even when our intentions seem good. It's hard to put into words what sin really is. Yet it's real, and we all know it. That's how the Catechism begins: with straightforward words, it announces the reality of sin.

I DON'T SEE ANY SIN IN MY LIFE!

Take an example from the destructive force of a tornado. When the radio announces that a tornado is headed toward your home, you don't stop to prove it. A man may clamp his hands over his eyes and declare that there is no tornado. But that doesn't change anything. The tornado keeps coming all the same, and unless he takes cover, it will engulf him in destruction. So a man may close his eyes to the reality of sin, but he can't get rid of it simply by saying that it doesn't exist. Nothing is more phony than the prattle of those who try to talk away sin.

As Christians we must learn again and again to take sin seriously. Not that we must take delight in hanging our dirty linen on the line. Not that we must preach sin. We can only preach against it, while preaching the "good news." Yet the conviction that we are sinners is a first step on the road to salvation and service, the road to Christian comfort.

A deep biblical sense of sin doesn't come easily these days. Men talk a lot about troubles, tragedies, mistakes, problems, poor adjustments—but never about sin. They usually try to brush aside all talk about sin or smooth it over. Evolutionists talk about it as a lack of perfection. Humanists talk about it as a limitation on human nature. Psychologists talk about it as a guilt complex. Sociologists talk about it as the influence of a bad environment, often giving the impression that the ghetto or suburbia, rather than the human heart, is the root of our trouble. But the truth of the Bible rings clear: "Out of the heart come evil thoughts, murder, adultery, fornication, theft, false witness, slander" (Matt. 15:19).

I DIG READING THE BIBLE.....

BUT IT CAN SURE MAKE ME **MAD**

IT'S TOO HONEST!!

The Bible is a very honest book. Let sin be sin, it says. We are pretty accustomed these days to unblushingly "honest" novels. No secrets are left unsearched. But the Bible is even more honest—honest-to-God and honest-to-life. It doesn't flatter us. It calls a sin a sin. It confronts us with a holy God so that we may realize that we are "dead in trespasses and sins" (Eph. 2:1). It reveals Christ, who comes as the Light to drive away our darkness. As a two-edged sword the Bible cuts through our pretense. It probes our heart. It exposes the sins of unbelievers, but no less the sins of believers—Adam, Noah, Jacob, Samson, David, Peter, and Paul who called himself the chief of sinners (I Tim. 1:15).

History tells us that President Coolidge was a man of few words. One day when he returned from church his wife asked him, "What did the minister preach about?" To which the President replied, "Sin." The First Lady countered, "What did he say about it?" The President's answer: "He was against it." I suppose being against sin is every Christian's business. Certainly the Bible and the Catechism take that stand. For sin is the problem behind all our problems. If you want to read the most up-to-date story of sin, scan the daily newspaper. Wherever you turn, there's corruption—graft, violence, murder, dope, sex perversions, vandalism, war, poverty, racism . . . .

Sin is found not only among down-and-outers, but also among up-and-outers. The old goody-goody talk about man getting better all the time, about a "war to end all wars," about a utopia or ideal world just around the corner—even die-hard liberals choke on that kind of talk after all the catastrophes of our times.

OF COURSE I'M HAPPY, I JUST DON'T THINK ABOUT WORLD PROBLEMS

Not to see that things are radically wrong is to be blind. But to see them as sin—for this we need the Bible. For only by the penetrating power of the light of God's Word can we get to the bottom of our trouble. Christ is the mirror of our salvation, but also the mirror in which we see our sins. His salvation is God's greatest compliment to us, showing how much He loves us. But it is also God's greatest condemnation of us, showing how much He had to do to save us from our sinful situation.

Our situation is so bad that the Bible cannot find words enough to describe it. At least there is no single word that covers sin. So the Bible marshals forth a host of words to make sure we will not miss the point. What is sin? It is disobedience to God's command. It is unfaithfulness to God. It is breaking the covenant. It is transgression of God's law. It is missing the mark. It is rebellion, wickedness, confusion. These are the charges against us; we are all delinquents. "If thou, Lord, shouldest mark iniquities, O Lord, who could stand?" (Ps. 130:3).

"Me? Am I that bad? There must be some mistake!" We are all inclined to react that way. We want to think well of ourselves. We don't like to be criticized, not even by God. But the Bible has the goods on us. "All we like sheep have gone astray" (Isa. 53:6). The Bible puts what should be our words into Paul's mouth: "Wretched man that I am!" (Rom. 7:24). We will all have to swallow our pride and quit acting like hypocrites. We must all listen as the Bible writes our biography—the biography of a sinner—in Psalm 51.

NOBODY'S PERFECT

5. OUR MISERY

Granted that sin is a tremendous power and an inescapable reality in our lives . . . what difference does it make?

It makes all the difference between heaven and hell. The Catechism takes this world of difference and wraps it up in a single word: *misery*. The Bible puts it this way: "God is not mocked; whatever a man sows, that shall he also reap" (Gal. 6:7). We sow the seeds of sin. We reap a harvest of misery. It's the law of in-put and out-put: put sin in at one end, and misery comes out at the other. Where there is fire there is smoke;

16

so where there is sin there is misery. Just as air pollution results from the fumes that pour forth from exhaust pipes, and just as water pollution results from industrial wastes dumped into our streams, so misery comes from sin. It's like a contagious disease, a virus. And we are all carriers.

Everywhere we turn there is misery. It has been that way ever since sin entered our world, but in our times misery seems to be reaching epidemic proportions. Men shake off the miseries of a hard life only to saddle themselves with the miseries of a soft life, exchanging the miseries of poverty for the miseries of wealth or affluence. For sin turns everything into misery, riches as well as poverty. Once we are under the influence of sin, we cannot escape misery.

The lines of misery are written large on people's faces. Stand back sometime on a downtown street, and watch as people walk by. They may swallow tranquilizers, throw wild parties, take vacations to get away from it all, drown their troubles in alcohol, take trips into a psychedelic world of drugs—but misery hangs on and haunts them.

Men may speak eloquently about pouring out the milk of human kindness, or creating a "great society," or fostering goodwill among races, or establishing a lasting peace among the nations. We may launch our war-on-poverty programs, anti-war movements, human rights actions, anti-crime campaigns, gun-control bills, open-housing laws, save-our-schools campaigns. The Bible has no quarrel with such things. But it also reminds us that such actions do little more than treat the symptoms of our sickness without getting at the source or cause of our misery, which is sin.

Christians have often spoken of our misery as pollution, like air pollution and water pollution. Because of sin, we suffer both guilt and pollution.

Think of a criminal in court. The judge declares him guilty. Then he lays down a penalty—say, six months in prison. As sinners before God's tribunal or court of justice, we are guilty—and thus we bring upon ourselves the penalty of misery and pollution.

Sin reveals itself in three ways: in our relationship to God, to man, and to the world. As the Catechism says, we are by nature prone to hate God and our fellowmen. Men turn their backs on God, they curse Him, or figure that He doesn't count for much. Men hate their fellowmen and trample them down. The misery and penalty of sin is this, that it makes men strangers to God, strangers to themselves, and to their neighbors, and strangers in God's world.

But the greatest misery is not what has already happened to the world, nor what can still happen in the future. The greatest misery of all is what *cannot* happen, namely, that because of sin, man cannot love God and cannot love his neighbor. Love rejected by hate—this is the misery at the bottom of all our miseries. We see it most clearly at Calvary, where hateful men nailed the Lord of love to the cross.

6. THE LAW OF GOD AS OUR TEACHER OF SIN

I FELT FINE UNTIL I STUDIED THE HISTORY OF MAN'S ACHIEVEMENTS

Education is big business these days. And it's getting bigger all the time. Millions of people seem to believe that the survival of our civilization depends on educating men in new ways of thinking and living. Otherwise we are doomed to become victims of war, racism, poverty, and the population explosion. So today there are more educated and highly trained people in the world than ever before in history.

But what has come of it all? Things are getting bigger and bigger, but are they really getting better? Men know more, but are they wiser?

We have all kinds of teachers—people, books, maps, teaching machines, newspapers, magazines, movies, television, data-processing centers, and more. But there is one teacher men seldom turn to, namely, the law of God. This is the only teaching guide that can help us learn about sin as a basic fact of life. God speaking to us in His law is the only teacher who can tell us the truth about ourselves.

Look at it this way. A man is arrested for some crime. Right there on the spot, even before his case comes to court, the law of the land is read to the guilty person so that he may know exactly where he stands before the tribunal of public justice. He must realize that anything he says about his criminal act may be used as evidence against him.

So we are all law-breakers before the court of divine judgment. God arrests us on our sinful way. He holds up before us His holy law to make clear to us that we are guilty. We may protest. We may claim that we are innocent victims. We may offer excuses. We may talk back under God's cross-examination. We may even try to win our case against God. But the plain truth of God's law, written large across the face of the whole Bible, convicts us beyond the shadow of any reasonable doubt. Listen: "Therefore, as through one man sin entered into the world, and death through sin; and so death passed unto all men, for that all have sinned"

18

(Rom. 5:12). "There is none righteous, no, not one . . . they have all turned aside . . . there is none that does good, no, not so much as one . . . . Now we know that whatever the law says, it speaks to those who are under the law, so that every mouth may be stopped, and the whole world may be brought under the judgment of God" (Rom. 3:11, 12, 19).

The law of God is like a mirror (Jas. 1:23-25). All of us spend plenty of time in front of a mirror. That's one way we try to find out what we are like and what is wrong with us. Ordinary mirrors, of course, do not even go skin-deep. The law of God, on the other hand, is like an X-ray machine that uncovers our deepest desires and intentions. There is nothing we can hide from the searchlight of God's law. It sets in sharp focus the testimony of the prophet: "The heart is deceitful above all things" (Jer. 17:9).

Only children of God, only disciples of Christ, dare to discover their true identity as sinners. For they know that this is not God's final word of judgment. The law not only exposes our sins and makes us sense our great need of salvation. It also points the way to the Savior, who by keeping the law for us also opens the door to forgiveness.

No one, however, calls in a doctor unless he realizes that he is really sick. As a physician the law spells out God's diagnosis of our fatal sickness— we are "dead through trespasses and sins" (Eph. 2:1). Thus the law drives us to seek the healing mercies of the great Physician.

Too often, however, like the Pharisees in Jesus' day, we pretend we don't need Christ's remedy. We try to disguise our real appearance before the mirror of God's law by putting on our masks of self-righteousness. We put up a false front of piety or religious devotion, though down deep we know we are phonies. We pass the buck in our desperate attempts to shift the blame for our shortcomings to someone or something else—to heredity or environment, to our family or friends, to our church or school, to our neighborhood, to bad times, or to just plain bad breaks.

SOMEHOW I DON'T THINK THIS FOOLS ANYONE . . .

But it's a masquerade, or disguise, and we know it. And we can't get away with it. God's law pins the blame squarely on us.

It comes down to this: Whose word are you going to take about who you really are? Your conscience? —it may be on the wrong track. Your experience?— it could be very misleading. What everybody is doing nowadays?—popular practice is certainly not an infallible guide. The Bible and the Catechism put an end to our guessing games: God's law sets the standard.

So let's accept God's verdict. That's our only hope. Our middle name is "Sinner." That's the honest-to-God truth about ourselves. But it takes a miracle of grace to confess it. Only if your real name is "Christian" can you accept "Sinner" as your middle name. So that's who you are: John Sinner Christian!

There is only one who ever kept the law of God perfectly, Jesus Christ. So even if you have only one sin that bothers you, take it to Him. In His presence your many other sins will also come to the surface. But don't let that scare you off. For though the law and the cross show up our sins, they also show us the way out.

7. THE LAW AND THE GOSPEL

Learning from the law as our teacher of sin, we now realize that we cannot reflect upon the "bad news" of the law without at the same time reflecting upon the "good news" of the gospel. The law locks us up in a cell on death row. Sin is the great tragedy of our lives. We must honestly confess it. Then, in response to our confession of sin, the gospel proclaims the message of release. That's the way the Bible works. It breaks us down in order to build us up. It never pronounces condemnation over our lives without in the same breath proclaiming victory through Christ.

Remember the tax collector and the Pharisee in the temple? The Pharisee paraded his phony piety before God. In contrast, the tax collector, out of his broken heart, could only press out the penitential prayer: "God, be merciful to me, a sinner." Jesus then clinches His point by telling us that the tax collector, not the Pharisee, went home at peace with God. "For everyone who exalts himself will be humbled, and he who humbles himself will be exalted" (Luke 14:11).

Right now we are discussing the law mainly as our teacher of sin. Later, under Part III of the Catechism, we will concentrate on the law as our guide for thankful Christian living. It's clear from all of this that the law never stands alone. It's our teacher of sin, our usher to salvation, and our guide to Christian service. When we realize this, we can echo the words of the Psalmist: "Oh how I love thy law! It is my meditation all the day" (Ps. 119:97). God's law is our key to Christian comfort.

Some will say, It's a long leap from sin to service. But really, it's not a leap at all. Or rather, it's a leap into the arms of Christ who takes away our sin in order that we may willingly and joyfully serve Him.

By misreading the law the Pharisees fell into a terrible trap. They made the law a thing in itself. For them keeping the law carefully in every minute detail was the only way of salvation. In their book there weren't just ten commandments, but hundreds of commandments—law upon law, precept upon precept, here a little, there a little. What an awful burden! For them the law was no longer a servant, but a hard-knuckled taskmaster demanding fearful submission. Their version of the law turned religion into spiritual tyranny, or oppression. They remade Moses into an enemy of Christ, and in the name of their do-it-yourself religion they rejected the Savior.

The self-willed intentions of the Pharisees were perhaps understandable. They wanted to make religious choices as easy as possible for the common

IF THE CHURCH WOULD ONLY MAKE MORE DECISIONS, I WOULDN'T HAVE TO THINK!

20

people by prescribing a code for every situation in life. But even good intentions and rigid morality are no substitutes for a Christ-centered faith. The Pharisees' interpretation of the law led to a concentration-camp style of life, because they failed to place the law within the context of the gospel of God's free grace in Christ.

Centuries later Martin Luther also suffered at the hands of religious leaders who misunderstood the meaning of the law of God. Crushed by a sense of guilt, he spent hour after hour pouring out his sins before his confessor-father. But he found no peace with God. For as Luther discovered at last, salvation cannot come by keeping the law. Indeed the law is good, for it is God's law; but we are evil. "The law is holy, and the commandment holy and just and good . . . . but I am carnal, sold under sin . . . . For I do not do what I want, but I do the very thing I hate. Now if I do what I do not want, I agree that the law is good" (Rom. 7:12, 14-16). Therefore the law serves as a hard reminder that we cannot save ourselves. It must lead us by the hand to Christ.

Thus the men of Heidelberg learned—for themselves and for us—that the righteousness of the gospel is no longer a righteousness that God *demands* of us, but a righteousness that He freely *gives* us in Christ. The law and the gospel are the two sides of a single coin. God gives what He demands. The gospel declares that God has done for us that which the law reminds us we cannot do for ourselves.

Nowadays there are some Christians who preach the gospel at the expense of the law, and then triumphantly sing: "Free from the law, O happy condition!" They tell us that once we have embraced the gospel we can get rid of the law. All the while they forget that the law comes into its own when it brings us to Christ and when there is born within us a desire to do what the law requires.

Recall the words of Jesus in the Sermon on the Mount. "Think not that I came to destroy the law or the prophets: I came not to destroy, but to fulfill" (Matt. 5:17). Christ then goes on to give examples from the Ten Commandments for His disciples. What must we do with the law of God? Cancel it? No! Listen: "You have heard that it was said to the men of old, 'You shall not kill' . . . . But I say to you that every one who is angry with his brother shall be liable to judgment" (Matt. 5:21, 22). And again, "You have heard that it was said, 'You shall not commit adultery.' But I say to you that every one who looks at a woman lustfully has already committed adultery with her in his heart" (Matt. 5:27, 28 RSV).

You see what Jesus is doing? Far from canceling the law, He proclaims the deepest meaning and fullest claim of the law upon us. Not only our outward acts but also our inner attitudes must be seen in the light of the law. On both scores we fall far short of the goal.

The gospel sets us free from the law because it tells us of the One who has fulfilled the law perfectly for us, and who has taken away the penalty of our sins. But it also sets us free to obey the law as an expression of our grati-

21

tude for this great salvation. Now we are running ahead of the Catechism story, however, for this is the theme of Part III. Just remember this: There is one law of God, which serves a twofold purpose in our lives.

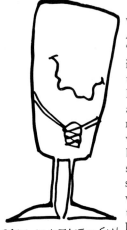

Taking the law seriously (the law of the land as well as the law of God) is not popular these days. A spirit of lawlessness is running wild in the world. "Freedom" is everybody's slogan. People are shouting madly, "I do as I please," and "Laws are made to be broken." But this certainly is not a lesson learned from the gospel. We can breathe the fresh air of gospel freedom only as we live within the atmosphere of God's law. Just as a fish is free only when it lives by the law of the water, and just as a bird is free only when it lives by the law of the air, so we as men are free only when the gospel leads us spontaneously to want to obey God's law in our whole life. For "where the Spirit of the Lord is, there is liberty" (II Cor. 3:17). Lordship and liberty, liberty and law, law and gospel—these go hand in hand.

BEING AN ACTIVIST IS FUN, YOU DON'T HAVE TO WORRY ABOUT ANSWERS !

8. THE LAW OF LOVE

It hurts to know the truth about ourselves. But only in this way can we be helped. Our sinfulness stares us in the face when we stop to measure our lives by the standard of God's law. To borrow the words of the Catechism: What does the law of God require of us? First, that we love the Lord our God above all else. Second, that we love our neighbor as ourselves. There you have the whole will of God in a nutshell. When all is said and done, it comes down to this one all-embracing obligation: *love* (Matt. 22:37-40; Mark 12:30, 31).

God lays our lives on the scales of His holy law. The needle swings over. The verdict is clear: weighed in the balance and found wanting. Lacking in love! For the power of sin within us robs us of our power to love.

Look at the Ten Commandments. The first commandment amounts to this: Thou shalt love! And the second commandment: Thou shalt love! And the third, fourth, fifth, sixth, seventh, eighth, ninth, and tenth: In each case it's the same story—Thou shalt love!

Love God above all! Yes, we give Him a few leftover tokens of affection. But is it real love? And above all else? This is "the first and great commandment." But do we really keep first things first in our lives? Often this first and greatest law of love comes last and least.

Love your neighbor as yourself! Yes, we toss the beggar a quarter. We contribute to a campaign for disaster victims and down-and-outers. We pray for the needy. But do we really love—not just tolerate? Do we love as we love ourselves? Loving ourselves comes quite naturally. But how about kindness toward our brothers and sisters, helpfulness to our parents, cooperation with our teachers and ministers, consideration of our friends? How about loving our rivals, those who have offended us, those who "get under our skin"?

These probing questions coming up out of the law of God cut as deeply as a two-edged sword into our often exaggerated sense of self-importance. With a single stroke the law of love lays bare all our pride, selfishness, meanness, anger, biting criticism, and just plain lovelessness. It's easy to say, "I love everybody." But the fellow next door whom we just "can't stand" is the real test of loving our neighbor as ourselves. And remember: "If a man says, I love God, and hates his brother, he is a liar: for he that loves not his brother whom he has seen, cannot love God whom he has not seen" (I John 4:20).

OH, PEOPLE ARE ALL RIGHT, ITS JUST MY NEIGHBORS I HATE!

You see, facing up to God's law of love is a pretty painful business. For the law is more than a series of "do's" and "don'ts." If it were only that, we might possibly come out looking pretty good. But it goes deeper. It's not merely negative. It carries in it a very powerful positive thrust that cuts through our pretense and reduces our inflated egos, or inner selves, to their proper size.

People do some very strange things with God's law of love. We Christians sometimes hate our fellowmen in the name of the God we claim to love, while humanists—those who put man on the throne—often engage in helpful actions for their fellowmen while denying the very God of love. Sin has made us terribly mixed-up people.

Think of the rich young ruler who came to Jesus with this question: What must I do to inherit eternal life? Jesus answered: Keep the law of God. To which the young Pharisee replied: I've done that since my youth. Then Jesus put him to the real test of the law, namely, love—self-sacrificing love. And the young man turned away downhearted (Mark 10:17-22). He might have earned an "A" in observing rules. But he got an "E" in love.

And we are by nature no better. Without Christ, we are all drop-outs from the school of love. But in Christ we see a perfect demonstration of self-sacrificing love. For the God who gave us the law also gave us His Son to fulfill it for us—the Perfect One dying for the guilty and polluted, the Altogether Lovely One giving His life for the unlovely and loveless. The gospel now calls us to be imitators of our Lord by walking in His footsteps.

9. OUR TOTAL DEPRAVITY

I can feel it: you're getting hot under the collar. You're about ready to blurt out: Why must the Catechism rub it in so hard? It rains hammer-blow after hammer-blow upon us. It keeps pounding us with our sinfulness—our misery—our lawlessness—our lovelessness. How much pressure does it take to prove the point!

Yet the Catechism hurls its accusations after us, one upon another. It says that we are inclined by nature to hate God and our neighbor, that we are wicked and perverse, that we have a depraved or corrupt nature, that we are incapable of any good, that we are inclined to all evil. It's a pretty sorry record, this devastating series of sins.

OF COURSE I'M
SATISFIED WITH
MYSELF......

IT'S EASY TO
BE SATISFIED
IN LIFE......

YOU JUST DON'T
THINK ABOUT ALL
YOUR FAILURES....

But don't forget, we are usually satisfied with ourselves sooner than God is. We also give up on ourselves sooner than He does. So God's Word takes all the time in the world to tell us the whole truth and nothing but the truth about ourselves. For there is no dawn without darkness and no great sense of salvation without a deep sense of sinfulness.

Well, where does all this leave us? There is a term we use to cover this truth about ourselves. We call it *total depravity*. We are not partly sinful, or even mostly sinful, but we are totally sinful. This doesn't mean that we are always as bad as we can be, for God in His grace restrains the evil in men's hearts. But it means that everything we are or say or do is discolored by sin. It means that sin lurks in every nook and cranny of our lives. From start to finish we are sinners.

Pretty strong language, you say? Yet that's what the Bible tells us. Sin has uprooted love in our lives, and sowed instead the seeds of hatred.

God is love, and yet—let's be honest—we tend to hate even Him. We cold-shoulder Him, and try to use Him to suit our purposes. We want to be the architects, and let God be the Builder to carry out our plans. When we hear the holy demands of His law to be perfect every hour of every day of our lives, we become even more angry with God, because then in utter frustration we know we have a lost cause on our hands—"unless we are regenerated by the Spirit of God." Only Christians are ready to confess, "I am totally depraved—infected by sin in every part of my being."

Men are always trying to rescue some remnant of personal goodness from the fire of God's judgment. For example, the church in which the men of

Heidelberg were born and raised had some very complicated teachings by which to sidestep the truth of total depravity. It taught that man's passions are sinful, but that his mind is still good, and his will is neutral so that it can do either good or evil, depending on whether a man chooses to follow his passions or his good reason. Living the good life therefore—the Christian life—means letting your intellect be your guide. But the Bible says of man that "every imagination of the thoughts of his heart was only evil continually" (Gen. 6:5). "Because the mind of the flesh is enmity against God; for it is not subject to the law of God, neither indeed can it be" (Rom. 8:7).

In our times liberals talk very easily about the inherent, or natural, goodness of man. There is a spark of the divine in all of us, they say. So we must live by the better self within us. After all, there is a little good

in the worst of us, just as there is a little bad in the best of us. Give man a little time and a fair chance and he will make something good of the world. Even World War I was part of this proud dream of creating a "kingdom of heaven" on earth. For remember, that was to be "the war to end all wars." But liberals aren't piping this tune so confidently anymore. In recent decades there have been more wars than years, plus countless savage and self-inflicted horrors. The bubble has burst.

The Bible says, "There is none that does good, no, not one" (Ps. 53:3). "All we like sheep have gone astray" (Isa. 53:6). Paul summarizes the whole ugly story in Romans 3:9-20. Man's whole existence has become twisted and depraved. By our sins we are defeating our purpose in life, namely, to glorify God and enjoy His blessings. Our lives have gone into reverse. As when a warped violin bow is drawn across the strings, our lives ring out with ear-piercing sound. We see how bent out of shape our lives really are when we measure them by the straight-edge of God's law.

So then it's all a lost cause? Are we a hopeless case? No—for where there is life there is hope, and Christ is our Life and our Hope. Our Judge is also our Savior.

10. WHOSE FAULT IS IT?

Sin stalks us like our shadow on a sunny day. But sin is not the *last* word about us. The last word is salvation in Christ Jesus. Is sin then the *first* word about us? Is this the way we came from the hand of our Creator? Did God bring us into the world as sinful creatures?

The Catechism uses this strange turn of questioning to get at the original truth about ourselves. It's a roundabout route, but it leads directly into the heart of the matter. The men of Heidelberg never seriously considered the possibility of an affirmative answer to their question: Did God then create man so wicked and perverse? In fact, to assume the possibility that God would create man wicked and perverse would make this a bad question. But the Catechism here uses this question simply as a teaching device to lead us to the right answer.

Countless critics of the Bible have used the very argument which the Catechism here rejects. It goes like this: If there is an almighty God of love and justice, why didn't He make a better world and better people? Why does He allow all this enmity and bloodshed? It's all His fault! Away with such a God!

So it's a real question we must face: *Did* God create man so wicked and perverse? Even serious-minded, well-meaning, believing people have fallen into this trap. Maybe in desperation you too have raised such questions: Couldn't God have prevented sin? Why did He permit it? Look at all the trouble God could have spared us!

You see what lurks behind these questions? They are subtle attempts on our part to shift the blame to God. Such practices go all the way back to our first parents. After Adam fell, God came to him in His judgment and grace with this question: Adam, where are you? What have you done? In self-defense Adam answered: It was the woman You gave me! She became a stumbling block to me. So, God it's really *Your* fault! Eve in turn tried to clear herself by passing the blame to Satan, whom God allowed to tempt her. So again it was God's fault. And we try the same tactics: I can't help it. That's the way I am. After all, to err is human. And I'm only human, you know. You can't hold me responsible!

Well, who then? Your parents? Adam? God?

That's the way our selfish minds twist the facts. We spoil things, and then look for sneaky ways to make God the scapegoat. The Catechism, however, reminds us in unmistakable language—"by no means"—that such thinking sets us on the wrong track. As the Negro spiritual puts it: "It's not my sister, nor my brother, not my father nor my mother [and we might add, 'It's not Adam nor Eve'], but it's *me, O Lord.*"

The history of the human race, however, did not begin on that note. At the dawn of creation God surveyed His handiwork, including man, and He said: It's all very good!

That's the way it was in the beginning.

But now, look at the mess we have made of it! And remember, it's *our* fault, not God's. As the Old Testament preacher says, "Behold, this only have I found: that God made man upright; but they have sought out many inventions" (Eccles. 7:29)—that is, man has sought out clever and ingenious ways of practicing sin. We've got a mess on our hands. But God sent Christ to organize a clean-up campaign.

I USED TO THINK THE HUMAN RACE WAS PRETTY GOOD...

THEN I REALLY STUDIED HISTORY IN SCHOOL......

ITS A RAT RACE !

11. MAN — THE IMAGE OF GOD

"To err is human"—that is, to be human is to be a sinner. This happens to be true of us the way we are now. But it will not always be so. Nor was it always so. Adam was truly human, but before the fall he did not sin.

You see, man was human before he became sinful. Sin is that "bad accident" that happened to us at some point in the long history of our race. Yet through it all we are still human beings; we are still men. John F. Kennedy, Mao Tse-Tung, John Calvin, Pontius Pilate, Abraham, Adam, you and I—we are all alike in this: we are human; we are men.

This means that all of us must somehow find an answer to this central question: Who am I? What does it mean to be a person? Our whole life is a search for self-identity. Where did we come from? Where are we going? What are we doing here? You may be a good student, a star athlete, an accomplished musician, a ham radio operator, a son, a daughter, an average Christian young person. But underneath all these differences, one thing is sure. We are all human beings. This is our life. And human life is the greatest thing in all of God's creation.

But what does it *mean* to be human? That's the big question. The answers are many. Some say we are highly developed animals. Others say we are descendants of the gods. Still others imagine that perhaps we are offshoots of some form of life from outer space. Whose word are you going

SOME SAY WE ARE DESCENDANTS OF GODS...

OTHERS SAY WE ARE JUST HIGHLY DEVELOPED ANIMALS...

I HAVEN'T DECIDED YET

to believe? God's Word states clearly: we have been created by God Himself, in His own image and likeness (Gen. 1:26-27, 9:6; I Cor. 11:7; Jas. 3:9).

Remember the second commandment? There God forbids us to make any images of Him or to worship images. For "God is a Spirit: and they that worship him must worship in spirit and truth" (John 4:24). Read Lord's Day 35 of the Catechism. God would not allow His people in Bible times to make images of Him made of wood or stone or metal. Many pagans, therefore, who worshiped images as idols, thought the Israelites had no God, that they were atheists. But they missed this wonderful point: God made His own image. He made man as His living image. Therefore, do away with dead images! And in the fullness of time God sent His perfect image into the world—Jesus Christ.

Man, the image of God—what does this tell us about ourselves? The Bible uses this language only in speaking about man. Man was given an exalted and unique position in the world. By a distinct act of creation (Gen. 2:7) God appointed man as His representative and ruler in the world (Gen. 1:28-30). Man was made sovereign over all creation, like God, yet

28

under God. For man is still earthy, a creature of time and space. He is not a little god, nor an angel, nor an animal. He is in a class by himself. Read Psalm 8. For man alone is made to be God's kingly servant, His prophetic spokesman, His priest in the temple of His world, His co-worker. At the level of a creature, man resembles God in his thinking and speaking and acting. Adam is even called "the son of God" (Luke 3:38). Being the very image and mirror of God, man cannot really know himself—his dignity and dependence, his character and purpose—without recognizing his reflecting relationship to God—like a son who resembles his father.

Again, Christ is central to a true understanding of ourselves. He is the key that unlocks the meaning of our lives. We learn to know ourselves by looking to Him. For He is the perfect God-man. Paul calls Him "the express image of the invisible God" (Col. 1:15). Therefore, Christ Himself could say, "He that hath seen me, hath seen the Father" (John 14:9). At the same time Christ is like us in every respect (Heb. 2:17). He is the key Person in understanding our key position in the world. For in His life we witness the perfect model of what our lives are meant to demonstrate —true knowledge of God, righteousness, holiness, perfect obedience to God's will, genuine love of fellowmen, and wise dominion over the powers of nature. That was our calling in Adam. That is now our calling in Christ. And through the indwelling of the Holy Spirit we receive power for this calling: Christ the Example, we His imitators; He the Master, we His disciples.

Being living images of God means standing in a threefold relationship.

First, we are related to God, called to love Him above all, and to make that loving relationship concrete in our worship, in our work, in our total style of life. Now this doesn't just happen. We must work at it prayerfully, believingly, obediently. Just as a mirror, for instance, doesn't automatically reflect. It must be polished. Therefore we must "walk with God" if we are to be His mirrors in the world. We must let His Fatherly discipline form the image of Christ Jesus within us.

Second, we are related to our fellowmen. They are all our blood relatives. All men are our neighbors. We are all branches springing from a single family tree. And God Himself came into this world in Jesus Christ, the supreme revelation of the image of God in man. Our lives, therefore, must image His life. He washed men's feet, healed the sick, fed the poor, preached the gospel, cast out demons, reclaimed the lost. Do you really want to be an image-bearer of God? Then hear the words of the Master: "I have given you an example, that you also should do as I have done to you" (John 13:15).

I THOUGHT I WAS PRETTY GOOD UNTIL I READ THE CATECHISM

Third, we are related to the world. Here we must live our lives. For it is our Father's world. We breathe its air, drink its water, bask in its sunlight, eat from its store of food. We are called to "subdue

29

the earth" by ruling it in the name of our overruling sovereign God. In harnassing the power of the atom, tilling the soil, generating electricity, painting pictures, building bridges, cooking meals—whatever it may be—we must act in obedience to God's cultural command to "have dominion over the earth."

In the name of *God*, for the good of our *fellowmen*, in the midst of the *world*—there you have the three dimensions of a God-imaging life. Are you up to it? No one is—not in his own strength. But God has given us the Holy Spirit to create in us a new life, and in the power of that Spirit we may begin to do the things He asks of us (John 14:15-17).

12. THE ORIGIN OF SIN

My little daughter, talking about herself, says, "Sometimes I'm naughty, sometimes I'm nice." Martin Luther put it into these words: the Christian is always both saint and sinner at the same time. Paul gives us a vivid description of this inner conflict between the old man of sin and the new man of righteousness in Romans 7:18-25.

For the good that is in us we have God alone to thank. He made us good. And even now He continues His good work in us. But for the evil that is in us we have only ourselves to blame. For in Adam we all walked right into the devil's trap. We fell for his line, swallowed his bait, and believed his lie.

That's the story of Genesis 3. Somewhere near the dawn of human history something disastrous happened, and as a result, everything went radically wrong. The man Adam—and in him all men—fell into sin. There is no sharper contrast in all the world than the contrast between God's evaluation of His handiwork in Genesis 1 and 2 ("very good") and His evaluation of the fallen creation in Genesis 3 ("cursed").

Like a jilted lover, God pleads His case in Isaiah 5: What more could I have done for My vineyard? Why then when I looked for it to bring forth grapes did it bring forth wild grapes?

God had every right to expect man to stand the test of religious faithfulness. It was not as though God set man on a religious fence, wavering between good and evil, with God wondering which way man would move. No, God made man good, able to stand up for the truth, dedicated to walk in obedience before the face of his Maker. But man deliberately jumped the fence from good to evil. The Catechism describes this awful act as "willful disobedience."

That was our downfall, and it was God's great disappointment. Yet God is still God, still sovereign, still in control. Man, the rebel, cannot dethrone God. He will not allow our sin to leave His masterpiece in ruins. Again He takes command. Our Maker becomes our Savior. In His judgment and grace God breaks through with His arresting question, "Adam, where art thou?" Christians, behold your God, who will not let you go, who stands there at the fork of the road that leads back from sin to salvation and renewed service!

First creation, then the fall, and now redemption—that's the way the Bible pictures God working out His plan for the world. There in Genesis 3 we meet Adam, not as a stranger to us, but as our father, our representative. As our representative he was choosing for us. When he chose to sin, he made the choice that we also have made. For we are like him, just as he was like us. Adam, you see, not only represented us, but in a real sense we were active in his sin. For we are all one family. Adam's sin was our sin. His fall was our fall.

Do I hear you complain? "Why hold me responsible for what Adam did? It just isn't fair!" But then think of this: if we are unwilling to recognize our involvement in Adam's sin, what about our involvement in Christ's salvation? For just as God counts us guilty of Adam's unrighteousness, so He now also counts us beneficiaries of Christ's righteousness. For Christ is our second Adam, who came to re-do what the first Adam had undone.

We stand here face to face with the mystery of sin and grace. For there are dimensions to the truth of Genesis 3 which we cannot measure. The very mind by which we seek to rethink that revolutionary turn of events in Genesis 3 is itself affected by the fall. Our only sure record of these events, then, is the revealing word of Scripture.

There we find two truths looming up large. First, we cannot point an accusing finger at Adam without also realizing that this same accusing finger is pointed directly at ourselves. Behind that finger we hear the voice of our Judge saying, "Thou art the man!" Second, we may never forget that the God of Genesis is also the God of Golgotha. It is in the saving work of the second Adam that the wickedness of our sin in the first Adam comes to fullest and clearest revelation.

Read carefully Genesis 3 and Romans 5:12-21.

Alas! and did my Savior bleed,
And did my Sovereign die?
Would He devote that sacred head
For such a worm as I?

Was it for crimes that I have done
He groaned upon the tree?
Amazing pity, grace unknown,
And love beyond degree!

Well might the sun in darkness hide,
And shut his glories in,
When Christ, the mighty Maker, died
For man the creature's sin.

Thus might I hide my blushing face
While His dear cross appears;
Dissolve, my heart, in thankfulness!
And melt, mine eyes, to tears!

13. OUR ORIGINAL SIN

From where we are in history, in this year of our Lord, we can look back over countless generation gaps. There are two great realities that bridge all those gaps, namely, our sin and God's grace. Here are two links forging together an unbreakable chain that unites us with our fathers' fathers, all the way back to Adam. We are all his children. His fall is ours. His guilt is ours. His misery is ours. Our sinfulness is related to his original act of disobedience. His sin repeats itself in ours. And our sins are living reminders of his. Here is the mystery called original sin.

No one can fully explain original sin. Yet it is terribly real. It is our spiritual birthright, for we are all conceived and born in sin. Our daily lives prove it. Original sin is our inheritance, and our whole life long we continue to make investments on this evil deposit.

MY SIN DOESN'T SEEM SO ORIGINAL

But in what sense can we speak of our present condition as *original* sin? Sometimes the way this word is used seems to suggest a sin that happened way back in some dim and distant past. This idea, however, is misleading. For original sin exposes what we are like here and now. It is as much a part of us as the air we breathe. Sometimes this word is used to suggest a sin that happened just once and is now finished. This idea too is misleading. For original sin is a permanent reality reliving itself in our daily experience.

Perhaps it will help to think of it this way. What happened in the life of Adam was the original—our daily experience is a copy. Remember, a copy always carries the original in it, just as the original places its stamp upon the copy. One can check out a message

32

by reading forward from the original to the copy, or by reading backward from the copy to the original. So Adam's original sin points forward to ours, and our original sin points backward to his.

But how does sin manage to keep itself alive from generation to generation? How is sin transmitted from our first parents down through all the succeeding generations, right down to the generation of youth who are living today?

About fifteen hundred years ago the great church father, Augustine, and another church leader, Pelagius, locked horns over this issue. Pelagius believed that Adam sinned only to his own hurt. There were no after-effects. So we, the descendants of Adam and Eve, come into the world as they did, good and with a clean record. But since the sins of previous generations have contaminated the world we live in, we lose our innocence as we live in this world, and we learn evil habits by following the bad example of others who have already adopted sinful ways. Sin, then, is rooted in our environment and is passed on by imitation. This is what Pelagius taught.

Augustine, however, looking back upon his own checkered career of sin in the light of the Bible, answered that sin is not learned, but inherited. The source of sin lies within man himself. Man is a sinner and therefore the world is sinful. So our salvation must come not by following some good example, such as the life of Christ, but by embracing the work of Christ which renews our hearts and lives.

Original sin is a term used by the Catechism to describe the sinful attitude behind our many sinful acts. We are guilty not only of *doing* sin, but we are also guilty of *being* sinners. Salvation, therefore, means not only cleaning up bad practices in our lives, but first of all having the principle of new life in Christ implanted in us through the power of the Holy Spirit. Only God's redeeming work can break the powerful hold of sin upon us.

The Bible uses many pictures to portray the power of original sin in our lives. Look at these three.

First: Sin is _missing the mark_. It's like an archer facing the target and aiming his arrows at the bull's-eye, but constantly missing the mark. So the Bible points out the God-given goals and standards for us to live up to. But sin throws us off balance, so that we stray from our purpose in life and fall short of our goal.

Second: Sin is _disobeying the law of God._ It turns us into law-breakers, rebels, revolutionaries. God's laws of love and justice are given to hold the world together and keep our lives in order. But sinful men reply, Laws are made to be broken! Is it any wonder, then, that our world is falling apart into hostile camps, the East versus the West, whites versus blacks, and haves versus have-nots? For sin breeds a spirit of lawlessness. And we find the telling evidence of it in our hearts and in our homes, in our streets and on our university campuses.

Third: Sin is _enslaving ourselves to wickedness_. Men want to be free, yet they choose the slavery of sin. This is the awful puzzle, the terrible riddle of our human predicament. We make ourselves the victims and captives of devilish forces within us and around us, and then have the audacity to call such bondage the good life! Complacency. Materialism. Drinking parties. Pot-smoking. Psychedelic drugs. Cut-throat competition in business. Vandalism. Dragging on main street. The more you sin, the more you want to sin. It's a vicious cycle.

By nature, that is the way we are: first, *misdirected;* then, *lawless;* finally, *enslaved.* No one can escape this divine judgment, for sin is universal. All men, says Paul, Jews as well as Gentiles (the two important classes of people at that time), are sinners (Rom. 3). Today we would say, all men, Americans as well as Russians, or whites as well as blacks—all men without exception are sinners. This is our common confession of guilt. But thanks be to God, there is a way of escape. "Who on earth can set me free from the clutches of my own sinful nature? I thank God there is a way out through Jesus Christ our Lord" (Rom. 7:24-25 Phillips).

14. OUR ACTUAL SINS

Few of us own an original great painting. But we probably see reproductions almost every day, at home, in school, or at church. Originals seem remote and distant to our everyday experience.

Perhaps you feel that way about original sin too. So now, as we turn our attention to actual sins, you probably have the uncomfortable feeling that things are coming closer to home. Actual sins are living realities—like greediness and hate, lying and cheating, stealing and cursing. All this is part of our daily world of experience. All this is real.

But must we then conclude that original sin is unreal? Surely this would be a big mistake. Original sin does have a very real hold on us. It describes our sinful *condition,* while actual sin describes our sinful *conduct.* Both are terribly real.

For example, being addicted to dope is a horrible condition, and this condition of life shows up in the actual use of dope. So original sin is, by nature, our real condition of life, which shows itself in actual deeds of sin.

We *are* sinners and this shows up in our sinful *acts*. Our sinful *hand* (or eye, or mouth, or foot) and our sinful *heart* work together to produce a sinful *life*. Both the attitude and the act are real, and both belong to us, and therefore God holds us responsible for both.

No man can escape the full force of this judgment. One and all, we stand as guilty sinners before the tribunal or court of divine justice. Yet only Christians know this and confess it. For daily sin is offense against God— we cannot see sin as our sin until we see God as our God. With Paul we must learn to say: "Jesus Christ came into the world to save sinners, of whom I am chief" (I Tim. 1:15).

Sometimes today, as in Jesus' day, people try to sit back and decide whether some men are greater sinners than others. Jesus says, in effect, That's the wrong question. The right question is this: Have you repented of your sins? (Luke 13:1-5).

When a preacher talks about sin in general, most people will nod approvingly. What great sinners we are! This awful sinful nature of mine! But if the sermon brings our daily, actual sins under the searchlight of God's Word, then the preacher is becoming too personal! But the Bible hits a man where it hurts: Abraham in his lying, Jacob in his deceit, David in his adultery, Thomas in his doubt, John Mark in his cowardliness, Ananias and Sapphira in their evasion of the truth. You in your . . . .

Sin, repeating itself day after day—this is our common enemy. Don't underestimate its power. We cannot stand up to it in our own strength. But don't overestimate its power either. We can conquer it through the power of Christ. "If we confess our sins, he is faithful and righteous to forgive us our sins, and to cleanse us from all unrighteousness" (I John 1:9).

Many people do indeed feel a heavy burden of misery resting on their shoulders—a burden that never gets beyond an overwhelming sense of despair. But with the Catechism it's different. The Catechism leads us to see how great our sin and misery is in order that we may learn to live and die *happily*.

To get on the road back home, we'll have to start by swallowing our natural pride and simply saying, "I'm sorry, God," and "Please, forgive me." These are the hardest words in the world to get across our lips, yet these are the very words with which our biography must begin. Listen to the confessions of David in Psalm 51—a plea for pardon pressed out of the man after God's own heart.

> Wash me thoroughly from my iniquity,
> And cleanse me from my sin.
> For I know my transgressions;
> And my sin is ever before me.
> Against thee, thee only, have I sinned,
> And done that which is evil in thy sight . . . .

How deep even the godly, like David, sometimes fall! Adultery, murder, deceit! So take courage. Don't give up on yourself—God doesn't. Seek, and you will find (Matt. 7:7). That's the promise of the Bible. And that's the point of the Catechism.

15. THE JUSTICE OF GOD

The central point of the Catechism comes through with ringing clarity: God is just in all His dealings with men, from start to finish. In the beginning God established His covenant with man. It was like a contract which He drew up with us. He made us partners in it. In the terms of agreement, God spelled out the condition under which we were to live in covenant fellowship with Him, namely, obedience to His law of love. He promised us countless blessings if we would obey Him, and warned us of the punishment that would follow if we disobeyed.

God lives up to His covenant. He is true to His word. He is just and fair. We can count on Him.

But through the sin of Adam and Eve, which is also our sin, we broke the covenant. We turned our backs upon the opportunity for wonderful fellowship. And so we brought God's punishment down upon us.

God is not like man, that He should break His word. God's warnings are as real as His promises. He is just in all His ways. He continues to uphold His law. So we can count on God to take sin seriously. The cross reveals just how dead-serious God is in His dealings with us, His sinful covenant people. So our choice now comes down to this: either we allow Christ to meet the demands of God's justice for us, or we must meet them on our own.

Judgment and punishment—these are certainly not welcome visitors in our lives. But God's justice is at stake. By meting out punishment He upholds His part in the covenant and satisfies the holy demands of His law.

God punishes sin already in this life. But punishment can also spill over into the life to come. The Catechism calls punishment that takes place here "temporal judgment" and punishment that takes place hereafter "eternal judgment."

Here and now, in this world, and in our lives, the evil results of our sins have a way of catching up with us. This is clear from the Bible. After the fall Adam and Eve were quickly driven out of Paradise. The utter wickedness of Noah's generation called forth God's judgment in the flood. Even after his confession and forgiveness, David experienced the bitter fruits of his sin throughout his lifetime. Israel was eventually led into captivity after having repeatedly trampled under foot the law of God. The hardheartedness of Jerusalem drew from our Lord bitter tears that spoke of coming judgment. Judas came to a tragic end because of his betrayal of Jesus.

But during this lifetime not even the world's worst sinner gets the full measure of judgment that he deserves. In this life God always tempers His judgment upon men and prolongs their day of grace. Otherwise life would hardly be livable.

In the life to come, however, God's just judgment will come to full expression against those who during this lifetime chose to love their sins more than His salvation. In the end God gives men what they want. If they want a life without Him, they will eventually get it. Separation from God! This the Catechism calls "eternal judgment." This is hell, the place where "the worm dieth not, and the fire is not quenched" (Mark 9:48). There God's justice takes over completely. The wages of sin are paid out in full. There the unrepentant and unbelieving —and may their number be few—will witness a

SOMEHOW I FEEL LIKE I'M GETTING OFF LIGHT IN THIS LIFE

total eclipse of every last ray of divine mercy and goodness. Let's stop at that. It's really too awful to think about. And the half has not been told us.

Hell or heaven—that's the choice. God's justice is at stake. For the believer it is heaven, eternal glory, with justice paid in full at the cross and the empty tomb, for Christ "was delivered up [to death] for our trespasses, and raised for our justification" (Rom. 4:25). For the unbeliever it is hell, eternal punishment, paying forever for the injustices of his sin.

For Christians, God's mercy has already lifted the awful weight of His justice from our shoulders in this life. For "there is now no condemnation to them that are in Christ Jesus" (Rom. 8:1). We are already free from the slavery of sin. Free from the tyranny of the law. Free from the accusations of a tormented conscience. Free to serve God and our fellowmen.

Even when the consequences of our sins overtake us along the way, we know they are not meant by God as harsh judgments. For Christ has taken our just judgment upon Himself. The effects of our sins serve rather as chastisements, by which with the firm and loving hand of a Father, God disciplines us His erring children.

It is wonderful to know that God is just in all His ways. For God's people shall be redeemed by justice—in Christ! There is something very urgent and compelling about this knowledge. To put it in the words of Paul: "Knowing therefore the fear of the Lord, . . . we beseech you on behalf of Christ, be ye reconciled to God" (II Cor. 5:11, 20).

16. "I OBJECT!"

It's not easy for us to take criticism, is it? Yet when it comes to sin, that is precisely what the Bible gives us—criticism—and what the Catechism gives us here too. But our Critic and Judge is God, and that should make a difference. For in our hearts we know that His criticism is true. We *are* sinners. Yet for that very reason, there is something in us that protests.

The men of Heidelberg shared our feelings. Like us, they also heard the voice of the old man of unbelief echoing within the chambers of their lives. Believer and unbeliever, both are alive and at work within us. Therefore

we find ourselves praying, "Lord, I believe; help thou my unbelief" (Mark 9:24). The voice of belief in us says "Amen." The voice of unbelief in us shouts "I object!"

The Catechism picks up three of our objections, puts them into words, and then proceeds to answer them from the Word of God. Let's listen to this little dialogue.

First: Isn't it unjust for God to expect me to do what I cannot do? My sin keeps me from obeying God's holy law of love. Yet this is what God requires of me. This simply isn't fair!

But is it really unfair? What does God's law ask of you? Just one thing—love. Is that an unfair and unjust requirement? Surely not.

But you say, since I am now a sinner I find it impossible to love God above all and my neighbor as myself. I find hatred welling up within me, instead of love.

But what brought this on? It was your doing, wasn't it, not God's? So you cannot accuse God of being unfair. He made you able to love. And He Himself is love. He still loves you. He has not changed. And He has not changed His law of love. You changed—therefore the fault is yours, not God's.

Suppose your father sent you to the store with a twenty dollar bill to pay a debt in the amount of $18.95. Along the way you met some friends who took you on a wild spending spree. At last you returned home with the debt unpaid and only $2.00 left in your pocket. Now you are really on the spot. Your father asks for the receipt. You try to cover up and excuse yourself by arguing: "How do you expect me to pay a bill for $18.95 with only $2.00 in my hand? That's not fair!" Well, who is being unfair? If your father were to ground you and make you work until you paid the debt, would that be unfair?

Second: Will God really insist on punishment for my sins? Isn't God free to overlook them? Can't God close His eyes a bit? If He is a God of love, can't I count on Him to discount sin? I'll take a chance on getting away with it. Somehow I'll get by.

You probably picked up these ideas by observing human affairs. For among men, wrong sometimes goes unchallenged. Right often has a hard time coming out on top. The rich buy their way out of trouble. The poor lose their day in court. Criminals go free. Robberies remain unsolved. Murder cases are never closed. Traffic courts overlook many violations.

In your own life too you probably get away with things, with sins that are never detected and punished. Maybe you think you can slip one over on God.

Punishment is not a popular idea these days. Men talk about crime as a sickness or a birth defect or an offense against society, rather than as breaking the just laws of God for human life. So the emphasis falls on rehabilitating a criminal, rather than on punishment. Justice gets watered down.

MAYBE GOD WON'T NOTICE ME

But remember, you are dealing here with God, not with men. Your sins offend Him. They ruin His good work. None of your sins escape His attention. God never has to throw a case out of court for lack of evidence. He never gets stuck with a hung jury. You can never bribe God into a favorable judgment.

I know you resent the idea of punishment. We all do. But in our hearts we know we deserve it. Yet we snatch at every straw to avoid it. All the while there is only one way of escape, the way of repentance, as the story of Nineveh demonstrates (Jon. 3:10; Matt. 12:41).

Third: But God is merciful, isn't He? Well, if He is so kind and compassionate, surely He will not be too strict about enforcing justice against my sins!

40

Yes, I see what you are driving at. Others have stated your argument even more strongly. Surely an almighty God of love will not sentence men to everlasting punishment in hell! But who are you to decide what God will or will not do? Jesus took a different view of these things. Punishment is for real, man! So don't try to sidestep the issue by playing off God's mercy against His justice.

HOW 'BOUT AN APPEAL

Thus the Bible and the Catechism overrule our objections. But not without giving us a message of hope. For in Jesus Christ, God's justice and His mercy meet together at the cross. Justice without mercy is hard. Mercy without justice is soft. God is just and fair. God is also merciful. In Christ He found a just and fair way of opening the door of mercy for repentant sinners.

17. THE MERCY OF GOD

Jehovah is merciful and gracious,
Slow to anger, and abundant in lovingkindness.

Ps. 103:8

That message was given to put a spring in the sinner's step as he moves along the road of salvation and service.

God's mercy is our bridge to the second part of the Catechism. After exploring our sin, this is music in our ears. There is mercy—thank God—there is mercy!

A certain liberal preacher who heard one of the first broadcasts of the Back to God Hour mounted his radio pulpit the following Sunday and said: "I heard a new program, The Back to God Hour. Back to what kind of God? Back to a God before whom we must bow as sinners and plead for His mercy? I tell you, I hate that God! I hate that God!" That preacher didn't know God, he had never learned to really read the Bible, and he didn't know himself.

To keep the record straight, the emphasis in Part One of the Catechism is on the terrible displeasure and just judgment of God as He views our sin. All you have to do is read the Bible texts listed under the answers in the Catechism. There are only two that highlight God's mercy, while at least twenty proclaim the divine sentence that rests upon our sins.

But don't forget, the first part of the Catechism is the shortest part. The best is yet to come.

"God is indeed merciful, but He is also just." You can also turn it around: "God is indeed just, but He is also merciful"—full of mercy!

There you have the gospel in a nutshell, the "good news." Sometimes we say, No news is good news. But that's not always true. Silence about sin makes us deaf to the sounds of salvation and service. The "good news" of God's mercy and the "bad news" of our sin go hand in hand. God's

Word must make us uncomfortable with ourselves if we are truly to seek and find our only comfort in Christ.

But the Bible does not expect us to tell and retell forever the story of our sin. Nor will the Catechism allow us to get stuck in the swamps or quagmires of sin. For God has set our feet upon a firm path, and put a new song in our mouths (Ps. 40:1-3). So now we must get going. Step forward, then, to a confession of our salvation in Christ (Part II) and our calling to Christian service (Part III).

PART TWO: SALVATION

18. SATISFACTION GUARANTEED

It's common to hear people complain, "You just can't get any satisfaction these days." A contractor orders steel. Late delivery. So the whole construction job is held up for two weeks. Your father brings in his car for repairs. The bill: $65. But the next day his motor is still knocking. Poor workmanship. Your mother calls a catalog house for a pair of jeans. But they send out the wrong size. You just can't get satisfaction—guarantee or no guarantee!

But hold on a minute. There is "good news" for you. With God it's different. You can count on Him to keep His word. Salvation means that full satisfaction is guaranteed—satisfaction for all our sins. God will settle for nothing less. But who can fully satisfy the demands of God's justice against our sins? Can we ourselves? Or some of the great Christian saints? Or the holy angels? All such attempts would end in failure. For no creature can pay the price of God's wrath against sin—and live.

God knows this even better than we do. So since there is no other way, in a tremendous act of love God sent His own Son into the world to make satisfaction for our sins and to create a new life within us, through His Spirit. There you have the heart of the gospel.

With this grand confession the Catechism makes the transition from Part One on "Sin" to Part Two on "Salvation."

Because the men of Heidelberg knew the Bible well, they never raised the question whether or not salvation has come to us. This was beyond doubt. Salvation was a living reality for them; they found the message of the Bible confirmed in their own experience. The only question left to be understood was this: *how* does God save us? From the pages of Scripture the answer came back: God stepped in. He Himself made satisfaction for us.

Christian comfort, you recall, is setting something good in the place of something bad in such a way that the good offsets the bad. Comfort and satisfaction go together. In fact, God's act of satisfaction in Jesus Christ is the basis for a Christian's comfort.

In our daily prayers we ask, "Forgive us our debts . . . ." In these words Christ taught us to confess that we stand as debtors before God. What an

42

incalculable debt we have to repay because of what we have destroyed by our sins! God is our Creditor. Time after time He comes knocking at our door to collect on our long overdue bills. Knocking, knocking . . . (Rev. 3:20). So we open the door. And there we stand, face to face with our great Creditor! But imagine the stunning news: God holds in His hand—and He hands over to us—our whole batch of bad bills, and across the face of every last one of them are these words: "Paid in Full," "Account Closed."

Only the man who has been over his head in debt really knows the enormous sense of relief that follows: Our debts paid in full! That's cause for celebration—a mortgage-burning ceremony! Full satisfaction guaranteed, signed, and sealed.

Again, only the person who has spent years behind bars, serving a well-deserved life-sentence in prison, can really experience deeply the joy of being pardoned. With tears of joy he watches the prison doors swing open to a new life of liberty.

The satisfaction of being a Christian is something like this. God made good for us. When it comes to our sins, however, payment is made not with a mere wave of the hand, nor with inflated money. There is nothing cheap or easy about it. To figure the cost of salvation, look at Christ and at His cross. That's God's way of satisfaction—justice matched by love!

The unbeliever says in his heart, "God hath forgotten. He hideth his face. He will never see it. He will not require it" (Ps. 10:4, 11). With an air of wishful thinking he brushes aside the realities of sin and satisfaction. The Christian, however, knows better, and in the words of the Catechism he confesses: "God will have His justice satisfied." The requirements of His holy will must be met. And it's God's will that counts, not our whistling in the dark.

Satisfaction for sin is the world's first need. Through Christ's finished work, that satisfaction is guaranteed to all who put their trust in Him.

As Paul says, "God was in Christ reconciling the world unto himself, not reckoning unto them their trespasses . . ." (II Cor. 5:19).

19. THE TRAIN OF THOUGHT

Suppose that in an orientation session at the beginning of a new school year all the students were asked to write an essay. This is the topic: "Your idea of an ideal student." That's a big order. How would you try to get

at it? There are different ways you could approach the subject. You might, for example, use the process of elimination. Following this train of thought you might explore such questions as these: Would an ideal student be one who takes shortcuts on his assignments? One who takes scanty notes in class? One who skips school? One who never takes part in class discussions? One who makes a habit of turning in his work late?

Obviously, the answer No fits all these questions. An ideal student is just the opposite. But do you see what you are doing? In a rather indirect, roundabout way, you are setting up the standards a person must meet to qualify as an ideal student. For without checking out all these standards for an ideal student, you already know what an ideal student is, because you know someone who strikes you as being an ideal student. So all the while you really knew the answer to these questions, even before you raised them.

The Catechism uses a train of thought very much like this. Can we ourselves satisfy for our own sin? Can a saint, or an angel, or some other creature satisfy for us? You see, we are being led to the truth in an indirect and roundabout way. The answer to each of these questions must be No. No "mere creature" can provide a way back to God. All such attempts are dead-end streets. Only Christ can satisfy for our sins.

The men of Heidelberg knew this before setting up this series of questions. They are really tongue-in-cheek questions. They are questions for learning—slanted questions, slanted toward Christ, the only Answer. They are questions aimed at helping us think backward from Christ to ourselves, and then from ourselves forward to Christ. Along the way the Catechism sets up the standards and conditions our Savior must meet, as revealed in the Bible, and then proclaims Christ as the One who fully satisfies every standard and condition for our salvation.

This train of thought is something like asking questions when you already know the answer, hoping in this way to help others find the right answer too. This process of eliminating the wrong answers in order to arrive at the right Answer is designed to help us confess in a meaningful way, "This I believe," and at the same time to say in a meaningful way, "This I do not believe." The Catechism is a good teacher.

20. HOW ABOUT PAYING YOUR OWN WAY?

They used to call it "Dutch Treat." You take your guests out to dinner, but each person pays his own bill. Impolite! Absurd! you say. Yet many people play up the idea of paying their own way through life. Fact is, by nature most people resent being dependent on others. Yes, I know, there is a spirit abroad these days that says, "The world owes me a living." Yet deep down no one really likes to live on handouts.

You go out with your friends to the "House of Flavors." You order a delicious sundae. When the waiter serves it, you discover you are broke. There you sit, unable to pay your own way. You're highly embarrassed. But happily you are with friends. So it all turns out quite well. Sally agrees to pay your way, and you agree to repay her later. Still it hurts a little, because we all like to pretend at least that we can make it through life on our own.

But now, a change of scenery. Imagine that you are haled into court and tried for a very serious crime. The jury finds you guilty and the judge passes the death sentence. Would you still want to insist on paying your own way? Chances are you would welcome eagerly some other way of settling the bill.

You see, our natural desire to pay our own way through life breaks down sooner or later. We all run into situations that we cannot handle alone. A prime example of such a situation is our bankrupt spiritual account with God. After all is said and done, we cannot satisfy for our own sins.

Still, we find that do-it-yourself religion is deeply rooted in the human heart. This is nothing new. From the beginning, self-centered religion has been a glaring sore spot in our lives. Look at the results—complacency in the lives of some; panic and defeat in the lives of others. Have you ever actually tried pulling yourself up by your bootstraps?

The history of mankind is an unbroken record of man's repeated efforts to blaze his own trail to glory. With sickening regularity the children of Israel tried to justify their living at ease in Zion by trusting in their temple, their sacrifices, and their feasts, rather than in God. The Pharisees turned religion into hypocrisy with their strict self-help programs of salvation. Saul of Tarsus thought he was winning the favor of God by his zeal in persecuting Christians. Only later did he learn to turn over his ill-gotten gains as losses, that he might gain the righteousness that God gives in Christ. Then only was he ready as a missionary to proclaim the gospel of salvation by grace alone, through faith, over against the works-righteousness religion of the Jews.

In the days of the Heidelberg Catechism, the Reformers—by learning to walk anew in the footsteps of Paul—found it necessary to protest the church's misplaced emphasis on good works as the way to earn salvation. But people forget so quickly. In our times modern liberals are still preaching a gospel of self-improvement.

Every form of do-it-yourself religion is doomed to failure. We are spiritually penniless; we cannot repay our debts to God. We are spiritually dead; so how can we make ourselves alive? All our self-generated attempts to satisfy for our sins never even get off the ground. If God were to abandon us to our own devices, we would only pile up new mountains of guilt every day. You know from your experience how that goes. We try to dodge one sin by committing another; we dig one hole to fill in another; we tell one lie in trying to escape another; we take on new debts to cover old ones.

So the question comes back: Can we satisfy for our own sins before the court of God's justice? Those who fail to take sin seriously answer, "By all means! Of course I can!" But the Christian echoes the confession of the Bible. "By no means! For if I am left to myself I only make things worse, rather than better. I cannot pay my own bills. I cannot buy my way into the kingdom of God."

We come to this realization not just because we have tried so often and failed, but more convincingly because this is the testimony of the Bible; and we realize it most clearly because we have caught a glimpse of that stupendous miracle of Christ's paying the price for us.

21. EMERGENCY . . . HELP!

So I cannot pay my own way. But don't think I'm giving up yet. Just give me a little time to work this thing out. I'll come up with something . . . .

I CAN'T PAY MY OWN WAY I GUESS . . .

BUT, I'LL COME UP WITH SOMETHING . .

JUST GIVE ME SOME TIME . . . . A LOT OF TIME

I've got it! If I'm too sinful to satisfy God and save myself, I'll find someone else to lend me a helping hand. How about the great saints of the church? Many of them lived holy, self-denying lives. During their lives they succeeded in building up a treasury of merits, which others could draw upon. This was the teaching of the church for many long centuries. Just think of Saint Mary, Saint Augustine, Saint Francis of Assisi, Saint Thomas Aquinas. Surely they can help me out. —No? . . .

Well, how about the angels then? They never suffered from the crippling blow of sin as we did. Their lives are perfect. They are powerful. They seem to have an inside track to heaven. Moreover, the Bible states clearly that they are "ministering spirits, sent forth to do service for the sake of them that shall inherit salvation" (Heb. 1:14). —No? . . .

All right, then, let's go back to Old Testament times. Thousands upon thousands of animals were sacrificed upon the altars of Israel. God Himself commanded this. So it must be good. Every year at the great Day of Atonement the high priest would offer a bull to satisfy for his own sins; then he would offer a goat to satisfy for the sins of the people. A second goat, called the scapegoat, would be saddled with the sins of the whole nation and driven out to die in the wilderness. And so, away with sin! Since a new lease on life comes by the shedding of blood (Lev. 17:11; Heb. 9:7), why can't I fall back on something like this to satisfy for my sinful life? —No? . . .

You can see through these arguments, can't you? By nature we are all like drowning men, thrashing the water, snatching at every straw afloat in our frantic efforts to save ourselves. We dash desperately up one blind alley after another. Our self-esteem leads us to try everything else first, and to follow God's lead only as a last resort. Christians, too, are often tempted to offer God some sacrifice—a tithe, regular church-attendance, doctrinal soundness—as token payments for their sins.

But not even the most clever or ingenious substitute can satisfy. Saints cannot help us (Luke 17:10). They stand where we stand as sinners over against God. Angels cannot help us. For God is just and will not allow any other creature to bear the burden of man's sin. Old Testament sacrifices have had their day. Even in their day they could not in themselves satisfy for sin. All the lambs sacrificed on Israelite altars were merely pointers to "the Lamb of God that takes away the sin of the world" (John 1:29). Christ is the way, the only way, the way that fully satisfies (John 14:6).

Moses learned this by hard experience. After the incident of the golden calf, in the wake of God's judgment upon this act of idolatry, we hear Moses the would-be mediator pleading with God: "This people have sinned a great sin, and have made them gods of gold. Yet now, if thou wilt forgive their sin—; and if not, blot me, I pray thee, out of thy book which thou hast written" (Exod. 32:32).

Moses was asking the impossible. No man can satisfy for his own sins, let alone the sins of others. Moses was tugging at the veil of the temple dividing the Old and New Testaments, the veil that could not be rent until the hour of Calvary. This was Moses' way of praying, "Come, Lord Jesus, come quickly!"

Paul, standing on this side of the cross, had the same idea. In a moment of anguish he cried out, "I could wish that I myself were anathema [cursed] from Christ for my brethren's sake, my kinsmen according to the flesh." Read Romans 9:1-5. Paul too was dreaming impossible dreams. And he knew it. For he had doubtless read God's answer to Moses, "Whosoever has sinned against me, him will I blot out of my book" (Exod. 32:33).

In Christ impossible prayers are answered, impossible dreams come true. The impossible is possible. No, it's real! He is the Way. So come, let's take a walk. Read Micah 6:6-8.

22. "CHRIST ALONE!"

In a stirring scene from the "Luther" film, Brother Martin gives up on all the traditional sacred relics of the church. His confessor-father von-Staupitz then asks him, "If you take away from the people all these spiritual helps, what will you give them instead?" For a moment Luther paces back and forth tensely. Then he stands erect and replies in his native language, *"Christus allein!"* (Christ alone!").

The Catechism has now brought us to the point of making that confession: "Christ alone!" We have looked at the alternatives and come back empty-handed. There are no two ways about it. Christ is our all—nothing else will help. As Jesus Himself said, "No one cometh to the Father, but by me" (John 14:6). And "The Son of Man came . . . to give his life a ransom for many" (Matt. 20:28). Entering our world of great need He satisfied His Father's will by fulfilling the words of prophecy,

> Sacrifice and offering thou wouldest not,
> But a body didst thou prepare for me . . .
> Then said I, Lo, I am come
> (In the roll of the book it is written of me)
> To do thy will, O God.
>
> Ps. 40:6-8; Heb. 10:5-7

There, Christian, behold your Savior and Lord, your Mediator, Son of God and Son of Man! That's the way it had to be.

The Catechism first sets up the conditions that someone must somehow meet to save us from our sins and satisfy God's justice. Then it introduces the only One who can meet all these conditions—but without at this point giving us His name. The Catechism holds us in suspense.

Look at the conditions. Our Savior must be true man in order to take our place. "Behold, the man!" (John 19:5). Morever He must be a righteous, sinless, perfect man. Listen to Christ's unchallenged claim: "Which of you convicts me of sin?" (John 8:46). To bear the awful load of our guilt He must be stronger than any "mere creature." Listen to the disciples' words of wonder, which are an eloquent testimony to the power of their Master: "Who is this, that even the wind and the sea obey him?" (Mark 4:41). To restore the broken harmony between man and God, our Savior must be truly divine as well as truly human. Looking back as an eye- and earwitness upon the total impact of Christ's mission, John writes, "These [things] are written, that ye may believe that Jesus is the Christ, the Son of God; and that believing ye may have life in his name" (John 20:31).

So now we have come to the end of our hunt. And who is the object of our search? It's the Man in the middle, on the center cross, Jesus Christ. He satisfies. He alone.

23. THE BRIDGE IS CHRIST

Tom, Dick, and Harry were fast friends. People called them "the inseparable trio." But somehow—nobody quite remembers how—something went wrong. Tom and Harry were no longer on speaking terms. All three were unhappy about it. But Tom would not give in. And Harry would not make the first move either. Finally Dick managed to get the unfriendly friends together again. Since both Tom and Harry had long forgotten what the fight was all about, without much trouble they patched up their differences.

You see what a mediator is? He's a go-between, an umpire or referee, a negotiator or arbitrator, a person who bridges the gap and settles disputes between two opposing parties.

Here are some examples. Parents often act as mediators in settling teenage quarrels in the home. Ministers often serve as mediators between estranged husbands and wives in broken homes. The government sometimes appoints mediators to enforce collective bargaining and to settle labor disputes. The United Nations must often act as a mediator between hostile powers.

Because of sin, God's creation has been turned into a divided world. You see gang against gang, whites against blacks, labor against management, Communist countries against capitalist countries. Who will deny that we live in a house divided against itself? As long as men continue to live at odds with each other, mediation remains the only way to maintain some semblance of peaceful relations in society.

But look, now, at the most divisive thing in all the world—sin. This is the division behind all other divisions—the great gap, the yawning chasm between a holy God and sinful man.

But sin is not the final act. The division between God and man is not permanent. The gulf is not unbridgeable. Christ is the bridge. He steps in as Mediator to heal the breach between the King and His rebels. God did not wait for us to act. He made the first move. For "God was in Christ reconciling the world unto himself" (II Cor. 5:19). Christ alone can span the chasm between God and man and close the gaps among men. Because He is truly God, He can reconcile God with man and bear the weight of divine judgment against sin. And because He is truly man, He can take our place in the plan of salvation and make atonement (at-one-ment) for us with God. Reconciliation (God's peace with man) and atonement (man's peace with God)—there you have the only solid foundation for peace in a divided world.

Paul puts this message in straightforward language to his spiritual son Timothy: "For there is one God, one mediator also between God and men, himself man, Christ Jesus, who gave himself a ransom for all" (I Tim. 2:5, 6).

24. SON OF MAN

"The Word became flesh, and dwelt among us [and we beheld his glory, glory as of the only begotten from the Father], full of grace and truth" (John 1:14). Jesus Christ, the God-Man, that's who Christmas is all about.

Early Christians did not have much of a Christmas Day by our standards. No celebrations, no decorations, no parties. Yet the truth of the incarnation stood out in their lives, even in times of persecution. For example, to identify themselves secretly they used the sign of the fish. Why a fish? Because the five letters that spell fish in Greek—I K TH U S—also stood for the first letters of the Christian confession: Jesus Christ, God's Son, our Savior. Early Christians inscribed the fish symbol on the walls of their meeting-places, something like this: ⊂◁

The confession that Jesus Christ is God's Son, our Savior, is the main hinge on which the message of the Bible turns. This is the heartbeat of the Christian faith and life. God and man in the one person of Jesus Christ! Who would have expected anything like that? But God's ways are higher than our ways.

But our Savior was also fully and truly divine; He was also fully and truly human. He started out in life where we start. After a nine-month pregnancy He was "born of a woman" (Gal. 4:4). He lay in a crib, help-less, dependent, no halo. Drop the myth about "no crying He makes." It was all very common. Like all Jewish boys, Jesus was circumcised the eighth day. He was a displaced person, living as an exile in Egypt. He placed Himself under the parental authority of Joseph and Mary. He worked and played. He probably went to a synagogue school. At twelve years of age He frightened His parents by staying behind in the temple—without their knowledge—in order to talk with the teachers. He grew up physically and mentally just as we do—but without the handicap of sin. Though He was perfect, He had to learn the full meaning of obedience through suffering (Heb. 5:8). He became hungry and tired. He was filled with righteous anger at "the Establishment." He cried real tears—at the grave of Lazarus, and over an unrepentant Jerusalem, and in the garden of suffering. He sweat and bled and died and was buried. From start to finish, He lived our life and died our death.

He could trace His family tree all the way back to David and Abraham and Adam. Look at the genealogies in Matthew 1 and Luke 3. In speak-ing of Himself, His favorite name was "Son of Man," a name rooted in Daniel 7:13. During His life on earth He endured our kind of tempta-tions. He knows our troubles. He can help us overcome them. For He has gone through them (Heb. 4:15, 16). Our life is not strange to Him. He knows all about us by experience. For He stood close to us. No, He took our place. He identified Himself completely with the mankind He came to save. Body and soul, inside and outside, words, thoughts, deeds —His life covers ours at every point. So, have no doubt about it, Jesus Christ is our perfect Mediator.

There have been Christians who lost sight of the real humanity of Jesus. Because they were deeply concerned with defending the full divinity of Christ, they tended to soft-pedal His full humanity. Holding a low view of human nature, they thought they would be insulting Jesus if they be-lieved He was really human, like us. Instead of having a real earthly body —so they argued—Christ took a heavenly body with Him when He came into our world. Others argued that He only took on the appearance of humanity and acted the role of a man.

In the name of the Bible we must set aside all such arguments. If Christ was not really like us in all things, sin excluded, then we are still burdened with our sins. For our salvation depends just as much upon the real and perfect humanity of Christ as upon His real divinity. He is our Immanuel, God-with-us, Son of God and Son of Man, the God-Man. Behold the Man of God! Look at the nail prints in His hands. Then, with Thomas, fall down and confess, "My Lord and my God!" (John 20:28).

25. SON OF GOD

A modern German philosopher, father of the "superman" idea, once said: "If I had been at Calvary that day, and watched Jesus hanging on the cross, I would have spit in his face and said, 'You weakling!' "

Another man, a Roman soldier—one who was actually there—spoke a different language: "Truly, this was the Son of God!" (Matt. 27:54).

These two answers stand worlds apart. But both men were answering the central question of human life, the question that Jesus Himself put to the men of His day: "What think ye of the Christ? Whose son is He?" Read Matthew 22:41-46. At a loss for words, they turned their backs on Him.

Jesus confronted His disciples with the same question. "Who do men say that I, the Son of Man, am?" Read Matthew 16:13-17. All kinds of answers were making the rounds. "But who say ye that I am?" Peter, always first with his words, then made his great confession: "Thou art the Christ, the Son of the living God!" That answer has stood the test of time. It is the rock upon which Christ still builds His church.

But for many this confession is a rock of offense. The apostles already discovered that the divinity of Christ was a stumbling block to Jews and foolishness to Greeks. For they were meeting the same forces of unbelief that their Master had met. "He came unto his own, and they that were his own received him not" (John 1:11). In Nazareth Jesus' fellow citizens were willing to give Him a hero's welcome as a hometown boy making good in the world. But as a prophet He had no honor in His own country. The Messiah? The Son of God? Who does He think He is anyway? He's the carpenter's son, and that's all (Mark 6:1-6; Luke 4:14-30). Throughout the long running controversy that fills John 8, the thing that offended the Jews was Jesus' claim that God was His Father. Absurd! Then He thinks He is the Son of God? Finally, when the debate was reaching its breaking point, Jesus forced the issue by saying, "Before Abraham was, I am" (John 8:28). That's when the hostile audience started picking up stones.

THERE ARE MANY STUMBLING BLOCKS IN MY LIFE ...

Well, when was Christ born? As Son of Man He was born, of course, in the fullness of time in Bethlehem at a certain hour of a certain day in a certain year. We today still mark time on our calendars from that date. But as Son of God His life reaches back eternally into the past and stretches out eternally into the future. In the beginning all things were made through Him (John 1:13). And looking forward, "he shall reign forever and ever" (Rev. 11:15). So we can count on Him, for "[he] is the same, yesterday, today, and forever" (Heb. 13:8).

Down at the Jordan River when Jesus was baptized, God said it clearly, "This is my beloved Son, in whom I am well pleased" (Matt. 3:17). But who listened to this voice from heaven? Even John the Baptist, an ear-witness, was plagued with doubt (Luke 7:18-20). Caiaphas the high priest turned a deaf ear. Placing Jesus under oath he asked, "I adjure thee by the living God, that thou tell us whether thou art the Christ, the Son of God" (Matt. 26:63). When Jesus answered in the affirmative, all Caiaphas could say was "blasphemy!"

That spirit of Caiaphas is still alive today. Jesus—a great Teacher, a wonderful Example, the Man for all men. But the Son of God? No modern man can believe such myths!

But then, what about Jesus' clear-cut claim, "I and the Father are one" (John 10:30)? Here a man must choose. Either Jesus thought He was divine, but was honestly mistaken—in which case He was suffering from delusions of grandeur. Or He knew He was not divine, but deliberately misled the people—in which case He was a fraud. In either event He is not worthy of our trust. Or Jesus actually *was* what He claimed to be, namely, the Son of God. Then there is salvation and comfort, hope and joy.

Christ Himself creates the moment of decision. Believe Me, He says, that I am the Son of God. Take Me at My word. Or otherwise believe Me because of the works I do (John 14:11). Look at His works: healing the sick, casting out demons, feeding the hungry, raising the dead, stilling the storm, forgiving sins, dying in your place, rising to make you right with God, ascending to heaven to prepare your place, sending His Spirit to rule in your hearts. Who but the very Son of God could do all that? Read carefully Philippians 2:5-11.

To any honest reader of the Bible the truth is inescapable: Jesus Christ is the Son of God. It's enough to make you sing! For now our salvation is sure. As Son of God and Son of Man, He could do what no ordinary man could do, namely, satisfy the eternal justice of God in one lifetime; bear all the punishment for all the sins of all God's people of all time. In short, He could do everything necessary for our salvation.

Dear Lord, thanks a million!

26. THE GOOD NEWS

Under new management! That's the "good news." Christ has taken over in our lives. Now we can go back and capture anew something of the deep meaning of the first question in the Catechism, "What is your only comfort?" Christ is our comfort, our strength. For He is our Mediator, Son of God and Son of Man, our wisdom, righteousness, sanctification, and redemption. In a word, He is our salvation. That's the new story of our lives.

Having made this great confession of faith, we now ask a question: Upon what authority do we rest our case? For faith always rests on some authority. It takes somebody's word for it. Whose word do we appeal to in support of the Christian religion? Where do we turn to learn the new truth about ourselves? The Heidelberg Catechism has the one sure answer, "the holy gospel." That is, the "good news" of the Bible.

But let's push this question a little harder. How did the gospel manage to work its way into our lives? Who brought us into contact with the "good news"?

Under God, many people play important roles in shaping our Christian lives. We think of parents, teachers, ministers. Or a neighbor, friend, or counselor. Perhaps the "good news" got through to us in a book, or a

THOSE CHRISTIANS
ALWAYS TALKING
ABOUT THE GOOD NEWS...

YOU KNOW WHY
IT BOTHERS ME?

IT MAKES ME
FEEL LIKE I'M
MISSING SOMETHING..

radio broadcast, or a television program. Every younger generation owes a debt of gratitude to the older generation for keeping the gospel alive, and every older generation in turn must look back thankfully to their forefathers for relaying the message of salvation to them. That's how Christ through His spirit works in history to keep the "faith of our fathers" alive in the church and in the world. In an unbroken line we can trace the story of the gospel back across the ocean to mother churches in Europe, and back through the Reformation to the early church fathers, and back through them to Paul, the first missionary to Europe, and to his fellow apostles.

The apostles heard the "good news" from the lips of Christ Himself and saw it enacted in His life and death and resurrection. They were observers on the scene. Their on-the-spot reports in the New Testament link us with the Christ of the gospel and establish a clear channel of communication between Christ and the church of all ages. This is still the firm foundation for the faith and life of the Christian community today.

Did the "good news" then begin its journey through history in the days of Christ and the apostles? Was Pentecost the birthday of the church? Was there no church and no "good news" before Christ?

To find answers to these questions, go back in your thoughts to the evening of the first Easter Sunday. Walk with me down the seven-mile road from Jerusalem to Emmaus. A few steps ahead we see the figures of two downhearted disciples of Jesus trudging along. Their sullen faces, their bewildered conversation, all betray their depressed state of mind. As we tag along, we see a Stranger come up from nowhere to join the wayfarers. He makes His way into their conversation. He asks questions about their experiences, and they assume that He is a stranger to these recent events in Jerusalem. But as the talk moves along He shows that He is no stranger to the Bible, the only Bible they had—the Old Testament.

As we listen in we hear the Stranger say, " 'O foolish men, and slow of heart to believe all that the prophets have spoken! Was it not necessary that the Christ should suffer these things and enter into his glory?' And

55

beginning with Moses and all the prophets, he interpreted to them in all the scriptures the things concerning himself" (Luke 24:25-27 RSV). Later the men from Emmaus exclaimed, "Was not our heart burning within us, while he spoke to us in the way, while he opened to us the scriptures?" (Luke 24:32).

Not only from Matthew to Revelation, but also from Genesis to Malachi, Christ is the key that unlocks the meaning of the Bible. Therefore Christ Himself could speak of searching the Scriptures and add that "these are they which bear witness of me" (John 5:39). His redeeming work binds all sixty-six books together into one all-embracing gospel of salvation. His coming, concealed in the Old Testament, is revealed in the New Testament. If in reading the Bible we miss Christ, we miss the point completely. For the "good news" revealed, published, and foreshadowed in the Old Testament reaches its high point of fulfillment in the New Testament.

What greater incentive could there possibly be for "searching the Scriptures"! So—what are you waiting for?

27. THE LAST WORD

Many people turn the Old Testament into a forgotten book. They think it has reached the age of retirement—that it's outdated. Good for Jews perhaps, but Christians have outgrown it. So they say.

Christ, however, never downgraded the Old Testament. He said it this way: "Think not that I came to destroy the law or the prophets: I came not to destroy, but to fulfill" (Matt. 5:17). The gospel in the New Testament is rooted in the gospel of the Old Testament; and the gospel in the Old Testament bears its fruit in the gospel of the New Testament. So it is all one gospel, all "good news," from the first word "In" to the last word "Amen." The Old Testament without the New Testament is like a foundation without its superstructure. The New Testament without the Old Testament is like a house without its foundation.

THE OLD TESTAMENT IS OUTDATED AND DOESN'T RELATE, MAN...

I HAVEN'T READ IT...

BUT THAT'S WHAT PEOPLE SAY...

The Catechism reminds us that there is only one way of salvation running through the whole Bible. Stage by stage the Old Testament advances this plan of salvation forward to its high point of fulfillment in Christ at the center of the centuries. As the rising sun dispels the predawn darkness, climbing ever higher into the morning sky, until at last it hits its zenith at noonday; so God's revelation in Christ emerges in the Old Testament with increasing clarity, until at last we stand face to face before our Savior and Lord.

You see now why Christ and the apostles make so much of the Old Testament? All the New Testament writings—especially Matthew's gospel —glean numerous pointers from the Old Testament and show how they came true in Christ. For example, Christ Himself recalls the awful three-day experience of Jonah as a sign to be fulfilled in His three-day experience from Good Friday to Easter (Matt. 12:38-40). Promise and fulfillment, that's the pattern. Circumcision becomes baptism, the Passover becomes the Lord's Supper, manna becomes the Bread of Life. Thus the temple becomes a church, the priest becomes a preacher, the altar becomes a pulpit, the people waiting in the outer court become a congregation actively worshiping inside the house of God.

And Christ looms up large at the center of it all. When Philip finally caught up with the Ethiopian in the chariot, who was studying the book of Isaiah, we read, "And Philip opened his mouth, and beginning from this scripture, preached unto him Jesus" (Acts 8:35). In Jesus Christ dreams come true (Joel 2:28; Acts 2:17), shadows become reality, faith becomes sight.

The opening lines of the letter to the Hebrews are a key passage for understanding the meaning of the Bible as a whole. There we read that in Old Testament times God spoke His "good word" in many different ways. But now in the fullness of time God spoke His last word in His Son, Christ Jesus. Generation after generation of Israelites stopped their ears to the never-ending stream of words uttered by wave after wave of prophets. But now God has spoken with finality in Christ, and that's the end of all contradiction. Everything God has to say to us He has said in Christ, His last word to the world. Read the parable of the wicked tenants (Matt. 21:33-46).

Jesus hit this point hard before the local congregation in His hometown of Nazareth. Being a "son of the church," He was asked to preach. As His text He chose Isaiah 61:1, 2. It was a familiar passage. Many knew it by heart. It was a favorite of all the people. So without much explanation, Jesus plunged directly into its application: "Today hath this scripture been fulfilled in your ears" (Luke 4:21).

Christ the Fulfiller! What a long time it took to fill up the cup of "good news" that was being handed down century by century through Old Testament times! Already in Paradise we hear the dim and distant strains of the "good news" in the so-called "Protevangel," the "first gospel," the "mother promise" (Gen. 3:15). According to Luther, this makes Adam the first Christian! After that the gospel was published by the patriarchs (Abraham, Isaac, Jacob, Joseph) and the prophets (Samuel, Elijah, Jeremiah,

Amos). By means of audiovisual instruction the gospel was foreshadowed in the sacrifices and ceremonies of the law.

All these things were previews of the full revelation, preliminaries to the main event. Christ is the One! He is God's last Word. What more could He say that He hasn't already said in Christ?

So you see, the Christian religion has very deep roots. It's as old as Adam. Yet as Christians we can always "think young." For we have "good news" that is as up-to-date as Christ Himself. He is the latest "Word" on everything.

28. WILL ALL BE SAVED?

As Jesus was making His way toward Jerusalem, someone in the crowd —like a reporter in a face-the-nation news interview—came up with the question, "Lord, are they few that are saved?" (Luke 13:23). That's a natural question for men to ask. I guess we have all asked it in one form or another. How many people will be saved? Ten percent? Twenty-five percent? Fifty percent? Seventy-five percent? A hundred percent? It's a haunting question. So few in every age seem to answer the gospel call.

How many? How few? The Bible will not allow us to turn this question into a mathematical problem. It's a matter of choice, not calculation; of decision, not statistics. To the questioner in the crowd Jesus replies, "Strive to enter in . . ." (Luke 13:24). Looking ahead to the judgment day, Jesus talks about believers as sheep on His right hand and unbelievers as goats on His left hand (Matt. 25:31-33). But this is not a problem in addition and subtraction. The point is not to give us some insight into the number of believers in comparison with unbelievers. But the point is this: make sure *you* are on the right side.

Is There A MIDDLE ROAD ?

Yes, the number of Christians in the world is small. We see the mysterious power of unbelief all around us and within us. Jesus was keenly aware of this too. In speaking about the narrow gateway to the Christian life He added, "And few are they that find it" (Matt. 7:14).

But thanks to God, the number of believers is also "a great multitude, which no man could number" (Rev. 7:9). As Christians we are "compassed about with so great a cloud of witnesses" (Heb. 12:1). For Christians make up that new humanity, of all times and all races, whom God is recreating in Christ Jesus. Census-takers may tell us that Christians are a minority in the world. But with God we are a majority—"more than conquerors" (Rom. 8:37).

The Catechism tries to get to the bottom of this question. Since in the first Adam all men are lost, will all men be saved through the second Adam? Does the second "all" follow from the first "all"? The answer comes back a painful No. Though all men choose for Adam, not all men choose for Christ. Many men do not welcome God's "good news." Many

58

men do not endorse God's "last word" in Christ. Instead they turn thumbs down on it. Facing the Christ of the cross, men fall into two camps—those who are for Him and those who are against Him.

Yet the will of God is perfectly clear: ". . . not wishing that any should perish, but that all should come to repentance . . ." (II Pet. 3:9). God "would have all men to be saved, and come to the knowledge of the truth" (I Tim. 2:4). That is God's will. And where there's a will there's also a way. God's way is as clear as His will. His way is Christ.

It's not for us to say that hell will be overpopulated; nor that hell will turn out to be empty, as some wishful-thinking universalists believe. Nor is it for us to decide whether the "many mansions" in the "father's house" (John 14:2) are spacious enough to hold all men. It's simply a matter of decision, of choice—to believe or not to believe, that is the question.

29. TRUE FAITH

However painful it may be, we'll have to face it squarely: not all men are saved. This is the testimony of the Bible, and our experience confirms it. But there is just one reason that men perish—and that is their unwillingness to accept God's way of salvation: faith in Jesus Christ.

God has gone all-out for our salvation. Now there is just one question left, the question of the Philippian jailer: "What must I do to be saved?" Today as well as then, Paul stands ready with the only answer: "Believe on the Lord Jesus, and thou shalt be saved, thou and thy house" (Acts 16:30, 31).

"Believe!" This one word captures the call of the entire Bible. The most common Old Testament counterpart is the word "fear," meaning reverence and trust. "The fear of the Lord is the beginning of wisdom" (Ps. 111:10). Thus faith is the starting point and foundation of our search for truth. "The righteous shall live by faith" (Rom. 1:17; Heb. 10:38; Hab. 2:4). It all comes down to believing in God, knowing Him, trusting Him. Being a Christian is basically a matter of commitment and loyalty.

But remember, Christians don't have a monopoly on faith. Other people have faith too. In fact, everybody believes in something or other. Some people believe in themselves, others believe in reason. Some believe in securities, others in science. Still others believe in the Party or the State or the Future. There are many faiths in the world, many religions, many idols in which men place their trust.

You see, it's really not a question of *whether* a man has faith, but *what* the nature of his faith is.

So the question of the Catechism is real and urgent: What is *true* faith?

The Reformers who helped to give shape to our Catechism realized clearly that Christianity stands or falls with true faith. When Luther rediscovered the words of Paul, "The righteous shall live by faith," then the windows of heaven swung open and the light poured in upon his open Bible. Now at last the Bible started to make sense. For faith is the key to the meaning of God's Word. Calvin came to the same conclusion: it is faith that holds the Christian life together. Faith is not just part of being a Christian, as the Roman Catholic Church was teaching. No, faith is the full commitment of our hearts to Christ, embracing our whole life. Faith is not trusting in religion, nor in personal piety or devotion, nor in good intentions, nor in noble deeds, nor in the church. But faith is trusting completely in Jesus Christ alone.

MAYBE IF I RUN FAST I CAN FIND SOME FAITH

Faith is not something we can come up with by ourselves. It is a gift of God. The very faith by which we trust in God must come from God Himself. You see how totally dependent we are on God? But you can be sure of this, that God is more eager to give us the faith we need than we are to ask Him for it. That's the "good news" for today and everyday: God for Christ's sake creates faith in us

60

through His Word and Spirit. Then we can say, "Lord, I believe; help thou my unbelief!" (Mark 9:24).

Faith is saying Yes to God's promises in the Bible. It is a step we must take. The Bible never denies that faith is an act on our part. But it does strip our active faith of every hint of self-merit or self-glory. For faith is self-denial. It points away from ourselves to Christ. It's the beggar's hand which gratefully accepts all that God stands ready to give.

The Catechism has all this and more in mind when it defines true faith as "a firm confidence." But there is also another side to the same coin. True faith is also "a sure knowledge."

True faith is not a leap in the dark. It knows what it is doing. It means turning ourselves over to God. Not to some strange supreme being, not to some god of the gaps—but to our Maker and our Father. Faith says, "I know him whom I have believed . . ." (II Tim. 1:12). But remember, faith is not just head-knowledge. It's heart-knowledge. Therefore by faith I entrust my whole self to God's control—my thinking, my feeling, my willing. So faith-knowledge is more than giving intellectual agreement to a number of facts about God; it's more than nodding approval to a mass of information about the Bible; it's more than memorizing Catechism answers. It's a matter of personal experience—a personal relationship with Jesus Christ. Otherwise we would not be much better off than the demons, for "the demons also believe, and shudder" (Jas. 2:19). Knowing God means knowing that He is *my* God; it means knowing that I myself am heir to all His promises.

"Sure knowledge" and "firm confidence" go hand in hand. With men it is often different. We sometimes find that the better we get to know a person the less confidence we have in him. Not so with God. If you really know Him, you will trust Him. To believe *that* God is my Father and to believe *in* God as my Father—faith as an *article* of belief and faith as an *act* of belief—these go hand in hand.

61

30. THE GIFTS OF FAITH

Pretend it's your birthday and your parents surprise you with a set of skis. What do you do? Start patting yourself on the back for earning such a wonderful gift? That would be stupid! There is only one thing to do: say "Thanks a lot!" and try to follow up with a demonstration of thanks-living.

That's the way it is with faith. It's a hand held upward to receive with thanks what God has promised to give. It means becoming children of our heavenly Father—childlike, not childish, being willing to take a helping hand from God.

Pulling together some of the biblical thoughts embedded in our Catechism, we can put it this way: By grace through faith we are engrafted into Christ and receive all His benefits on the basis of His merits. Let's take a quick look at the four new ideas in this sentence.

A. THE GRACE OF GOD. That's what Luther was looking for. Somehow he could not free his mind of the image of God the harsh judge, as he remembered it from the stained-glass windows of the cathedral. How could he escape an angry God? Then he stumbled upon the answer in the Bible. God is a God of grace who turns His anger into friendship through the work of Christ. Now we are right with Him. He is on our side. Nothing can really hurt us.

B. GRAFTED INTO CHRIST. In Palestine in the days of Jesus, farmers had to make the best of the trees they had. Grafting was a common practice to improve production. A farmer would take a small branch from one tree and by means of surgery set it into the larger branch of another tree. There it would take hold and grow and bear its good fruit. So God takes us as living branches together with other living branches and unites us, by faith, with Christ. Thus we draw upon His life and bear His kind of fruit. He is the Vine, we the branches (John 15:1-11). In this way we begin a new way of life.

C. THE BENEFITS OF CHRIST. When God gives, He gives all He can. He gives unsparingly: "He who spared not his own Son, . . . how shall he not also with him freely give us all things?" (Rom. 8:32). It's something like an insurance policy. The holder of the policy turns the benefits over to his beneficiary at the appointed time. So Christ makes us the beneficiaries of all the blessings of His saving work. Our lives were empty until He came to fill them. We were poor, but He being rich became poor to make us rich. Every favor in our lives comes through the cross of Christ.

D. THE MERITS OF CHRIST. By faith we stake our claim upon the merits of Christ. We disown any personal merit. What we could never earn for ourselves He earned for us. Christ, as it were, writes out a total security check and deposits it to our account. Now all we have and are and hope to be is based upon His finished work. You can count on that.

31. THE BIBLE — THE REVEALED WORD OF GOD

The Bible is still the world's best-seller. It has gone through hundreds of translations. It has touched the lives of more people than any other book. Nevertheless, the Bible is also too often "the book that nobody knows."

Few people really take the time to read it. It gathers dust on the shelf. It is banned from public schools. After ten years, wedding Bibles show no signs of wear. Millions never give the Bible a second thought. They live as if it doesn't count.

Little wonder, then, that three astronauts orbiting the moon took the world by surprise when they relayed the Word of God to earth from outer space.

You can shun the Bible. But you can't shake it off. As Jesus said, "Heaven and earth shall pass away: but my words shall not pass away" (Luke 21:33). Standing upon this solid foundation, the Christian finds firm footing for confessing with Luther, "Here I stand! I cannot do otherwise! So help me, God!"

God's revelation and our response: there you have the two basic ingredients of the Christian religion. God speaking with authority and man listening in obedience—where that happens, at that point of interaction, there you find Christian faith and life. It begins with an opening of our hearts to the Bible. For the Word of God is our standard for Christian principles and Christian practices. That Word lays its claim upon every part of our lives—in the privacy of our room, in the family circle, in studying, in earning money, in working around the house, in watching television. At every turn along the way God wants us to make His Word a lamp to our feet, and light to our path (Ps. 119:105).

The Bible must take first place in our lives. But we should not forget that God's first revelation came in that "most elegant book" (see the Belgic Confession, Article II), the world of His creation. The whole universe is a mirror reflecting the glory of its Maker. We usually call this God's general revelation. If only we have eyes to see! But sin has blurred our vision. We look at God's work of creation and call it natural evolution. We see His providence in operation and call it luck or fate or the law of averages. Our spiritual eyesight is badly distorted.

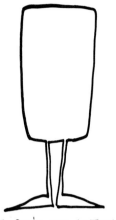

I DON'T SEE ANYTHING IN THE BIBLE ♫ ♫

But God did not leave us in the dark. To correct our faulty vision, He gave us the Bible as glasses to refocus our eyesight, to cure our spiritual blindness. We usually call the Bible God's special revelation. It is not, however, a substitute for God's general revelation. Rather, it helps us see the world for what it really is—God's handiwork, the arena for His great acts in history, the stage for working out the program of His coming kingdom. The Bible helps us see Christ as the one through whom all things were made (John 1:3) and in whom all things hang together (Col. 1:17).

The central meaning of revelation lies in the idea of unveiling. Think of unveiling a statue on dedication day, or of a bridegroom unveiling his bride at the marriage ceremony, or of drawing the curtains aside at the opening act of a play. So God unveils the meaning of things that were previously unknown or only vaguely known, and which would still be unknowable if God did not step into our lives. All that we know is dependent upon revelation. True knowledge comes not by inventing ideas, but by discovering God's works, retracing His ways, and rethinking His thoughts.

God's revelation is actually His powerful Word, a Word that does what it says. In the beginning God spoke His *creative Word* to bring the world into existence. This was not just a pious wish, but an active command. "For He spake, and it was done; He commanded and it stood fast" (Ps. 33:9). Progressively God spoke His *redeeming Word* through the prophets and the apostles. Eventually He saw to it that the message of salvation was set down in His *written Word.*

In the fullness of time God sent forth His Word in flesh and blood, as the *incarnate Word,* Jesus Christ. Christ is the epitome or ideal expression of all God's revelation to man. In the Bible we meet Him clothed with all the promises of the gospel. Today God still speaks through the *Word of proclamation* in the preaching and teaching of the church.

32. THE BIBLE — THE INSPIRED WORD OF GOD

In our Catechism there is almost complete silence on the doctrine of Scripture. This is a striking gap in our confession. But there is a good reason for this. In the sixteenth century there was almost total agreement on the Bible as the inspired Word of God. There were indeed many sharp controversies among Roman Catholics, Lutherans, Calvinists, Zwinglians, and Anabaptists. But they stood together in their views of Scripture. So the men of Heidelberg felt no great need to spell out their common faith on this point of doctrine.

But the atmosphere is far different today. A new spiritual climate has set in. Modern men with their critical minds and scientific methods have

SURE I'M CRITICAL OF THE BIBLE...

WHAT DO I BASE MY CRITICISM ON?

IT'S CRITICAL OF **ME**, MAN!

launched all kinds of attacks upon the Bible. That's where the Compendium comes in. It is based on the Catechism. But it's an updated version of the Catechism for modern times to help us face contemporary challenges. It devotes two questions and answers to the doctrine of Scripture, giving a brief summary of how the Bible views itself. You see, even our view of the Bible must be drawn from the Bible itself. For we have no higher authority. This is our confession: the Bible is the revealed, inspired, infallible Word of God.

How was it possible for God to reveal a heavenly message through earthly means? How could a holy God speak His Word to us through sinful men without the truth and purity of the gospel getting lost? The answer lies in the mystery of inspiration. Through the power of the Holy Spirit, who guided and stimulated and controlled the human authors, the Bible now comes to us as the Word of God in the words of men.

Its divine inspiration means that the Bible stands in a class by itself. It is the only book in the world with a double authorship—divine and human. Dozens of men wrote these sixty-six books over a span of nearly fifteen hundred years. So there is great variety in the Bible. Yet it hangs together consistently. There are indeed strange turns along the way from Genesis to Revelation. Yet an underlying unity runs through every book and chapter and verse. All this points to the triune God, the primary author of the Bible. The Spirit molded the minds of the human authors into a unified team of writers so that all the books find their focal point in Christ. This happened by divine inspiration. How else could it have happened! This unity in diversity is what makes the Bible so unique—the only book of its kind.

How can we give an account of the Bible's double authorship, divine and human, God's word in the words of men? There are three leading views that try to help us get at the meaning of this mystery of inspiration.

First, there is the dictation view, which rules out the real personal involvement of the human authors. According to this view, human authors were just passive instruments in the writing process. They were like tape recorders, with the Holy Spirit doing all the talking. Therefore all variations of style, vocabulary, and point of view in the Bible are due to varying moods in the overriding work of the Holy Spirit.

Second, there is the dynamic view, which cancels the divine dimension in the Bible. According to this view the Bible is great religious literature written by pious men with valuable insights. It ranks high among the masterpieces of human literature—but that is all.

Both of these views fail to do justice to the Bible. Both dissolve the mystery of inspiration—the one by eliminating the human factor, the other by eliminating the divine factor.

Only the organic view of inspiration honors the fullness of the Bible as the inspired Word of God. It confesses the Bible as fully and truly divine and at the same time fully and truly human. According to this view God used the human writers—with all their varied backgrounds, personalities, and insights—and made them His active servants in revealing His Word in their words, under the sovereign direction of the Holy Spirit.

Since the Bible is its own interpreter, let's look at two classic passages on inspiration. II Timothy 3:16-17 tells us that all Scripture is "God-breathed." This is no abstract point of doctrine. It's a very practical truth. For inspiration makes the Bible useful for our believing ("for teaching, reproof, correction, instruction in righteousness") and for our living ("unto every good work"). The Spirit's work of inspiration covers "all Scripture," in all its literary forms, whether history, psalms, proverbs, laws, prophecies, symbolism, or parables. Scripture is inspired in its full extent (plenary inspiration) from Genesis 1:1 to Revelation 22:21, and in all its parts (verbal inspiration).

II Peter 1:19-21 makes the same sweeping claims for the Bible when it declares that the word of prophecy came as an act of divine initiative ("from God"). In the process of inspiration, the human authors were swept along by a Spirit-energized thrust ("moved by the Holy Spirit"), thus making them active communicators of the message of salvation ("men spoke").

That's why the Bible will never let you down.

33. THE BIBLE — THE INFALLIBLE WORD OF GOD

For a long time it has been a favorite game among unbelieving scholars to try to shoot holes in the Bible. They comb the Book from cover to cover, looking for inconsistencies and contradictions. They come up with strange rivalries: prophets against priests in the Old Testament, the God of the Old Testament against the God of the New Testament, Jesus against Paul, John against Matthew, Peter and Paul and James all at odds with each other.

Some Bible critics set out deliberately to discredit the trustworthiness of the Bible. Others are working out their honest doubts. But they all start

at the wrong end. For no one can handle aright the Word of truth (II Tim. 2:15) unless he takes his starting point in a believing acceptance of the Bible as the infallible Word of God.

For centuries, enemies of the Bible have been predicting its early death and the death of Christianity with it. Yet here we are as Christians, still very much alive! Facing these attacks, can we still confess the infallibility of the Bible in our times? It all depends on whose word you choose to believe—the word of the critics or the word of Christ. Christ never expressed any doubt about the reliability of God's Word. He accepted it at face value. He never warned against placing our full confidence in its message. Listen to what He said: "Verily I say unto you, Till heaven and earth pass away, one jot or one tittle shall in no wise pass away from the law, till all things be accomplished" (Matt. 5:18).

Anyone who downgrades the Bible had better remember that he can count on no support from Christ. Our Lord's position is clear: "Scripture cannot be broken" (John 10:35). In all things on which the Bible claims to speak,

it speaks without error. There is nothing misleading or deceiving about it. You can follow it with confidence for it will never lead you astray. The infallibility of the Bible means that it is trustworthy—worthy of our trust.

Anyone who opens the Bible looking for errors had better reexamine his motives. Anyone who thinks he has found errors in the Bible may be sure he is looking with the wrong kind of glasses. This should stop us in our tracks. For all of us are tempted to pass judgment on the Bible from our twentieth-century scientific points of view. But this is not fair. For while the Bible gives guidelines for our study of science, it is not itself a scientific document. Nor should we expect the Bible to speak with mathematical precision or to tell its story according to present-day standards of historical exactness. The Bible speaks to us in the language of the times in which it was given. Therefore we must always pray: "Lord, teach me to read thy Word aright." For it is not the words and syllables in themselves, standing in isolation, for which the Bible claims infallibility. But as His listening children we hear the voice of our God speaking to us in the Scripture within the living flow of its total message.

So here is one Book that will never lose ground. It will unfailingly stand you in good stead as you reflect on your Christian faith. Take it with you as your faithful guide in Christian living.

34. THE BIBLE AND THE CREEDS

There is an old worn-out slogan that goes like this, "No creed but Christ!" Scrap all the creeds, it means to say, for they are only human statements. Christianity is just a personal relationship with Christ. So forget about truths. Just give us *the* Truth. Away with all doctrine. Ban all confessions. Make Christianity a personal experience. Eliminate instruction. —That's the anti-creedal line of reasoning that some Christians take.

Such talk sounds pious. But actually it filters out the words of Jesus Himself and discounts the plain teachings of the Bible. Besides, this slogan is self-contradictory. For to say "No creed but Christ" is itself a creed.

Any church that intends to be a truly confessional church (standing up for its faith) and a truly confessing church (witnessing to its faith) must take its creeds seriously. This is clear from the word "creed" itself. It comes from the Latin word *credo,* which means "I believe." No Christian is worth his salt if he is not willing to stand up and say, "This I believe." And no church is worthy of the name Christian if it fails to proclaim for all to hear, "This we believe." That's the language of the Apostles' Creed.

Down through the centuries the Christian church has rallied round the banner of the Apostles' Creed—the most ecumenical or universal creed in the world. For nearly two thousand years this creed has stood as the most enduring symbol of Christian unity. Our church shares this confession of faith with countless other Christian churches around the globe. Standing solidly within this long and deep tradition is what makes a church truly ecumenical.

Besides the Apostles' Creed, our church also confesses its faith in three other creeds that arose in the time of the Reformation—the Belgic Confession, the Heidelberg Catechism (with its shorter version, the Compendium of the Christian Religion), and the Canons of Dort. All these creeds serve two main purposes in the life of the church. First, they serve as confessional ties to bind us together in the Christian faith. Second, they serve as a creedal basis for our Christian witness to the world.

The question arises again and again: what kind of authority should we attach to our creeds? Some people view them as nothing more than historical documents which come down to us from the past, which we should keep safely in our church libraries as reminders of what Christians used to believe. Others view them merely as forms to be used in the liturgy—that is, valuable parts of our worship services. Still others view them as infallible decrees of the church which are as binding on the consciences of Christians as the Bible itself.

None of these views can stand the test of Scripture. Some make too little of the creeds; others make too much of them.

SOME MAKE LITTLE OF THE CREEDS...

OTHERS MAKE MUCH OF THE CREEDS...

I WISH I COULD MAKE SOMETHING OF THEM...

As Reformed Christians we use these creeds as confessions of our Christian faith because they are faithful summaries of the teachings of the Bible. They are restatements of the central truths of God's Word to meet the needs of our day. As such they are reliable standards for faith and life. But they should not be used as substitutes for the Bible. Nor may we ever place them above the Bible. When we recite the creeds, including the Catechism (which contains the Apostles' Creed as a creed within a creed), we mean to say to each other and to all our fellowmen: *"credo"*—"This I believe," and *"credimus"*—"This we believe," because this is the truth of the Bible.

35. THE APOSTLES' CREED

Names sometimes prove to be quite misleading. Maybe this is true for you when it comes to the Apostles' Creed. Chances are you are so familiar with the name "Apostles' Creed" that you never really think of what it means. Why is this creed adorned with the name of the apostles of Christ?

Have you ever asked yourself that question? Well, what's your answer? Take a guess. Was it because the apostles wrote it? Was it because they handed it down to the church? Or what?

Your guess is probably about as good as the general opinion that prevailed in the church for many centuries. Generation after generation the story of the Apostles' Creed was told in the following way. At the time when persecutions broke out in Jerusalem the twelve apostles gathered in the upper room for their final meeting. Very soon, they realized, they would be scattered around to different countries. So, standing at the parting of the ways, they decided to draw up a creed as their last will and testament for the churches. There were twelve apostles. So each of them contributed one article of faith. Thus the twelve articles of the Apostles' Creed were born.

That's a very appealing story, isn't it? It seems almost cruel to have to explode it. But honesty demands that we tell it like it is. Careful study shows that this story was one of the many medieval legends that held an honored place among Christians for a long time. But that is not the way it went.

The facts of the case seem to be that the Apostles' Creed was built up gradually piece by piece from about the second to the fifth century. In its earliest form it was probably a very simple confession of faith in the Trinity, "I believe in God, the Father, the Son, and the Holy Spirit." It kept this trinitarian form through all the stages of its development. But as the church faced new questions that called for new answers, and as heresies arose in the life of the church, one new element after another was added to fill in the church's confession of faith. Finally, about the turn of the fifth century, the finishing touches were added. Since then it has been used by churches everywhere in the form in which we know it today.

Perhaps you still find the older story more appealing. I don't really blame you much. Except, of course, that we have to face reality. But you may continue calling it the Apostles' Creed in the sense that it reflects the *teachings* of the apostles.

More important is what the Apostles' Creed has to say to us and for us today. So let's turn to that now.

36. OUR TRIUNE GOD

About fifteen and a half years ago you were baptized. That was one date you didn't miss. Your parents saw to it that you got to church on time. I guess you don't remember that red-letter day in your life very well. But the past few years you have been a witness to many baptisms. As you recall, the key words in baptism—yours too—are a confession of faith in the great One-in-Three and Three-in-One: "I baptize you into the name of the Father and the Son and the Holy Spirit."

The whole Apostles' Creed is built up around this testimony to the triune God. The truth of the Trinity also holds a prominent place in the Catechism and the Compendium. It's enough to take your breath away: one God, living and active in three Persons! Down through the centuries Christians have looked hard for illustrations of the truth of the Trinity: illustrations such as past-present-future, faith-hope-love, father-mother-child, root-tree-fruit. Even the three points in a sermon! But the Trinity is not an invention of the church. Nobody in the world could have come up with an idea like that. We would never have come around to confessing our faith in God as Father, Son, and Holy Spirit if God had not revealed Himself to us that way.

So with that we are back to the Bible. In speaking on the doctrine of the Trinity, as on every other point of Christian doctrine, we must try to say no more than the Bible says, for that is speculation; and we must say no less than the Bible says, for that results in a weakening of God's Word.

In the Old Testament the central emphasis falls on the oneness of God. "Hear, O Israel, Jehovah our God is one Jehovah" (Deut. 6:4; Mark 12:29). God had to bring this truth of His absolute uniqueness to the attention of His people as a constant reminder, because Israel found itself among pagan nations who superstitiously served more gods than all their priests and people could possibly remember. Recall the altar Paul found in Athens dedicated "to an unknown god," which was meant to cover any forgotten deity. There were gods of spring and summer and winter, gods of earth and sky and sea, gods for the sun and moon and stars, holy cows and sacred reptiles. Repeatedly Israel had to choose between Jehovah and the Baals, Molochs, and Asherahs that were worshiped by the world of that day. One of the important by-products of the Babylonian captivity and of Israel's scattering among the nations was that the monotheism of the Jewish religion (belief in one God) helped to break down the awful polytheism (belief in many gods) of the ancient world.

In the Old Testament, therefore, the message rings forth clearly: Jehovah God stands all alone. But He is not lonely. From all eternity He was there, living, planning, working as a fellowship of three divine Persons —Father, Son, and Holy Spirit. The light of this truth begins to dawn already in the Old Testament. That's why Jesus and the apostles could appeal to it in support of their testimony that both Christ Himself and the Holy Spirit are truly God, together with the Father. The Old Testament was the Bible of the Jews; therefore the Jews too could have seen the beginnings of this truth of the Trinity, if only they had had eyes to see and ears to hear. Note Psalm 33:6: "By the word of Jehovah were the heavens made, and all the host of them by the breath of his mouth" (where "word" is a preview of the Word-become-flesh, and "breath" suggests the Wind of Pentecost). Note also Isaiah 61:1: "The Spirit of the Lord is upon me . . . ," where the Spirit and the Father stand out clearly, and later Christ applies the "me" to Himself (Luke 4:18, 21).

The truth of the Trinity is clearly portrayed in the fuller light of New Testament revelation. Still there are those who deny that God is Three-in-One—such as Liberals, Unitarians, and Jehovah's Witnesses. We can only conclude that they are guilty of twisting the teachings of the gospel to fit their false, preconceived notions about God. So Jehovah's Witnesses are not witnesses of the God of the Bible at all. They are witnesses of man's attempts to be wiser than God's Word.

Look at the biblical evidence. At the baptism of Jesus at the Jordan River the Spirit descended in the form of a dove and the Father identified Jesus with these words, "This is my beloved Son, in whom I am well pleased" (Matt. 3:16, 17). In giving His apostles the great commission, Jesus told them to baptize believers "into the name of the Father, and of the Son, and of the Holy Spirit" (Matt. 28:19). Paul gave his apostolic benediction to the church at Corinth in these words: "The grace of the Lord Jesus Christ, and the love of God, and the communion of the Holy Spirit, be with you all" (II Cor. 13:14).

You will look in vain for the word "trinity" (tri-unity) in the Bible. This word was first used by the church father Tertullian about A.D. 200. But the truth of the Trinity is firmly rooted in the Bible. Therefore, in the face of various heresies, the early church confessed the doctrine of the Trinity in clear-cut terms at several early ecumenical councils, Nicea (A.D. 325), Constantinople (A.D. 381), and Chalcedon (A.D. 451). You should take time to read the Nicene Creed and the Athanasian Creed.

The gospel of salvation stands or falls with the truth of the Trinity. Without God the Father there would be no Christmas, for He gave His

Son as our Mediator (John 3:16). Without God the Son there would be no Easter, for He arose for our justification (Rom. 4:25). Without God the Holy Spirit there would be no Pentecost, for He was sent to be our Comforter (John 14:16).

It's a matter of practical Christianity. We come to the Father through the work of the Son, and we come to the Son through the power of the Holy Spirit, who comes to dwell in us as His temples (I Cor. 6:19).

It's a matter of personal Christianity and of communal (group life) Christianity. We confess our faith in God the Father and our creation, God the Son and our redemption, God the Holy Spirit and our sanctification.

37. THE FATHERHOOD OF GOD

I can't read your mind. So I don't really know what you think about your father. Ten years ago you probably thought he was the greatest guy in the world. Ten years from now you will probably look upon him with great respect. But right now?

A prison chaplain was talking with a teen-age convict about God as Father. The youthful prisoner became very angry. "If God is a Father like my old man—the drunken brute!—forget it!" Earthly fathers often spoil for their children the image of the heavenly Father.

Jesus talked about both the sunny and shady side of fatherhood. To His disciples He said, "If ye then, being evil, know how to give good gifts to your children, how much more shall your heavenly Father give the Holy Spirit to them that ask him?" (Luke 11:13). Standing face to face with hypocrites, however, Jesus openly called them children of their rightful father, the devil, who is the father of lies and murders (John 8:44).

The Bible holds a high view of earthly fatherhood. Earthly fatherhood is called to be a reflection of the fatherhood of God. In this life, therefore, fatherless children become the special objects of God's care. As adopted children of God, we learn to pray, "Our Father who art in heaven . . . ." We also learn to confess, "I believe in God the Father . . . ."

The fatherhood of God is the central thread running through the first article of the Apostles' Creed, as explained by the Catechism and the Compendium: the eternal Father of our Lord Jesus Christ . . . is my God and Father for Christ's sake. Being my almighty God, He is *able* to help me. Being my faithful Father, He is also *willing*.

God is Father in three different, yet related, ways.

First, He is the eternal Father of Christ, the Son of God. There never was a time when God was not the Father. This goes beyond our understanding. As young people growing up, we hope in a few years to become parents. But God is Father from everlasting to everlasting. So He has plenty of experience in fatherhood, without playing the game of hit-and-miss or using the trial-and-error method. He is the perfect Father. So you never have to doubt His fatherly love and care.

Second, God is the Father of all creation. Think of the vast universe we read about in astronomy books, the realms of outer space, and all the unknown worlds beyond—it's all "my Father's world." He is the Maker and Sustainer of every atom. So remember that "though the wrong seems oft so strong, God is the Ruler yet." Nothing can slip out of His control. As the popular spiritual puts it, "He's got the whole world in his hands . . . ."

Third, in a special way God is the Father of all Christians. We all started out in life as prodigal sons and daughters. But the Father sent out Jesus Christ to track us down, to bring us back home, to take us back into His family. Now that we are back in our Father's family circle, now that we have the mind of Christ (Phil. 2:5-11), we have a new "Father image." He asks us to serve Him in obedience as reliable children and counts on us to do our part in His church and kingdom.

38. OUR CREATOR GOD

"In the *beginning* . . . ." Nobody knows exactly when the beginning was. It stands there in the opening verse of the Bible as a dateless date at the very dawn of time. But one thing is sure: however long ago this universe came into existence, God was there. He made all things. He was behind everything that came into being. He made the first move.

> Before the mountains were brought forth,
> Or ever thou hadst formed the earth and the world,
> Even from everlasting to everlasting, thou art God.
>
> Ps. 90:2

"In the beginning *God* . . . ." That's the way the Bible breaks the "good news." It doesn't waste time on introductions. Nor does it lift a finger to prove the existence of God. Nor does it make a case for the possibility or probability of God. Nor does it define the nature of God. Nor does it even state that there is a God. God *is*—that's the major basis on which the whole Bible rests. For once we've heard the voice of God speaking tc us from the cross, what further need is there for proofs and arguments?

Once we've seen Christ, we have seen the Father (John 14:9). The Creator of the world is our Father for Christ's sake.

"In the beginning God *created* . . . ." Perhaps you have some creative ability in art or music or poetry. But this is altogether nothing compared with the artistry God displayed in putting together our world. Talk about originality! Ours is only a dim reflection of His. Once there was "nothing" —"nothing" at all, "nothing" but God. Then, like a massive surge of electrical energy, lights started blazing everywhere!

Of course, there were no observers there to watch in breathless amazement. There were no eyewitnesses—at least no ordinary people. Just three Persons—the Father, the Son, and the Holy Spirit. And a little later, swirling choirs of angels (Job 38:4-7). God didn't have to call in outside help. He created the world on His own, by the Word of His power, the Word that became flesh in Christ Jesus, the Mediator of all creation (John 1:3). A catechism book used by a former generation asks this question, "What does it mean to create?" The answer: "To make something out of nothing by the act of an omnipotent will." Such things belong to God alone.

"In the beginning God created *the heavens and the earth.*" This statement makes you want to sing doxologies with the psalmist:

When I consider thy heavens, the work of thy fingers,
The moon and the stars, which thou hast ordained; . . .
O Jehovah, our Lord,
How excellent is thy name in all the earth,
Who hast set thy glory upon the heavens!

Ps. 8:3, 1

Genesis makes just a passing reference to the creation of the heavens— the nearer heaven of wind and clouds, the farther heaven of galaxies and outer space, and also that heaven which is the special dwelling-place of God Himself. Then Genesis turns its full attention to the earth, the development of its raw materials into a finished product, the rise of the plant and animal kingdoms, and finally the making of man as the crown of God's creation.

Genesis 1:1—unfolded step by step above—gives us the central theme of God's creating work. This theme is then worked out as seven acts (days) in the drama of creation. In the great theater of the universe, God—as the Director of the drama and the leading Actor in it—displays His powerful creative artistry. Late in the drama, man makes his entrance on the stage of history. But before it's all over, man is drawn into the act and is given a significant supporting role as co-worker in God's creation.

Looking back on His mighty work, God said, "It is very good" (Gen. 1:31). At the close of six days of creation, unwearied, yet desiring a change of activity, "God blessed the seventh day, and hallowed it; because that in it he rested from all his work which God had created and made" (Gen.

2:3). Built into the original structure of things is the divinely established pattern for our weekly cycle of worship and work.

39. THE GOD OF PROVIDENCE

The God of creation is also the God of providence. For the Maker of the universe never deserts the works of His hand (Ps. 138:8).

The closest you come to the word "providence" in the Bible is in Genesis 22:8: "God will provide . . . ." But the reality of this truth is written large on every page of the Bible—even in the Book of Esther, though it never mentions God. And it fills every chapter of our lives. Our word "providence" comes from the Latin word *provideo,* which means to look after something, to care for someone. That "someone" is you and me and all men. That "something" is everything in the world. Even the falling of a sparrow and the loss of a hair from our head are under the watchful eye of our Father (Matt. 10:29, 30). Such biblical faith gives strength and direction to our lives. When men refuse to confess "My times are in thy hand" (Ps. 31:15), they still see God's providence in action, but they call it destiny (Hitler) or natural law (atheism) or the law of probability (scientism).

God's work of providence picks up immediately where His work of creation leaves off.

That's the way the Catechism tells the story. It talks about creation and providence in a single breath. Creation flows over naturally into providence. "In the beginning"—at the very first split-second of creation—providence goes into operation. Creation, both in its origin and in its continuation, is wholly dependent on God. The world cannot run on its own power, as though it were a clock wound up and then left to tell its own time (deism). Moment by moment every force in the universe and every spark of life in the world is upheld by the everlasting arms of our Father. "O Jehovah, thou preservest man and beast" (Ps. 36:6).

The original acts of creation often seem far removed from our world of experience, hidden in the mists of ancient history. But actually that's not true—our beliefs about creation determine our view of God and man and the world here and now. We usually feel, however, that providence is much closer to our everyday lives—as close as the air we breathe, the food we eat, the clothes we wear. Looking at all these things we confess as Christians that they come to us, not by chance or by a stroke of good or bad luck (secularism), but from the fatherly hand of our God (Matt. 6:30-34).

Providence is not a problem to be solved by processes of logical thought. It's our solid starting point for Christian living, an article of Christian faith. For only by faith can we know God's hand in history and sense His guiding presence in our lives.

The inner workings of God's providence come into sharp focus in the experiences of Joseph. To his father he was the favorite son, to his brothers the dreamer, but to God he was the preserver of His people. In Joseph's life we see the providence of God breaking through the sinful acts of men

76

—those of his brothers, Potiphar's wife, the chief baker, the chief butler—bending evil into good. Looking back on his ups and downs, the victim-who-became-a-victor puts his whole life story into perspective in these words, "You meant evil against me; but God meant it for good" (Gen. 50:20).

In the light of the Joseph episode, read thoughtfully Questions and Answers 26, 27, and 28 of the Catechism. It's all there—our full confession of faith in the providence of God and all its rich meaning for our lives. The language is incomparably beautiful. The wording is lifted directly from the pages of the Bible itself. Now it is our task to translate our faith in the providence of God into attitudes and actions that honor Him as King of our lives. Try this: think of yourself as Joseph and look at your life in the light of his.

40. MIRACLES

Do you ever wonder where our sense of wonderment went? Our world is bursting with amazing happenings—moon shots, heart transplants, live television from the other side of the globe via tel-star—and we take it all in stride. Yet all these inventions are just discoveries of powers and applications of laws that God built into the universe from the beginning. For centuries these great potentials for good and evil have been out there waiting to be explored and developed.

But what if a real miracle were to happen? Would that fill us with wonder? Would we even recognize it as a miracle? There's a lot of talk nowadays about "miracle drugs." But isn't this just a figure of speech?

Well, what are miracles anyway? We all have a pretty clear feeling that we know what miracles are, but when we are asked to answer the question in clear words, we find this most difficult. How could it be different! Here we are, mere creatures of time and space, trying to account for God's supernatural work in the world.

The place to start is by listening to the words of this song: "It took a miracle to put the stars in place; it took a miracle to hang the world in space; but when He saved my soul, cleansed and made me whole—it took a miracle of love and grace." Salvation is the greatest miracle known to man.

As the Compendium says, miracles are for the purpose of *redemption*. That involves you and me as Christians, the whole Christian community, and God's world which Christ is busy redeeming. Miracles are also for the purpose of *revelation*.

This much is clear: miracles, like all God's acts, are part of His providential care for the world. The Bible never makes a sharp distinction between the natural—the things that happen according to the ordinary operations of the laws of nature—and the supernatural works of God in history. Actually there is nothing "natural" in anything God does. All His works are wonderful, powerful, meaningful. That holds for miracles. But it holds no less for God's ongoing control of the whole order of creation (Rom. 1:20; Col. 1:16, 17).

Miracles are special acts of God that rise above the laws of nature. Frequently they were performed to counteract the forces of evil in the world and to overthrow the pretended powers of false gods. For example, think of God's mighty hand in the history of Egypt in the ten plagues. Miracles demonstrate in dramatic ways God's intervention in human affairs for the benefit of His people.

Miracles are linked to faith: they call forth faith, they are performed in response to faith, they aim at strengthening faith. That's why Jesus refused to show spectacular signs as displays of sheer force, just to satisfy the curiosity of unbelieving bystanders (Matt. 12:39). He always looked for a faith that was ready to embrace His mighty deeds (Matt. 15:28). His works and His words, His miracles and His message go hand in hand (Mark 6:5, 6).

The prophets and apostles also performed miracles. But always in the name and power of Another (Acts 3:12-16). Jesus, however, displayed His power with personal authority (Mark 2:9-11)—yet always in dependence upon His Father (John 5:19).

The central miracle in the Old Testament was the exodus, of which Israel was reminded year after year in the Passover. This miracle of the exodus—the deliverance from Egypt—finds its fulfillment in the outstanding miracles of the New Testament: the supernatural birth, resurrection, and ascension of Jesus Christ. It is especially the Easter miracle that stands out in the gospel. For without this greatest of all miracles, our faith is empty (I Cor. 15:17).

So you still want a miracle? The place to start is by looking at Christ and what He has done in your life. For the resurrection miracle must find its counterpart in our lives today. As Christ was raised from the dead, so we also are raised to newness of life in Him (Eph. 2:4-6).

41. JESUS: "NO OTHER NAME"

"What's in a name? A rose by any other name would smell as sweet." The feelings that gave birth to these words, penned by Shakespeare, crop up continually in our lives. A name is just an ID or identification tag to distinguish one person from another, a label, a mass-produced number on a punch card to run through a computer. Names tell us nothing about the personality of people. They just serve some practical purposes—such as calling cards to identify visitors, and nameplates to keep your belongings from falling into other people's hands.

Your name, for example, probably says nothing meaningful about your character. Perhaps it's a name that has been in your family for several generations. More likely your parents chose it simply because they liked it or it happened to be popular at the time you were born. Maybe there are several young folks with the same name in the school you attend, or at church, or among your relatives. Confusing, isn't it?

In Bible times, however, people took names more seriously. They tried to find names for people, as well as places and things, that would say something important about them. One boy was called Moses because he was "drawn from the water." Another was called Samuel because he was "asked of the Lord." A certain early Christian named Joseph was renamed Barnabas because he proved to be a "son of encouragement" (Acts 4:36 RSV).

A name was a revelation of the nature of the person bearing that name. To put it stronger, the name *was* the person. To take someone's name in vain was therefore an act of character assassination. No wonder the Bible warns us against taking God's name in vain! What we do to His name we do to Him. This is true of Jesus too. There is something very special about His name.

We know that many people in the Bible failed to live up to their names. Absalom means "son of peace," yet in reality he was a disturber of the peace in David's family and in the nation. Judas means "God be praised," yet how he dishonored God!

With Jesus it is different. At Jesus' birth, Joseph and Mary didn't have to choose a name out of a long list in a book. The angel who announced His birth gave these instructions, "Thou shalt call his name Jesus, for it is he that shall save his people from their sins" (Matt. 1:21; Luke 1:31). And angels don't make mistakes. "Savior"—that's what the name Jesus means. And that's who He is: the Savior of the world. He fulfilled that name perfectly, something no one else could do.

Not that Jesus was a brand-new name, coined especially for Him. No, this name linked Him with Israel's forefathers, showing once again that He is the fulfillment of the whole Old Testament. For "Jesus" is the New Testament form of the Old Testament name "Joshua," which means "God saves." This name was certain to bring to the mind of every believing Jew the memory of the earlier Joshua who led Israel into the promised land of Canaan and the later Joshua who led the exiles of Israel out of the Babylonian captivity back into their homeland. Both of these rescue missions pointed forward to the saving work of the New Testament "Joshua."

Jesus was our Lord's personal name. Mary probably used this name in scolding the twelve-year-old Jesus in the temple, and in calling Him in to dinner. It was a rather common name among the Jews. In a town the size of Nazareth there were probably about twenty boys running around with that name. So sometimes, perhaps, Jesus too got mixed up with others. But that's why He came into the world: He became like us in all things, including His name. He became involved in all our down-to-earth human affairs, so that He could really take our place. Nothing human was foreign to Him.

Now we understand the words of Peter in his sermon before the Sanhedrin: "For neither is there any other name under heaven, that is given among men, wherein we must be saved" (Acts 4:12).

Jesus, the *only* name! Many view this as the great stumbling block in the Christian religion. "Why so exclusive?" they say. Or, "Don't be so narrow-minded! Sure, Jesus made a great name for Himself. But so did many others in the world. Don't tell me that Christianity has exclusive rights to salvation!"

But the logic of the Catechism rings true to Scripture. Either Jesus is not a complete Savior—and then we must look for other saviors besides him: patron saints, for example, or guardian angels, or self-sacrificing martyrs, or our better selves. Or else He is what He claims to be, the one and only and perfect Savior (John 14:6; Heb. 7:25). Really, it's not a hard choice to make, is it?

There's no doubt about it: "The church's one foundation is Jesus Christ, her Lord . . . ." He will not share His name with any other.

42. CHRIST: "THE NAME ABOVE EVERY NAME"

The apostle Peter was a born leader. He overshadowed his brother Andrew by far. Still, it's wonderful to be an Andrew. For Andrew was one of the first to follow Jesus. He quickly recognized Jesus' true identity. Then he dashed off to find Peter and introduce him to Jesus. Listen to Andrew's words: "We have found the Messiah (which is, being interpreted, Christ)" (John 1:41).

Our Lord's *personal* name is Jesus, Savior. His second name is Christ, the Messiah, the anointed One. This is His *official* name, His title, which describes His position of authority and the office He holds.

It's something like the nameplate on the office door at school: D. R. Henry, Principal. Or the sign on the big door in the city hall: J. B. Peters, Mayor. You see, Mr. Henry has the right to serve as principal because he was appointed to that position by the school board. And Mr. Peters has the right to act as mayor because he was elected to that position by the citizens. Otherwise neither Mr. Henry nor Mr. Peters could speak with authority.

So also with Jesus. He is not a free-lance operator, going off and working on His own as some religious leaders do today. He was chosen, appointed, and sent out by His Father to do His work in the world. He was a Man under orders. He came not to do His own will, but the will of His Sender (John 6:38). For His name is Christ. This links Him with the Messianic hope of the Old Testament. This is His office. This gave Him the authority and power to establish His kingdom. This official name, Christ, covers everything our Lord did under His personal name, Jesus.

In Bible times men were installed in special offices in a ceremony of anointing with oil. This happened to Aaron, David, Elisha, and others like them. In line with this practice, "God anointed Jesus with the Holy Spirit and with power" (Acts 10:38). No one else could share His anointing. So also, no one else can bear the name Christ. For "God gave him the name which is above every name; that in the name of Jesus every knee should bow, . . . and that every tongue should confess that Jesus Christ is Lord, to the glory of God the Father" (Phil. 2:9, 10).

Christ holds a single unique office. But as a prism splits a single beam of light into several rays, so we recognize in Christ's one central office of Mediator several special offices—those of Prophet, Priest, and King. All three special offices exist in one Person, indivisible, in unified interaction, embracing Christ's whole life. As *Prophet* He proclaims His *kingly* message with all the compassion of His *priestly* heart. As *Priest* suffering on the cross He testifies in a *prophetic* way, and with *kingly* authority He opens the door of Paradise to a repentant sinner. At the time of His *kingly* ascension to glory, as a *Prophet* He gives His apostles their marching orders, and as a *Priest* He lifts His loving arms in benediction over that little nucleus of the early church.

Is it any wonder that Christians prize the name of Christ so highly and call themselves by His official name?

43. CHRIST: OUR PROPHET, PRIEST, AND KING

If the Master walked into town today and people stopped to ask Him, "What's your name?" what do you think He would answer? Would He use figurative language like "I am the Good Shepherd," or "I am the Door," or "I am the Alpha and the Omega"? All these, and many more like them, would be true names. Such names are recorded in the Bible. But chances are, people would shake their heads at such names and walk away.

I think Jesus would probably hit the modern man-on-the-street with the straightforward answer, "I am Jesus Christ"—His personal name and His official name.

Let's take a little closer look at His name as Man-in-office—Christ, the Messiah, the anointed One. He is Prophet, Priest, and King, all in one Person.

This threefold office comes to clear expression in the way men reacted to the life and work of Christ.

After the "Amen" at the close of the Sermon on the Mount, the crowd buzzed with excitement. They were astonished at Jesus' masterful teaching for, as they said, "He teaches as one who has authority, not as the scribes" (Matt. 7:28, 29). Yes, Christ is the Prophet, and we are His disciples.

When Jesus walked up to John the Baptist at the Jordan River, John exclaimed, "Behold, the Lamb of God, that taketh away the sin of the world!" (John 1:29). Jesus is the Priest, and we are His redeemed people.

Out of the calm after the stilling of the storm we hear the awed cries of the disciples, "Who then is this, that even the wind and the sea obey him?" (Mark 4:41). Jesus is the King, and we are His servants.

Let's dig into each of these three special offices of Christ a little more deeply.

Christ is our chief *Prophet*. An ordinary prophet is one who speaks *for* God. But Christ speaks *as* God. A prophet *speaks* God's Word. Christ *is* God's Word in the flesh. All the Old Testament prophets, right down through John the Baptist—as messengers, spokesmen, and ambassadors of God—all of them came to a head in Christ. Moses' prediction, "The Lord thy God will raise up unto thee a Prophet from the midst of thee, of thy brethren, like unto me" (Deut. 18:15), came true in Christ (Acts 3:22). But in their stubborn unbelief the Pharisees would never admit this. In a spirit of reluctant courtesy they condescended to call Him Rabbi. But they would not go an inch further. The truth of God incarnate? Blasphemy! A false prophet! That's all these critics could say. This fatal mistake is being kept alive by Modernists who prattle about Jesus as the "great teacher," but nothing more. They would never confess Him as the Truth personified.

Christ is our only *Priest*. A priest is one who sacrifices and prays for His people. Take Abraham, for example, climbing Mount Moriah with the wood and the fire and his son Isaac. His heartrending duty stared him in the face: he was to take his son, his only son, whom he loved, and offer him as a sacrifice. In a surprise ending, as you recall, God provided a substitute. But the real substitute came nearly two thousand years later, almost on the same spot, when God sent His Son, His only Son, whom He loved, to take the place permanently of Isaac not only, but of Abraham, and of all believers (Matt. 3:17; John 3:16). During those long centuries between Abraham and Christ, wave after wave of priests offered drove after drove of animals on Jewish altars. But the once-for-all sacrifice of Christ brought an end to all those rivers of blood (Heb. 7:26, 27; I Pet. 1:19)—with this added dimension, however: that Christ was both priest and offering at the same time (Heb. 9:14). Upon this firm foundation Christ now carries on His priestly prayers for all His people (John 17:20).

Christ is our eternal *King*. Rulers are servants of God. They are responsible to God for the exercise of their God-given authority. They are called to rule for the welfare of their people. In Israel and Judah many kings were far from this ideal. One after another, in wearying succession, the rulers came and went, until finally after the captivity the days of the kings were numbered. Yet God preserved the line of the house of David. So in the fullness of time Christ, the Son of David, came into the world as Lord of lords and King of kings. In the power of His royal triumph at Easter, He now rules in the hearts and lives of His loyal subjects. He defends us in the salvation He earned for us.

But His rule is even bigger than that. He holds the scepter of world government in His hand. Yet He rules as a Shepherd who lays down His life for the sheep; as a King who became poor to make His people rich; as the Prince of peace. His kingdom has already come, but it is also still coming; one day it will come in all its glory. We can therefore pray with confidence, "Thy kingdom come." But then we must also be prepared to put our prayers into practice by seeking our place in the program of His coming kingdom.

44. CHRISTIANS AS PROPHETS, PRIESTS, AND KINGS

Do you hold any office—in your class, perhaps, or in your society at church, or in your club, or band, or choir? There are special offices in each of these organizations. But there is one office we all hold—the office of Christian.

Our Lord's official name is Christ. He bore this name in fulfilling His public office as our chief Prophet, only Priest, and eternal King. Now He calls us to be His prophets, priests, and kings. For we share in His anointing by the Holy Spirit. Christ does His threefold work *for* us and *in* us. Not that we take over His three offices. But Christ does exercise His threefold office *through* us. That's what it means to be a Christian. And that's why we talk about Christian homes, Christian churches, Christian schools, Christian publications, Christian labor organizations—all these activities serve as channels for exercising our office as Christians.

83

The name Christian is pretty commonplace nowadays. But it got off to a strange start. The story goes back to the city of Antioch in the days of the apostles. It was there that believers were first called Christians—not Jesuits, not Disciples, but Christians. These early believers apparently made so much of Christ that the citizens of the city dubbed them "Christmen"—which was intended as a title of scorn. But the believers accepted it as a title of honor, and so it stuck. That's how we inherited the name Christian.

By the time of the Reformation, however, the church had pretty well forgotten that being a Christian means holding a threefold office. The Roman Catholic Church of that day was sharply divided into clergymen and laymen. Only the priests were viewed as holding an office. Thus most Christians were robbed of their sense of Christian calling.

The Reformation set out to recapture the biblical view of all Christians as prophets, priests, and kings. The men of Heidelberg set forth this truth clearly. As prophets we are called to confess the name of Christ, as priests to offer ourselves as living sacrifices of thanksgiving, as kings to "fight the good fight of faith" (I Tim. 6:12) and thus to reign with Christ forever.

The church at Antioch not only *bore* the name Christian, but *lived* it too. As prophets they were active in evangelizing their neighbors (Acts 11:20-26). As priests they demonstrated the compassion of Christ in collecting funds for the needy in Jerusalem (Acts 11:27-30). As kings they sent forth the first missionaries to conquer the world for King Jesus (Acts 13:2, 3). They went all out to exercise their office as Christians on the home front in Antioch. This equipped them for front-line duty in the forward march of Christianity throughout the world.

Today, too, our official name is "Christian." As Christians we all hold an office. It should be clear, then, that there is no room for second-class citizens or for third-rate members in the Christian community. Being a prophet, priest, and king covers every situation in life. Antioch is our example. It's just a matter of *becoming* what we *are*. We *are* Christians, aren't we? Well then, we must increasingly *become* what we *are*—Christians, in our whole way of life.

45. CHRIST OUR LORD

A quick look will convince us that there are all kinds of children in God's family. Some pretty rare characters too. Some that we might not expect to find there. Yet God's family room is never over-crowded. And there is still plenty of room at His dinner table. You want to know roughly how many children there are? Well, go to the beach and let the sand run through your fingers. Can you count the grains? Or scan the skies on a starlit night. Can you count their hosts? Well, God tells us that His children shall be more in number than all these (Gen. 15:5). And remember, these are all adopted children. Yes, God's adoption laws are wide open for children of all races, colors, nationalities, and dia-lects. For to all who believe He gives "the right to become children of God" (John 1:12).

THOSE CHRISTIANS ARE SURE STRANGE ♫

But look carefully. One Child is in a class all by Himself—God's natural Son, His "only begotten Son." This Son towers head and shoulders above all the adopted children. In fact, He opened the door to let the adopted children in. Yet "he is not ashamed to call them brethren" (Heb. 2:11). Who else could this be but Christ our Lord? How wonderful it is to have such an older Brother as our Guardian and Friend!

In praying to our older Brother we often say, "Lord Jesus . . . ." But do we really understand what we mean when we say that He is both our Lord and our Savior? For often we behave too little like children of God, and too much like children of our times. False notions of democracy have a way of rubbing off on us. We blurt out, "Nobody is going to lord it over me!" But this is really a form of rebellion. For this Lord has every right to rule in our lives, and He also rules us through the authority of parents, teachers, ministers, judges, police officers, and government officials.

We may ask, how did Christ gain His lordship? In the past some men became lords over others by birthright. Others got this power as a gift. Others bought it. Others took it by fraud. But Christ became Lord of lords in a unique way. He earned this right by scoring a decisive victory over all the enemies that stood in His way—sin, death, the devil, and hell. By freeing us from the stranglehold of these evil powers, He made us His pos-session. Now we belong to Him. He paid the full price to make us His brothers and servants. With Thomas, the only true response we can make to Him is to say, "My Lord and my God!" (John 20:28).

We are His double possession, you see. First, it was He who made us. Then, after we became lost in sin, He found us and bought us back. We are actually twice-born people. Christ has a double claim on us. So when the devil tugs at your heartstrings, tell him off: "You have no right to me, for I belong to Jesus!" In the house of our lives the devil is still a nasty tenant in the back room, who often goes on a rampage. But Christ is the Landlord. It is He who gives the orders.

The price of ownership that Christ paid was so high that money couldn't touch it. How we ought to ask God to forgive us for acting as if the mighty dollar can buy anything in the world! For here is something more precious than silver or gold. And it's a gift; you can't buy it. After all, the best things in life are free—free for all, except for Christ. He carried the price of blood on His head.

But now Christ is Victor. The devil is fighting a losing battle. He doesn't give up easily. He keeps launching his counterattacks. But it's a lost cause. For Christ has bound the strong man and spoiled his goods (Matt. 12:29). He Himself saw Satan fall as lightning from heaven (Luke 10:18). The power of darkness has been broken. Christ wields all authority in heaven and on earth (Matt. 28:19). The final campaign is underway. But Christ is still calling up recruits to fill His ranks. There is still time to enlist.

So the choice is clear. Either unbelief which says, "We will not that this man reign over us" (Luke 19:14). Or belief which says, "Lead on, O King eternal!"

46. THE MYSTERY OF CHRISTMAS

If a visitor from some distant world were to drop in on us at Christmas, he could hardly avoid the impression that we want to turn it into a gay event, and that we are ready to spend ourselves to the limit to keep it that way—a yuletide spectacular, with pageantry and parades, toys and tinsel. We turn on the glittering lights for all the world to *see*. Is there anything of the mystery of Christmas left for us to *believe?*

What a generation gap from the first Christmas to ours! Look through the eyes of the shepherds. There He is, Son of David and Son of God, born in the lowliness of a backyard building, amid the stench of a stable warmed only by the breath of oxen—no room for Him in the inn. Little wonder that many early Christians forbade the celebration of Christmas. They hated to think of the misery and shame that our sins had heaped upon our Lord.

It's a strange combination when you think of it: Christmas—God's greatest *compliment* to man, for look how much He loved us; yet Christmas also reveals God's greatest *condemnation* of us, for see the awful depths of humiliation to which Christ had to descend to save us.

In Israel the arrival of a first-born son was viewed as a great status symbol. But not with this son! Perhaps many assumed that He was an illegitimate child, and it is not difficult to imagine the wild rumors, the staring eyes, the whispers, and the scoffing that attended His birth. Mary herself— the virgin mother—would feel the sharp edge of a sword piercing her soul as public opinion questioned who the father of her child might be.

But this was God's way of working salvation at the crossroads of history. Coming up out of the Old Testament times was that long unbroken line of descendants going all the way back to David and Abraham and even to Adam (Matt. 1:1-16; Luke 3:23-38). Time after time the "great red dragon" (Rev. 12:1-6) tried to prevent the coming of Christ—Pharaoh's conspiracy to drown the Jewish boys, Saul's javelin hurled at David, Athaliah's attempted purge of the house of David, Haman's plot against the Jewish race. Often it was a narrow escape. But God kept the line of Christ alive until Christmas in Bethlehem, "for salvation is from the Jews" (John 4:22). Then and there it happened, the hope of the world, the fulfillment of Isaiah 7:14: "Behold, a virgin shall be with child, and shall bring forth a son, and they shall call his name Emmanuel" (Matt. 1:23).

This was God's way of becoming man without ceasing to be God. The Spirit who was active in creation (Gen. 1:2) now became active in an overshadowing way for our re-creation (Luke 1:35). In Jesus' birth God bypassed Joseph, so that the full emphasis might fall on the mystery of the incarnation as God's sovereign act of salvation.

For us this means total coverage from the cradle to the grave—and even beyond. Christ's sinless birth covers even our sinful entrance into life. Not that sex is sinful in itself. It is God's good way of reproducing human life. But sex, too, has fallen under the corrupting power of sin. Therefore marriage as life's most endearing relationship cannot be our salvation. In Christ's birth, God stepped in to overcome sin by the overshadowing power of the Holy Spirit in the life of the virgin Mary. The virgin birth points out, however, not only how different Christ is from us in His sinlessness, but especially how much He is like us in all things in His true humanity. He was "born of a woman" (Gal. 4:4). That's how down-to-earth Christianity really is.

So "thanks be to God for his unspeakable gift" (II Cor. 9:15).

47. HAIL, MARY!

"Hail, Mary, full of grace, the Lord is with thee. Blessed art thou among women, and blessed is the fruit of thy womb, Jesus. Holy Mary, mother of God, pray for us sinners now and in the hour of our death. Amen."

Ever heard that before? Millions of Roman Catholics offer this prayer daily. Their broadcasts beam it across the country. Catholics regard Mary as the holiest of all the saints. Therefore, they worship God through her, and pray to Christ through her. Veneration of the "Forever Blessed Virgin" has grown mightily in our times. This has been called the "Century of Mariology," the climax of nearly two thousand years of doctrinal development. Two of the most important highlights along the way came in 1854, when the Vatican declared the doctrine of the Immaculate Conception of Mary (that Mary was born without an earthly father), and in 1950, when a recent pope declared the doctrine of the Heavenly Assumption of Mary (that Mary was taken bodily to heaven).

In view of these beliefs we must face the question, What role does Mary play in the Bible? Many of the words in the Catholic prayer to Mary are found in the angel's announcement of Christ's birth. But there is a world of difference between an announcement and a prayer.

The angelic messenger sweeps Mary off her feet with these words, "Hail, thou that art highly favored, the Lord is with thee" (Luke 1:28). In humble obedience Mary accepts her place in God's plan with these words, "Be it unto me according to thy word" (Luke 1:38).

Mary is indeed a saint, as every believer is a saint. But more than that, we honor her in a special way because of her great faith, her simple obedience, her wonderful part in the plan of God. We gladly join all generations of Christians in calling her "blessed" (Luke 1:42, 45, 48).

MARY IS BOTH SAINT AND SINNER. THAT MAKES ME FEEL BETTER ♫

But like every believer, Mary is both saint and sinner. She had to be cleansed by the same blood as we. Often she too was very slow of heart to follow her Son. She found it very hard to exchange the mother-son relationship for a relationship in which she was called to trust Jesus as her Savior and Lord. At twelve years of age Jesus had to remind His mother that she could serve Him best by cutting the apron strings and giving Him the freedom to go about His Father's business (Luke 2:49). At a critical point in Christ's career, His family apparently became concerned about His state of mental health and physical well-being. They tried to exert a special claim upon Him. But Jesus told them to seek their place within the ranks of His disciples. "Who is my mother? And who are my brethren? And he stretched forth his hand towards his disciples, and said, Behold, my mother and my brethren! For whosoever shall do the will of my Father who is in heaven, he is my brother, and sister, and mother" (Matt. 12:46-50).

Mary misunderstood Jesus whenever she tried to stand on His side, over against mankind, to help Him. She finally understood Him only after learning at the foot of the cross to stand with us on the side of sinful mankind (John 19:26, 27). In the early church, Mary and Jesus' brothers found their place within the circle of Christian believers, joining the one hundred and twenty in awaiting the promised outpouring of the Spirit (Acts 1:14).

Our Christian comfort, therefore, lies not in extolling Mary's virtues, but in blending our voice with hers in singing her doxology, "My soul doth magnify the Lord . . ." (Luke 1:46).

An early church council called Mary the "mother of God." Roman Catholics view this as good ground for their adoration of Mary. The point of this council, however, was not to highlight the holiness of Mary, but to declare the true humanity of Christ. Christ is central. We cannot divide our allegiance between Christ and Mary. We owe Mary honorable mention, for she is a mirror reflecting the glory of Christ. But our hope and trust is in Christ alone.

48. CHRIST'S LIFELONG SUFFERING

It was a mixed group of people around the cross that Good Friday, making their entrances and exits, moving in and out across the stage, playing their roles in the drama of salvation. There you see Judas, Caiaphas, Herod, Pontius Pilate, Peter, Simon of Cyrene, John, Mary, the Centurion, and Nicodemus, to mention only a few. But in it all Christ is central. He is the leading Player, up stage, under the floodlights of God's revelation. It was His hour that had struck.

If ever anyone was born to die, it was Jesus. The darkness that enshrouded Calvary cast its shadow all the way back into Bethlehem's crib. As a child, Jesus barely escaped the mass murder at the hands of Herod's soldiers. He lived as a fugitive. As a twelve-year-old boy He already shouldered the great responsibility of His Father's business (Luke 2:49). In His youth He could hear the thunder of Calvary rumbling along the horizon of His life. An artist has tried to capture on canvas something of Jesus' intense suffering, painting Him as a young man in Joseph's carpenter shop, lifting a beam whose shadow fell across the wall in the shape of a cross. He had to learn the meaning of obedience under a foster parent of whom it could not be said, "Father knows best." This was the way it had to be (Luke 24:26; Acts 2:23, 24). Yet Christ walked the road of suffering willingly.

As He began His public career the passion plot thickened steadily, without relief. Jesus was baptized in the waters of the Jordan, symbolizing His submersion into the filth-laden stream of human iniquity. In rapid succession, within three short years, He experienced the attacks of Satan in the wilderness, the attempt on His life by His townspeople, the unfaithfulness of His disciples, His family's misgivings about His sanity, the hostility of both church and state, the bloody sweat in the garden, the betrayal by Judas, the denials by Peter, the injustices of Herod and Pilate, the mistreatment at the hands of the Roman soldiers, the weight of the cross, the blood-drenched hill, and at the climax of it all the bitter cry, "My God, my God, why hast thou forsaken me?" (Matt. 27:46).

All in all, it's a picture of the Man of sorrows (Isa. 53:3). Yet people in some circles, who fail to read the Bible clearly, have gone out of their way to change this picture, painting instead the picture of a smiling Christ.

I READ ISAIAH 53 : 2-5

THEN I SAW ONE OF THOSE SICKLY, SWEET, SENTIMENTAL PICTURES OF CHRIST...

YOU'D THINK ARTISTS DON'T READ THE BIBLE

A robust, laughing Hero! A noble Crusader who suffered an untimely death! Strangely, though—yet perhaps not so strangely—while the Bible shows Christ weeping, it never describes Him smiling or laughing. Yes, He probably smiled at times, for He was like us in all things. Yet the undercurrent of His whole life was one of ceaseless suffering.

Behold the One who carried the greatest burden of sin in all the world. Christ "bore our sins in his body upon the tree" (I Pet. 2:24). For God "laid on him the iniquity of us all" (Isa. 53:6) and "made him to be sin on our behalf" (II Cor. 5:21). Indescribable, incomparable suffering! For Christ carried upon His back the total weight of God's wrath against all the sins of all God's people of all times and places. We must not think of this as suffering inflicted by a vengeful God upon His innocent Son just to make Christ's life as wretched as possible; rather, we must think of it as a revelation of the justice and mercy of a God who so loved the world that He gave His Son to be the sin-bearer for that world. In the garden, Christ endured affliction that no man could inflict—affliction that only a loving Father could lay upon His Son to satisfy for the sins of His people.

Christ stands all alone as the world's greatest Sufferer. For all our suffering is really nothing next to His. For Him there was no mercy, only justice, so that for us there might be grace abounding to the chief of sinners. No one could lighten His load, neither the comforting angel in the garden nor Simon of Cyrene carrying His cross. The humiliation of it! A thirty-three-year-old Man unable to carry His own cross as other criminals did! Even His divine nature did not ease the burden; it only supported His human nature so that it would not collapse under the awful pressure, thus making possible an infinite sacrifice. For every ounce of strength Christ received, another ounce of toil was added, until the full wages of sin had been paid, to the last penny.

How shall we respond? Pity will not do. What Christ wants is our love, our faith, our obedience, our all (I Pet. 2:21).

49. PONTIUS PILATE

By what right does a spineless, weak-kneed judge like Pontius Pilate deserve a place in the Apostles' Creed? Ever stop to think of that? We have no trouble giving honorable mention to Mary. But Pilate! That's another story—even though it's only dishonorable mention. Why take this infamous name upon our lips Sunday after Sunday?

Well, remember first of all that Pilate is there for the sake of Christ. We are not making a confession of faith about Pilate. Rather, we are confessing our faith in Christ who suffered under Pontius Pilate. Pilate has no value in himself. In his own way—like Mary—he is a mirror reflecting the saving work of our Lord.

There are two points we must keep in mind.

First, this reference to Pilate reminds us that God's plan of salvation in Christ did not happen in some imaginary world. No, Christ's suffering for us is tied down to a definite time and place and person in history. Christianity is based on fact, not fancy. It is as real and down to earth as a Roman court of appeals with a jellyfish judge.

Second, Pilate represents a human court of justice, the voice of world law passing judgment on Jesus. Courts are ordained by God to uphold righteousness and give every man his due reward (Rom. 13:1-4). But what a judgment this tribunal handed down! What a mockery of justice! The mobs on the street, whipped into a frenzied state of mass hysteria, exploding with their blood-curdling cry, "Away with him! Crucify him!"—these are enough to shake one's confidence in popular democratic rule.

But that the Roman court of justice should declare this Man guilty and sentence Him to death after finding Him innocent—this shows how little legal standing Christ had in the halls of human justice. He was denied a fair hearing. Even the Roman court, the best legal institution of the day—so good in fact that people today still study Roman law—made Jesus the victim of a terrible miscarriage of justice. See how the collective sin of mankind overtook Jesus with awful vengeance? And don't forget, Pilate's guilt is ours too. Just think of how often we try to compromise with the Truth, as he did.

Courts of justice are God's appointed way of defending the rights of the innocent, so that the strong shall not trample on the weak. In recent years our courts have gone a long way to assure the rights of the accused. But when Jesus had His day in court, justice was blind.

I'M GLAD I DIDN'T HAVE TO GO TO COURT IN CHRIST'S DAY...

Sensitive Jews, even at this late date in history, have offered to reopen the case of the people versus Jesus. They want to go over the trial, and right the wrongs. Such noble gestures, however, fail to plumb the full depth of the judgment that fell upon Christ's shoulders. For behind the savage condemnation of the crowd and behind Pilate's cowardly indecision we must also hear the voice of divine judgment.

O mystery of redemption! For God's judgment agrees with man's—but for reasons which are worlds apart. Listen, the Father breaks His silence: "You, My Son, are guilty! I concur in Pilate's judgment. I, too, sentence You to death. Remember, You came to earth for no other purpose than to give Your life a ransom for many. Though You are sinless, I made You to be sin for all My people. Your undeserved guilt makes up for their well-deserved guilt. To the cross, My Son!" (Mark 10:45; II Cor. 5:21).

50. THE OLD RUGGED CROSS

Some Christians tend to turn the cross into a popular status symbol. Roman Catholics make the sign of the cross. Protestants wear little golden cross-pins on their coat lapels. Hippies build their peace symbols around the cross.

Sometimes we glamorize the cross. We come close to worshiping it. We sing, "In the cross of Christ I glory . . . ." We may indeed translate our faith into music in these words borrowed from Paul (Gal. 6:14), but we had better know what we are saying. We must see something of the awful meaning of the cross for Christ before we confess its glorious meaning for us.

In our day the tide of public opinion is turning strongly against capital punishment. In Bible times, however, the death penalty was common and public execution of criminals was general practice. Whenever men forget God's law, life becomes cheap and death quick and easy.

Crucifixion as Christ suffered it is a horrible way to die. But keep this in mind, Christ died our well-deserved death. And He did this by suffering the slowest, cruelest, most agonizing form of death the Roman world had devised—the death of the cross.

Today the death penalty is meted out by a firing squad, or a gas chamber, or an electric chair. In the ancient world it was different. Greeks used a drink of hemlock (Socrates). Jews used stoning (Stephen). The cross was a typically Roman form of execution. Roman citizens, however, did not suffer such disgrace. Death by the cross was reserved for slaves and outlaws.

In the eyes of the Bible, the cross represented the height of God's curse upon human sin. A Jew who committed a crime worthy of death was usually killed by stoning and then his body was hung on a tree until sundown (Deut. 21:22, 23). Paul later quoted this law as a pointer to the Christ of the cross: "Cursed is every one that hangs on a tree" (Gal. 3:13). Christ took this curse upon Himself, turning the tree into a cross.

Of course, the important thing is not the cross itself: the history of the world has seen thousands of crosses. Nor is the important thing that Christ endured a lifetime of cross-bearing: thousands of Jews can testify to such suffering. Nor that an innocent Man died on the cross: crosses have taken the lives of other innocent victims too. It is the Christ of the cross who counts. The "old rugged cross" basks in the reflected glory of Christ who there "humbled himself, becoming obedient even unto death, yea, the death of the cross" (Phil. 2:8). With the cross as His pulpit Christ proclaimed, "It is finished!" (John 19:30), meaning "Debts paid in full" and "Justice fully satisfied."

No wonder the gospel is called the "word of the cross" (I Cor. 1:18). No wonder Paul was determined to preach nothing but "Christ crucified" (I Cor. 1:23; 2:2). And no wonder cross-bearing is a leading mark of Christian discipleship (Luke 14:27; Mark 8:34). The middle cross on Calvary's hill was unique. It was a once-for-all cross. The crosses we bear for Him stand in the shadow of His cross for us. We must remember this when we are called to suffer for righteousness' sake (Matt. 5:10). Our crosses derive their meaning from His. And this is our comfort: if we bear the cross of shame we shall also share the crown of glory.

51. THE LAST ENEMY

Have you ever been to a funeral? Have you ever looked death in the face, ever looked down into a grave? I mean in person, not on TV. Surely you have at least walked through a cemetery.

The experience of death arouses sadness in our hearts. But for Christians there is comfort too—a smile that breaks through our tears. For Christ has met death ahead of us. He has conquered death and the grave.

A funeral is for real, and we all know it. We may try to make a corpse look lifelike and dress it up with flowers. Yet we all need to recognize that death is the final effect of our sins (Gen. 2:17). The prophet says, "The soul that sinneth, it shall die" (Ezek. 18:20). And Paul adds, "The wages of sin is death" (Rom. 6:23). The grave is for real, but it is not for keeps. Christ conquered it! So now we can look death in the face defiantly and say, "O death, where is your victory?" (I Cor. 15:55). The grave is our *last* enemy. But it is not our *worst* enemy. Sin is that. But we have a Friend who has broken the power of all our enemies. He gave us new life and put a spring into our step. So now death is not the worst thing in

I JUST DON'T LIKE TO THINK ABOUT DEATH...

IT'S SO, SO, SO, SO ......

SO PERMANENT...

the world. The worst thing is life without Christ—for that means death without Him too.

The Catechism says that Christ was buried to prove that He was really dead. Well, that's true. Before a burial some public official must sign a death certificate. So, upon the testimony of the soldiers, Pilate assured himself that Jesus was really dead before giving permission to Joseph of Arimathea and the other disciples to take down the body of Christ from the cross and lay it in a tomb (Isa. 53:9; Mark 15:42-47).

To this day, however, skeptics still try desperately to peddle their theory that Christ merely fainted on the cross and so was later revived again. If they are right, then the power of this last enemy is still unbroken. Then death has still not lost its sting (I Cor. 15:55).

But the gospel record is clear. Christ really surrendered His spirit to His Father (Luke 23:46). His body was really dead; it was wrapped in real linen, and was laid in a real tomb. A real rock was rolled to the mouth of a real cave. The Catechism is right about Christ being really dead.

But there is more to it than that. Christ paid the "high cost of dying" in full. He suffered the wrath of God for our sins. Our well-deserved judgment—"Dust thou art and to dust shalt thou return" (Gen. 3:19)—fell upon Jesus. His conquest of this last enemy means that we were buried with Him through baptism into death, that we might be raised with Him in newness of life.

But if Christ overcame this "last enemy" (I Cor. 15:26), why must we still die? There is something haunting about that question. We cannot settle it to our full satisfaction. For Christians, death is still serious business, because sin and its effects are serious business. But we have been released from paralyzing fear. For death has died—death in the sense of condemnation and separation from God. True, we must still experience the separation of soul and body. But the sting of death is gone. For the sting of death

94

is sin, and the strength of sin is the law. But he who believes on Christ "hath eternal life, and cometh not into judgment, but hath passed out of death into life" (John 5:24). If we could see those who have gone on before, we would hardly recognize them, so little are they dead anymore. For they live with Christ in glory. And for us who remain on this earth the prospect of physical death is actually the firm hand of God's grace, to make us come across to His side by means of one last hard pull.

For the believer, death is no longer a penalty to be paid. For Christ has paid the full penalty of sin for us. It is rather the last stopping-off point, the final bridge on the road from grace to glory. And remember, Christ crossed the bridge ahead of us and He will cross it with us. In that day we will discover that there is nothing left to fear beyond the grave. For what lies before us is a full and perfect life. In the cemetery we see the sign of Jonah, who went down and under but came up again; and in Jonah we look to Christ; and then we lift two fingers in a "V for Victory" sign! As for those who have died in the Lord, we do "not grieve as others do who have no hope. For since we believe that Jesus died and rose again, so also, through Jesus, God will bring with him those who have fallen asleep" (I Thess. 4:13, 14 RSV).

52. YOU ARE MY WITNESSES

The truth of the gospel is on trial in our world. Or rather, all men stand on trial before the truth of the gospel. We Christians, therefore, are called to take the witness stand, place our right hand on God's Word, and testify to the reality of Christ's redeeming work.

You remember the monument Israel erected along the bank of the Jordan, as they entered the promised land of Canaan. There on the river bank the leaders set up twelve large stones. In the future, when the younger generation would ask, What do you mean by these stones? the people of Israel were to bear witness by repeating the mighty acts of God (Josh. 4:1-7).

A few years later the twelve tribes set up another altar along the Jordan, this time to settle a heated dispute among brothers. They called the altar "Witness." For as they said, "It is a witness between us that the Lord is God" (Josh. 22).

Centuries later in the continuing struggle between Jehovah and the foreign idols, God reminded His people, "You are my witnesses" (Isa. 43:10). It was Israel's often forgotten duty to stand up in a pagan world and declare by word and deed that Jehovah is God, and He alone, and that idols are just imaginary gods.

In the New Testament Christ draws upon these same words in sending His disciples into the world: "You shall be my witnesses" (Acts 1:8). The Greek word for *witness* is the same as the Greek word for *martyr*. Christian martyrs, like Stephen, were witnesses to the saving work of Christ. But let's not stop at that. Every Christian is a witness.

Witnesses are people who have seen and heard something important and who then stand up and say, "We know this is true." Of course, we are not firsthand witnesses of the ministry of Christ. But we have the trustworthy record of the life, death, burial, and resurrection of Christ from the first-hand witness of the apostles. They were actually there. They saw it happen. They heard it personally. In the New Testament they tell it like it is. Our witness is rooted in theirs.

Today, still, the whole world is a courtroom. There are still false witnesses who stand up to deny the claims of Christ. Therefore we as Christians, in all kinds of ways, must take the witness stand, and under the solemn oath of the gospel, testify by word and deed that the benefits of Christ's work in our lives are real. We know these things from experience. Christ was crucified, and we were crucified with Him to break the terrible power of the old man of sin in our lives. Christ was buried, and we were buried with Him, so that evil desires may no longer hold unbroken control over our lives. Christ arose, and we arose with Him, so that we may now offer our lives as sacrifices of thanksgiving in obedience to Him.

In the words of the spiritual: "Were you there when they crucified my Lord? Were you there when they laid Him in the tomb?" Yes, I was there. For my sins nailed Him to that accursed tree. I was deeply involved in it all. I know it from experience. The benefits of Christ's suffering are for real. I am His witness. Come, and I will tell you what the Lord has done for me! (Ps. 66:16).

53. THE DESCENT INTO HELL

In 1917 the French freighter Mont Blanc exploded after a collision off the coast of Canada. Seventeen hundred men lost their lives. One of the few survivors, reflecting on his rescue, made this comment, "I guess there wasn't room enough in hell for me that day."

People who outlived the attack on Pearl Harbor in 1941, or the Nazi concentration camps of World War II, those who have endured the terrors of modern warfare since then, as well as those who are hopelessly sunk in the frustrations of ghetto life, often describe their experiences as "hell on earth."

We understand something of that kind of language. Nevertheless, hell is more than a figure of speech. It's an awful reality. And it happened only once on earth. That was in the living death that Christ went through.

Once we've sensed something of the hell of agony that Christ suffered for us, how can we stand by calmly as men punctuate their sentences with "hell, this" and "hell, that"? They don't know what they're saying! For hell is more than a bad four-letter word. And if you think there is glamor and bravado in that word, you're dead wrong. For hell means existing in separation from Him who is the source of all light and life. It means experiencing forever God's just judgment and wrath.

I USED HELL AS A COOL CUSS WORD...

THEN I WAS TOLD IT MEANT SEPARATION FROM GOD...

THAT SURE TOOK THE FUN OUT OF THAT HABIT...

In the mind of Christ an appropriate symbol of hell was the city dump at Jerusalem (called "gehenna")—desolate, filthy, disease-ridden, worm-infested—where the smoldering fires never died and the low-hanging clouds of dirty smoke made you cough your lungs out (Mark 9:48; Matt. 8:12; 24:51). No wonder the rich man in Luke 16 pleaded for a drop of water to soothe his burning tongue! No wonder Christ cried out in anguish, "I thirst!" For throughout His life He had suffered the torments of hell in growing intensity, until at last all hell broke loose upon Him on the cross, wringing out of Him the bitter cry of forsakenness: "My God, my God, why hast thou forsaken me?" (Matt. 27:46). That's what hell is—God-forsakenness, a total blackout of every last ray of divine favor, the full force of the righteous wrath of a holy God. All this Christ absorbed in every part of His spirit, in every nerve and muscle of His body.

And still the half has not been told. Words fail us. All we can do is to move gingerly along the outskirts and look on from a distance. Only Christ and those who die turning their backs on heaven really know what hell is all about. And now that Christ has conquered hell, we can turn our backs on it for good.

Christ descended into hell for us—this is the way the Apostles' Creed (in one of the last articles to find its way into that creed) expresses His torment. Christians from the fourth to the sixteenth century apparently believed that Christ actually went to the place called hell. The Reformers, however, could find no biblical grounds for this position. So the writers of the Heidelberg Catechism felt compelled to make a choice. They could drop this article from the creed—but that would mean breaking with a long-standing Christian tradition. So they decided instead to pour into this article of Christian faith a new biblical interpretation. Rather than saying that Christ went down to the regions of hell literally, they confessed that hell, as it were, leaped up to envelop Christ on the cross in all its terrors and tortures.

Hell is no joking matter. It's high time that we quit toying around with this kind of fire, that we stop using this fearful word lightly. Why should we Christians burden our vocabulary with a word that has lost its terror for us? For hell can no longer touch us or hurt us. Heaven is our final home—a home Christ has purchased for us.

54. FOR WHOM DID CHRIST DIE?

This question can be answered only in a face-to-face encounter with the gospel of Jesus Christ. The answer is born from experience. For when we say, "I am a Christian," this is an abbreviated way of saying, "Thanks be to God, Christ died for me!"

But are all men Christians? Would to God it were so! This burning desire lives in the heart of God, as it should live in the hearts of all believers. "As I live, saith Jehovah, I have no pleasure in the death of the wicked; but that the wicked turn from his way and live . . ." (Ezek. 33:11). God is patient with men, "not wishing that any should perish, but that all should come to repentance" (II Pet. 3:9). Once we've turned to Christ as our way of atonement (at-one-ment), we too will desire that all men walk with us along that way.

Our daily experience teaches us, however, that not all men seek salvation in Christ.

But now we still face the question: did Christ actually die for all men, even though only those who believe in Him will be saved? Or did Christ die only for believers?

This much is clear, Christ died for *all* God's chosen people. For this is the only doorway to the Christian life. But did Christ die *only* for believers? Or is there some sense in which the Bible leads us to say that Christ also died for the whole world and for all men?

There are passages in the Bible that point toward an affirmative answer to the last question. "For God so loved the world, that he gave his only begotten Son . . ." (John 3:16). "God is the Savior of all men, especially of them that believe" (I Tim. 4:10). "He is the atonement for our sins, and not for ours only, but also for the whole world" (I John 2:2).

It is clear that every blessing in the world comes through the cross of Christ. Thus God keeps His claim on all men. In view of the cross, men are inexcusable for their unbelief. The call of the gospel comes to all men as a command, You must believe! If all men were to obey that call, Christ's atonement would surely be great enough to cover the sins of every last man in the world.

Yet not all men accept the salvation that is offered them in Christ. On his missionary travels Paul experienced that "as many as were ordained to eternal life believed" (Acts 13:48). Before this Christ had said, "I am the good shepherd: the good shepherd lays down his life for the sheep" (John 10:11). Paul describes God's mighty acts of salvation in this way: "Whom he foreordained, them he also called: and whom he called, them he also justified: and whom he justified, them he also glorified" (Rom. 8:30).

When a person takes his place within the Christian community, he can confess joyfully, "Christ died for me!" Such faith puts solid ground under our feet and gives comfort and assurance. For the death of Christ is the power of God unto salvation in the life of His chosen people. Then we may share in the confidence that we stand in a special relationship of love to God and that the special benefits of Christ's atonement are ours.

But the atoning death of Christ is also the source of a powerful witness to our fellowmen. As we brush shoulders with others we can face them with the gospel in these words: "God calls upon you to believe that Christ died for you." In talking with people who doubt the love of God, we may say: "God shows His love for you right now by appealing to you to be reconciled to Him."

The love of God as revealed in the death of Christ is both a standing offer and a standing claim for all men—but it is also a standing ultimatum, or final demand. So, before it is too late for them, we must urge men to come over to the Christian side. "Turn back, turn back from your evil ways; for why will you die?" (Ezek. 33:11b RSV).

55. GOD'S ELECTING LOVE

With the minister's morning mail came this little letter:

"Dear Pastor,

This is the end. I'm done. My faith is gone. But it doesn't matter. I'm a born loser anyway. So I'm calling it quits. Please don't bother to call. It's a waste of your good time. I'll make out somehow.

Sincerely,
Richard."

What's the answer to a letter like that? This: No, Richard, you're not a hopeless case. God still cares. These full-grown seeds of doubt and despair are sown by the devil. As Luther said, the devil is at his worst when he climbs up on your shoulder and whispers his taunting words into your ear, "So you think you're a Christian? Forget it!" But remember, Richard, God is greater than all your desperate doubts. So give the tempter the big brush-off: "Begone, Satan!" For your life has a firm foundation— God's electing love. In Christ there is a way out, a way to find assurance and security and comfort.

I LIKE THE SECURITY OF MY NEIGHBORHOOD

I guess that one of the things we all want most in life is a sense of security. A feeling of insecurity is a terrible thing. Most of all, we need to be sure where we stand with God. Peter impressed this point on his fellow-Christians with these words: "Wherefore, brethren, give the more diligence to make your calling and election sure: for if you do these things, you will never stumble" (II Pet. 1:10).

But how do we find such security? After all, popularity can wither. Health can fail. Friendship can go sour. Education cannot guarantee security. Wealth can be wiped out by inflation or depression.

When all is said and done, the only thing you can count on to see you through the ups and downs of life is the unfailing grace of God. Christ is God's chosen Savior (Luke 9:35). And in Christ, God elects us from before the foundation of the world to be His children (Eph. 1:4). God will never go back on His decision. Even when we give up on life, God never gives up on us.

> The work Thou hast for me begun
> Shall by Thy grace be fully done.

Election involves great privilege but it also involves great obligation. Not only did God choose us so that He could give us the highest dignity that can be given and benefits beyond imagination, but He also claims us for Himself. And He asks that as debtors to His love, we bear the fruits of loving service in His kingdom. Christ reveals this clearly to His disciples: "You did not choose me, but I chose you, and appointed you, that you should go and bear fruit, and that your fruit should abide" (John 15:16).

We could never earn this great privilege. Salvation-unto-service is anchored securely in God's unmerited favor to us, His undeserving children. It's a good thing God did not wait for us to make the first move,

for we would have made the wrong move. So God stepped in and took the initiative. Now, if we love Him, it's because He first loved us. God chooses us, and He remains faithful in His decisions, even when we are unfaithful and stumble through life.

> When I fear my faith would fail,
> He will hold me fast;
> When the tempter would prevail,
> He will hold me fast.

God's electing love is the solid ground for our security and comfort. For if God chooses for us, who can choose against us? Who can bring any charge against God's elect people (Rom. 8:31-35)?

This reassuring truth is a central theme running through every chapter of Bible history. The entire message of the Old Testament is based on the belief that Israel takes its place among the nations as God's chosen people. In a world filled with idolatry, God reached out and chose Abraham to become the father of believers (Isa. 41:8-10). Years later God intervened in the life of Egypt to call out the children of Israel to become a chosen people (Ps. 105:6, 43; Acts 13:17). In an overwhelming act of grace God set His love upon Israel (Deut. 7:6-8), so that their election might become a source of blessing to the whole world. For in choosing Israel (Hos. 11:1), God was really looking forward to His choice of Christ (Isa. 42:1), and in Christ God chose the members of His church (I Pet. 2:4-6).

So now we are called to settle the question of security in our lives by a face to face encounter with Jesus Christ. He is "the mirror of our election" (Calvin). You want to be sure about your life? Then look into the Mirror! As Christ chose His disciples to serve as founders of the church (Luke 6:13), so He now chooses the church for loving service in the world.

When people lose sight of the fact that election is God's way of personalizing His love to us, they turn this source of comfort into a fearful doctrine. God, they say, treats us like pawns on the chessboard of divine fate. For our eternal destiny is determined even before we see the light of day. There is nothing we can do about it. Thus men speculate wildly about God's eternal decrees. Or they sidestep the truth of God's electing grace, as though it were a dark cloud hanging like a threat over our lives, blocking out the sunlight of God's love.

HOW CAN A GUY BE SECURE AND STILL LOOK IN A MIRROR

But such thinking is not true to the Bible. It robs us of the security that Christ came to bring into our lives.

So never turn election into a "new problem" that must somehow still be solved after the question of faith in Christ is settled. Christ is the final answer to every question in our lives. What we do with Him settles the question of election. For if we trust in Christ as our Savior from sin, then we may be assured that His love for us is eternal.

He chose us, in Christ, before the foundation of the world (Eph. 1:4), and none shall pluck us out of His hand (John 10:28). Election means that we owe all that we are to Him, for as Paul said, "By the grace of God I am what I am" (I Cor. 15:10). And it means, further, that we will return His love in lives of grateful service.

Postscript: As you recall, the Heidelberg Catechism was written to promote unity between Lutherans and Calvinists in Germany. But because the Lutherans had difficulty with the truth of God's election, the men of Heidelberg soft-pedaled this biblical teaching to avoid offending the Lutherans. In a passing way the Catechism calls Christians "chosen" people in Questions and Answers 52 and 54. The Compendium, arising later out of a Reformed community, helps us fill in this gap in the Catechism.

56. EASTER POWER

It's a power-hungry world we live in. Millions live by the creed, "Might makes right." Look at the lineup: Black Power, White Power, Student Power, Flower Power. Paul cuts through this massive power play with the Christian alternative: "That I may know Christ, and the power of his resurrection" (Phil. 3:10). Easter Power is the Christian's victory. It offers the only real hope for true peace in the world.

What's the good of Christ's resurrection? This: it puts into our hearts and on our lips a song that soars with these joyous words:

> Love's redeeming work is done,
> Fought the fight, the battle won;
> Death in vain forbids Him rise,
> Christ has opened Paradise. Alleluia!

This note of victory is the heartbeat of the gospel. It turned men who were ready to go back to their fishing boats, defeated, into enthusiastic fishers of men. It gave the disciples a new lease on life and set free in their lives the power of a kingdom program that went out to turn the world right-side

up. What made the difference? Not the failure of Christ's followers to find what they expected—a dead body—but their coming face to face with the risen, living Lord. He was still the same, their Savior and Lord, like them and us in all things human (except for sin)—but now glorified!

The resurrection is one of the most well-attested facts in history, confirmed by hundreds of witnesses. Yet even in those days "some doubted" (Matt. 28:17). Thomas took the position that "seeing is believing," until the Christ who overcame death also overcame his doubt (John 20:27). At first all the disciples brushed aside the early reports of the women at the tomb as idle talk (Luke 24:11). The soldiers on guard at the tomb took bribes to pass the rumor that "his disciples came by night, and stole him away while we slept" (Matt. 28:13). Greek thinkers extolled the immortality of the soul, but mocked the resurrection of the body (Acts 17:32).

Christianity, however, is unique in that it takes the body as well as the soul—the whole man—seriously, simply because God does. The incarnation, reaching its climax in the resurrection, proves this beyond the shadow of doubt.

In spite of this, however, some early Christians still tended to downgrade the importance of the body, and therefore questioned the reality of the resurrection. To meet this challenge Paul fills a whole chapter, I Corinthians 15, with careful, convincing arguments for Christ's resurrection and ours. Literally everything depends on Christ's triumph. Because of lingering doubts and disputes, however, the church later confessed its faith clearly in the Apostles' Creed: "I believe . . . [that] the third day he rose again from the dead." Yet to this very day liberals talk easily and superficially about a resurrection faith, without a resurrection fact. The modern poet, John Updike, states the biblical case pointedly in these words:

> Make no mistake: if He arose at all
> it was as his body;
> if the cell's dissolution did not reverse,
> the molecules reknit,
> the amino acids rekindle,
> the church will fall.

Thomas Jefferson left us a Bible with every reference to the divine power of Christ scratched out. Why he did this is not clear. But the results are clear. For then the gospel ends on this note: There then—in the tomb— they laid Him (Luke 23:55). If that is all, then as Paul says, "we are of all men most pitiable" (I Cor. 15:19). Then we may as well close up shop and quit playing church.

But the goal of the Christian faith is not death, but life—life abundant here and now, and life eternal.

The story is told of a schoolteacher's son who had died. The next Sunday was Easter, and the teacher was in church. Afterward, at home, one of her young students said to his mother, "The teacher believes, doesn't she?" "Believes what?" asked the mother. "You know, the story of the resurrection and all that," replied the boy. The mother answered, "But, of course, we all do." To which the boy responded, "Yes, but the teacher *really* believes it."

Christ was "raised for our justification" (Rom. 4:25)—to justify our joy and hope, to justify the spring in our step and the smile on our face. For Christ is risen—He is risen indeed!

57. OUR ASCENDED LORD

What's the best you've done in high-jumping? Four feet? Five feet? Six? The world record is over seven feet. What makes high-jumping so challenging is the formula, $s = \frac{1}{2} gt^2$, which expresses scientifically the law of gravity—a built-in law of God's creation. This law is what keeps the furniture in place and makes walking possible. It's also the basic rule of the game in baseball, ping-pong, basketball, and such sports.

As you recall from Genesis, man was given the task of ruling over all creation. In spectacular ways we are now busy overcoming the magnetic drawing power of the earth. Hundred-mile orbits, moon shots, a probe toward Mars and Venus—what next?

From all these space explorations, unbelievers are already drawing their conclusions. Since none of the astronauts or cosmonauts has located heaven, faith in the Christ of the ascension—so unbelievers say—is just a myth.

How narrow-minded and shortsighted can you get!

No, we're not sure just where heaven is. But we know this: it's part of God's created universe. We don't understand fully what "up-there" or "out-there" or "down-here" means. But we do have the straightforward testimony of eyewitnesses who were there on Mount Olivet when Christ ascended. This is the way it happened: "As we were looking, he was taken up; and a cloud received him out of our sight" (Acts 1:9). That's why the church sings with confidence: "O Lord, thou hast ascended on high in might to reign" (Ps. 68:18). So, go ahead with all those rocket shots to the planets. In the end, it's still the ascended Christ who "calls the shots" in this whole universe.

Christ chose His own date for the ascension: forty days after Easter. That gave Him the time He needed to demonstrate His resurrection victory and to empower His disciples for their mission in the world. Then the hour of departure struck. Not that the apostles were completely prepared for this event. They still labored under some pretty false nationalistic ideas about the kingdom (Acts 1:6). But Jesus, as it were, says to them: You've got enough to get started; and when the Holy Spirit comes, He will fill in the rest. So be My witnesses! (Acts 1:8; John 16:12-15).

Yes, Christ ascended into heaven. And now what? Out of sight, out of mind? No, that would be impossible. Gone, but not forgotten. For Christ the ascension meant a great homecoming, a great reunion, the day of coronation. And what about the one hundred and twenty disciples in the upper room? Well, what happens to most movements when their leader drops out? Usually that means defeat. But not so here. There in their headquarters they closed ranks. Within their fellowship, expectation mounted. They awaited their promised marching orders. Sometimes, you see, a leader must withdraw in order to develop maturity in His followers (John 16:7).

Christ's ascension is both the great separation and the abiding presence all in one. "I go away," yet, "Lo, I am with you always, even to the end of the world" (Matt. 28:20). For "where two or three are gathered together in my name, there am I in the midst of them" (Matt. 18:20). Look at the disciples. Instead of being bored, they got busy. Having received the parting benediction from the pierced hands of their Master (Luke 24:48-53), they passed it on quickly from Jerusalem through Judea and Samaria to the farthest parts of the earth.

As the Bible tells us, Christ ascended into heaven bodily. This bodily ascension is a pledge of our complete redemption—a down-payment. The payment-in-full will follow. Christ took our human nature with Him to glory, and He gave us His Spirit in return. That brings heaven a lot closer home to us. For now there is direct contact, daily communication between heaven and earth. Christ's Spirit moves between both realms. Our prayers ascend to heaven and the answers return to us. Our dead go to heaven, but one day they will return when Christ comes back, bringing them with Him. We ourselves are told by the apostle to seek the things that are above, which are not yet on the earth.

Postscript: the Heidelberg Catechism was written for Calvinists and Lutherans in the German Palatinate. They held differing views, however, on the meaning of Christ's ascension. The Lutherans viewed His ascension as a change of condition, rather than a change of location. It was not, they said, that Christ ascended bodily into heaven, but that at the ascension His human nature became everywhere-present, just like His divine nature. So Christ, they explained, is present invisibly, also in His human nature right where you are at this very moment. This view of the ascension is related to the Lutheran view that Christ's real body is invisibly present in, under, and with the bread and the wine of the Lord's Supper.

The Catechism, however, follows the teaching of the historic Christian faith as embodied in the Calvinist beliefs. Do you see now why the Catechism pays so much attention to the meaning of the ascension? The reality of Christ's human nature is at stake. The Lutheran view tends to deify, or ascribe divinity to, Christ's human nature on this one point of omnipresence. If that were so, then we would have no assurance that we are really linked with the real Man, Christ Jesus, in heaven. We would have no assurance that our real selves, our real flesh and blood, are united with a Christ who is really like us in all things—now glorified in heaven.

58. AT GOD'S RIGHT HAND

During most of His trial, under brutal cross-examination and in the face of false witnesses, Jesus kept silence. Hypocrisy, after all, doesn't deserve an answer. But finally, under oath, Jesus revealed His true identity —He is the Christ, the Messiah, the Son of God. With a forward look, He then delivered this telling blow, "Hereafter you shall see the Son of Man sitting at the right hand of Power, and coming on the clouds of heaven" (Matt. 26:64). *At the right hand of God!* That was the breaking-point. Blasphemy! "He is worthy of death!"

Just a few years later Stephen caught a vision of Jesus standing in majesty and power above that cruel scene in which he was involved. Turning to the bloodthirsty mob he testified to this heavenly vision: "Behold, I see the heavens opened, and the Son of man standing *on the right hand of God*" (Acts 7:56). Again, this proved to be the breaking-point. They threw him out of the city. The stones began to fly.

King Jesus—not only *sitting* in majesty, but also *standing* in power at God's right hand! The Jews caught the point of this language. It meant that Jesus was taking over as supreme Commander of heaven and earth. That very thought filled them with uncontrollable rage. For if this were true, then they had still not gotten rid of Jesus. They would have to face Him again as their Judge.

From rags to riches, from peasant beginnings to glory beyond compare— that's the story of Christ's career. He stooped to conquer. Paul develops this theme beautifully in Philippians 2:5-11. Talk about your VIP's (Very Important Persons)! Christ tops them all by the biggest stretch imaginable. And what's best of all, He now rules in glory for us—for you and for me— for the good of His church and for the welfare of the whole world. No, He is not retired or unemployed. He is busy pressing forward the program of His coming kingdom.

So, let me ask, Who runs your church? Your minister? The synod? Some board? Your elders? Or do the people at the congregational meeting run it? Paul sets us straight: Christ is the head of the church (Col. 1:18). He is the policy-maker. Yet He exercises His authority as the Good Shepherd. Ministers are His under-shepherds. In the pulpit, they are servants of God to all God's servants in the pews. In this way Christ shows His special care for His church (Eph. 1:22).

But Christ also calls His church to be a blessing in the world, just as He rules the world for the good of His church. Put them together and you have a picture of His kingdom. God now rules the whole world as His domain through King Jesus, who is "far above all rule, and authority, and power, and dominion, and every name that is named, not only in this world, but also in the world to come" (Eph. 1:21). There is not a single square

THE WAY SOME PEOPLE RUN THE CHURCH....

WOW

I'M SURE HAPPY CHRIST IS THE REAL HEAD

inch of the entire universe of which Christ does not say, "This is mine!" It is our calling to honor that claim and to help make that claim come true wherever and whenever we can.

But don't think that Christ's interests are so big that you as a person don't count. Through the inner workings of His Spirit, Christ adapts and personalizes His blessings to fit all our needs. We are children of the King. Not just to be on the receiving end of things. His benefits call for willing obedience to His commands. For it is in Christian service that we find that Christ defends and preserves us against all opponents. Outgoing Christian service, engaging in labors of love in the name of Christ (Matt. 25:40; I Cor. 15:58)—this is the way to be right-hand servants of our Master. And He will see us through to the end.

59. CHRIST IS COMING AGAIN

I remember well that little old lady waiting at the trolley stop. As she climbed the steps laboriously, the conductor gave her a hand, with the remark, "Lady, you've seen your best days too!" To which she replied, with a twinkle in her eye, "No, sir, my best days are still coming!" She was on the right track.

A certain grocer also had a good sense of what the Christian life is all about. In his store window he put up a little sign with these words: "Live every day as though Christ died yesterday, arose this morning, and is coming again tomorrow."

Christians are people with a forward look. Yes, they also cast their glances back across their shoulders to Christmas, Good Friday, Easter, Ascension Day, and Pentecost—Christ's redeeming work, which happened during God's great day of victory about two thousand years ago. But now we are moving forward toward a still greater day. Looking ahead we see one last red-letter date still open on the calendar of the coming kingdom of God —Judgment Day. By keeping the windows of our lives open to the future, the second coming of Christ, we can also keep the doors of our lives open to the present, always ready for Christian service in the world.

With "uplifted head" we look for our Lord's return. There's no need for long faces. "Maranatha!"—the Lord is coming (I Cor. 16:22). So keep your chin up. Or don't we really live in great expectation? In the past many Christians were filled with an outstretched, tip-toed hope. Congregational prayers often closed on this climactic note, "Come, Lord Jesus, come quickly!" (Rev. 22:20). As a boy, when I heard such prayers, I used to say to myself, "Okay, but not too quickly, Lord, because I've got a lot of living to do yet." Amidst the luxuries and securities of our high standard of living, many Christians act as if our "Great Society" will serve quite well as a substitute for God's "New Order."

Do we really want the new earth under a new heaven? And how shall we get ready for it? As the year 1000 dawned, people were sure they saw the handwriting on the wall. But once the year was past, their fingernail-biting anxiety made way for wild celebrations. Again in 1843 and 1844 William Miller set the date for Christ's return. But it proved to be just another false alarm! Paul had a similar problem on his hands with Christians at Thessalonica (I Thess. 4:1—5:11; II Thess. 2). He reminded them that the way to get ready is by staying at their post and doing their duty. The hope of Christ's return is never an excuse for lying down on the job. It's a stirring call to active Christian living (Matt. 25:31-46). A Christian always keeps an eye out scanning the horizon, looking for the return of his Lord. But he also keeps his mind on the tasks at hand, so that at the trumpet call his Master may find him a faithful servant.

It's not for us to set the date (Acts 1:7). This lies securely in God's hand. But the signs are out—wars, racial tensions, world crises, spiritual indifference, moral decline, anti-Christian spirit (Matt. 24; II Tim. 3:1-5). These, Christ said, should remind us that He is coming again.

That day need not strike fear into our hearts. The coming Judge is our Savior and Friend. But what a difference! No longer is He the Man of

Sorrows or the humble Servant. With irresistible power and unquestionable justice He will right every wrong.

JUST THE MENTION OF A LAST ROLL CALL GETS ME ALL TENSE 🎵🎵

At the moment life runs out, every man faces a personal judgment at God's court of justice. But there will also be a public tribunal at the end of time—a grand climax, a last roll call—when God will openly demonstrate His righteousness and mercy for all to see. There are only two exits leading from that judgment hall, one to heaven and one to hell. The path you take then depends on the decision you make in this life—for Christ, or against Him.

This second coming of Christ as Judge, at the end of time, will be sudden and unexpected. As lightning streaks from horizon to horizon (Luke 17:24), so instantly God's judgment will cut across all the lines of human history. When that last hour strikes, it will strike with unmistakable clearness. So if at any time people say, "Look, He is here!" or "Look, there!" don't bother to check it out. Get on with your calling in life. When Christ returns, you will know it—with absolute certainty.

For His return will be universal in its sweep. It will bring about a renewal of the whole creation (Rom. 8:20-23). All men, the great and the small, those of times present and those of times past—yes, even those who pierced Him (Rev. 1:7)—will face Him as Judge of all the earth (Matt. 25:32; Mark 13:27; Phil. 2:10, 11).

60. THE WORK OF THE HOLY SPIRIT

The spirit of our times is punctuated with question marks. All kinds of time-honored truths seem to be up for grabs. As we live among people

I'M AT A LOSS FOR ANY ANSWERS...

GOD, THE WORLD AROUND ME...

I CAN'T EVEN ANSWER FOR MYSELF

who are at a loss for answers about God, themselves, and the world around them, it's great to be able to say: "I believe . . . in God the Father . . . in God the Son . . . and in God the Holy Spirit."

By ascending to heaven, Christ opened the way for the coming of the Spirit and made room for the Spirit's unlimited follow-up work. But Pentecost was not the Spirit's first work. As we trace the progress of revelation through the Bible, we see the accent falling first on the work of the Father, then increasingly and climactically on the work of the Son, and then, after the fiftieth day, on the energizing and transforming work of the Spirit. This division of labor in the Trinity leads the Catechism to set our sights first on God the Father and our creation, then on God the Son and our redemption, and now on God the Spirit and our sanctification.

Yet even within this triple pattern of divine specialization, there is harmony, cooperation, and unity of effort in all the acts of God from start to finish. The Holy Spirit did not stand by idly, unemployed until Pentecost. From the very dawn of history He was ever on the move as the life-giving principle of creation and renewal (Gen. 1:2; Ps. 104:30), setting things in order and putting on the finishing touches (Ps. 33:6; John 16:13), and continuously recreating the joys of childbirth (Job 33:4). At every turn along the way, we feel His inescapable stirrings at the mysterious depths of human life (Ps. 139:7). He is the breath of God, the glowing fire that kindles a flame in every believing heart, the rushing wind that swept men off their feet at Pentecost. Throughout the Old Testament times He quietly pursued His secret ways (Ps. 51:10-12; 143:10; Isa. 61:1, 2; 63:11; Acts 7:51), awaiting His mighty outpouring on Pentecost Sunday. Today the Holy Spirit is the Christian's "vital breath," his "native air." His work in our lives is the heartbeat of Christian faith and action. In hidden and humble ways, yet with powerful persuasion, His hand in our lives makes us willing to stand up and be counted as disciples of Christ.

Fulfilling the ancient promise (Isa. 11:2), Christ carried out His earthly mission filled to overflowing with the power of the Spirit, from the cradle to the grave (John 3:34; Luke 4:18, 19)—in fact, even before the cradle, for He was conceived by the Holy Spirit (Luke 1:35); and even beyond the grave, for He was raised by the power of the Spirit (Rom. 1:4). The unity between the second and third persons of the Trinity is so perfect that Paul can say, "Now the Lord is the Spirit" (II Cor. 3:17).

The work of the Holy Spirit is a clear pointer to the work of Christ. He stands in the wings, while Christ stands at center stage. The Spirit keeps saying in effect: "Don't look at Me; keep looking at Christ; I am just a Finger pointing the way to Christ and pointing out the way to live for Christ in the world." So any spiritual experience that does not draw us closer to Christ is not an outpouring of the Spirit of Pentecost.

Through the workings of the Spirit within us we are brought into living fellowship with Christ. To be "in the Spirit" is to be "in Christ." But you ask, how is it possible for us to live in unity with Christ, since we live two thousand years after Christ and half a world away from where He lived? The answer is the over-arching bridging power of the Spirit. He links us to Christ. He is the pulsating bond within the body of Christ—the muscles, the nerves, the tendons, binding Christians together as members of the body of Christ. And this happens not through some out-of-this-world, mountaintop experience on cloud nine; no, it happens in the common affairs of everyday Christian living.

This ingoing, ongoing, outgoing power of the Holy Spirit creates a new community of Christians, who are doing the work of the Lord in the world. The Spirit enlightens our minds so that we can test the spirits of our times. He is the power behind the church's proclamation of the gospel. He propels us out into the world to be Christ's witnesses in our daily lives.

You see, Pentecost happened on a particular day hundreds of years ago. Yet it was not a one-day affair. It's for today too—and for always. Once having come to live in the hearts of His people, the Spirit will never forsake us. He never drops His work. All the benefits that follow from His presence in our lives—regeneration, conversion, fellowship, forgiveness, resurrection, and life eternal—all these are living proofs of His abiding presence. Where does His presence show up? In a Christian style of family life, in forgiving each other, in Christian teaching and learning, in public declaration of faith, in being willing to suffer wrong for Christ's sake. All these are evidences of the Spirit. If we dishonor the Holy Spirit, we will be guilty of resisting Him and putting out His fire in our lives. "Do not grieve the Holy Spirit of God, in whom you were sealed for the day of redemption. Let all bitterness and wrath and anger and clamor and slander be put away from you, with all malice, and be kind to one another, tenderhearted, forgiving one another, as God in Christ forgave you" (Eph. 4:30, 31 RSV). Total surrender to the Holy Spirit—that's the secret of power in the Christian's life.

61. REGENERATION

As you grow up, you will find yourself filling in all kinds of forms—registration forms at high school, application forms for jobs, a social security number, driver training, and so on. In these forms there's always a blank asking for your date of birth. That's easy enough—a certain day of a certain month about fifteen years ago.

But now, how about the date of your rebirth? That's not so easy to fill in, is it? Yet that's what regeneration is all about—our new life in Christ. *Generate* means to cause someone to be born. *Regenerate* means to cause someone to be born again. Well, when did that happen to you? When were you "born again"? That's a pretty impossible question to answer. Fact is, no one can really fill in that blank, no one but the Holy Spirit. For regeneration takes place at a level deeper than our conscious mind. It takes place in our innermost heart, when the Holy Spirit creates in us a new life in Christ. Regeneration is the starting point of His great work of salvation in us.

Just as a child cannot remember the moment of his physical birth, so the child of God cannot name the exact hour when he was born again by the Holy Spirit. Both dates escape our memory. Yet they are real. Christians are twice-born people. As Christ Himself said, "Verily, verily, I say unto you, Except one be born anew, he cannot see the kingdom of God" (John 3:3, 7). Just as sin began in the heart of man and results in a living death, so salvation begins there too, and results in a living life.

This salvation that God works in us is not just a little touch-up job. It's a major overhaul. For God never does half-work. In order to make

I KNOW MY NEED...

AND IT'S MORE THAN A TOUCH-UP...

MAJOR OVERHAUL!

us right with God, and set us straight, and put our lives back in order, the Spirit reaches all the way down to our heart of hearts, where things first went wrong. He sows the seed of God's Word in our hearts and sees to it that it bears fruit in a new life of faith and love, of repentance and obedience. That's how the benefits of Christ's work become ours to have and to hold. Christ, as it were, sets up a checking account in our name. The Holy Spirit now draws upon that open account and gives us our daily allowance.

Our whole Christian life is therefore rooted in the renewing work of the Spirit who implants in us the new life that we have through fellowship with Jesus Christ, in His death and resurrection. Without this, we are still "dead in trespasses and sins." But with it, life starts all over again. For Christians, life begins at forty—or thirty—or twenty—or ten! Life in a new direction, in a new spirit! (Col. 3:10).

Although the origin of our new life is hidden from view, it cannot remain hidden for long. For just as the seed sown in good soil and covered over with sand for a while, springs up and cracks the earth's crust to produce new life, so too the power of the new life within us eventually bursts its bounds and demonstrates the dynamic force of Christian principles put into practice (Rom. 12:2).

Footnote: The biblical doctrine of regeneration is not singled out for special attention in the Catechism, as it is in the Compendium. This difference is probably due to the fact that in Reformation times Christian thinkers did not distinguish as sharply as we usually do between the various aspects of God's work of salvation, such as regeneration, repentance, conversion, and sanctification. They viewed salvation as being basically of one piece. This is a truth we may never forget. Otherwise we run the risk of staring ourselves blind at the trees, without ever really seeing the woods as a whole. From beginning to end, salvation is one grand ongoing work of God in Christ through the power of the Holy Spirit. The spark that touches it off is regeneration.

The next point of discussion in the Compendium is conversion. But the Catechism turns to this biblical truth later. So let's wait till then.

62. GOD'S ONE CHURCH AND OUR MANY CHURCHES

How many churches or denominations are there in your neighborhood or in your town? Five, ten, twenty, or more? Now just try adding up all

the churches or denominations that have come and gone over the past two thousand years. Yet we still confess: "I believe one holy catholic church." For in the final analysis, as God sees things, among our *many* churches there is really just *one* church. This universal church embraces the whole body of true Christ-believers all around the world. This is a biblical view that often escapes our attention. We tend to look at the parts, rather than the whole. Only by faith do we catch a glimpse of the full picture.

The permanent foundation for this ecumenical church was laid way back in Caesarea Philippi, when Peter confessed his faith in these words, "Thou art the Christ, the Son of the living God." At hearing this, Jesus' heart must have sung for joy. This confession of Peter's was a high point in Jesus' earthly ministry. In response, He called Peter blessed, for this confession was not the product of human insight, but was born out of faith as a gift of God. Then looking ahead, Jesus added this grand prediction: You are Peter, the Rock, and upon the solid rock of your confession I will build my church (Matt. 16:16-18).

Pentecost was the first big step forward in making that promise come true. The young church made front-page headlines! In one day its mem-

114

bership jumped from one hundred and twenty to three thousand. And the church has been moving forward ever since. Sometimes the going has been pretty rough. Stephen was stoned, James beheaded, Peter imprisoned, Paul executed. But the word of Christ stands: the powers of hell shall never overthrow the church. In every century the blood of the martyrs—those who gave their lives for Christ's sake—became the seed of the church. You as young members of the church are living proof that to this very day Christ continues to gather, defend, and preserve His church. It's great to be on a

winning team. Not that we ourselves picked the right side. God in His electing love takes the first step. He chooses those whom He has ordained to eternal life, giving them grace to repent and to believe on Jesus Christ. The church is truly a chosen company of Christ-believers.

The story of the church of Christ goes back to the beginning. There was Adam, Abel, Seth, Enoch, Noah, Abraham, Moses, David, and the like. By looking forward, these Old Testament saints shared our faith, and belonged with us to the household of Christ-believers. With us they were members of the one holy catholic church that spans all the ages. You see, it's really a never-ending story. For by His Word and Spirit, Christ will not fail to push forward the program of His church until the final curtain falls on world history. All of world history is really kingdom history, with the church of Christ at the center.

In our view of the church, as in everything else, we live by faith, not yet by sight. We *believe* that there is basically one church—but what do we *see?* We see the church torn apart and splintered into a thousand and one almost unrecognizable fragments. Yet above the noise of disagreement we hear Christ's prayer, that Christians may all be one (John 17:21). Christ is calling us to put His prayer into practice by urging us as Christians to draw closer together. We *believe* that the church is holy—but what do we *see?* Sins and shortcomings in terrible abundance. But who ever said the church would be perfect this side of heaven? Saints are only forgiven sinners. We *believe* the church is catholic—universal, worldwide, embracing all of human history—but what do we *see?* Often it looks like a little hole-in-a-corner movement, afraid to show its face on main street, suffering from an inferiority complex. How we ought to pray, "Lord, help us to dream big dreams. And then help us make them come true."

The strength of the church—its oneness, its holiness, its catholicity—rests on Christ alone. Not in its smooth-running organizations, not in its big budgets, not in its good reputation, not in its piety. Our comfort is Christ alone (Eph. 2:19-22). He is the church's one foundation—Matthew 16 again! Take "Christ" out of "Christ-ianity," and what's left isn't worth keeping.

63. THE COMMUNION OF SAINTS

Mr. Stevens was a Christian gentleman. But something went wrong. For years he never showed his face in church. He lived as a loner, seldom mixing with people. One day the local minister paid him a visit. As they sat together in front of the open fireplace, the minister steered the conversation around to every man's need for friendship, fellowship, communion. But nothing he said seemed to make much impression on Mr. Stevens. Finally the minister took the tongs and lifted a live coal from the fire and laid it off by itself on the hearth. Within a few moments it lost its glow and died. This little illustrated lecture got through to Mr. Stevens. He caught the point.

The apostle Thomas had to learn this lesson too. And he learned it the hard way. That first Easter Sunday, when the risen Lord appeared to His disciples, Thomas was absent. We don't know why. But we can imagine him sitting alone in some gloomy corner, nursing his heartaches. At any rate, he skipped church. So he missed Easter. And all because he decided to go it alone.

Man was not made to stand alone in life. None of us is an island. God created us together like branches in a family tree, so that we might support each other, giving strength to each other.

But then sin entered, driving all kinds of wedges between men. When we turned our backs on God, we also turned our backs on our fellowmen. We lost contact. We became bored with each other. We've turned mankind into a lonely crowd. Just read the newspapers: over and over again, people are left in a bad way by their neighbors with the lame excuse, "I don't want to get involved."

But Christ has established a place to bring people back together again. That place is the church. For the church is not first of all a building or an organization. Most of all it is people—all kinds of people, people like you and me, people with problems and hopes and talents. The church is a family affair, a place for God's children to feel at home. It's a friendship house where the welcome mat is always out. It's a circle of friends, a fellowship of believers, a communion of saints. And you know who saints are— forgiven and renewed sinners.

In the company of Christians we learn to keep the law of love by bearing each other's burdens (Gal. 6:2). There Christ gives the gifts of the Spirit —love, joy, peace, patience, hope—so that these gifts may spill over into our homes and schools, our recreation spots and working places. The church is the place to start working out Christ's command to do good to all men, especially to those who belong to the household of faith (Gal. 6:10). Paul lays down the ground rules for putting Christian faith into action in Romans 12:3-13. This kind of fellowship in the life of the first Christian community made a deep impression on the people of Jerusalem (Acts 2:44-47). How does your church measure up by these standards?

Despite all our differences and shortcomings, the unity of the church is simply amazing. In the early church we meet fishermen, tax-collectors, farmers, a doctor, merchants, statesmen, prostitutes, housewives, children. What did they all have in common? Today, too, as we look over the congregation, we see people from all walks of life. Yet there is unity. Not that our fellowship is everything it should be. It's perhaps a little too middleclass, too white, too much of a clique, so that artists and intellectuals, blacks, the down-and-outers and the up-and-outers don't quite feel at home among

us. The call to fuller Christian communion is a challenge we must work at, something that must grow on us and within us and among us. We must more and more grow up into Him who is the head, even Christ. (Eph. 4:15).

64. THE CHURCH AT WORK

There isn't a fish-eye lens wide enough to give us a total view of the whole Christian church, from the inside out, across the centuries, and all around the globe. Only God can capture that full picture in one sweeping glance. And He alone can search our hearts to separate hypocrites and pretenders from true believers.

From our point of view, we can judge the church only by its sights and sounds. We who seek to find our place within its fellowship can only go by experience. But what about those who stand outside the church, who never darken its doorway? What do they have to go by in making up their minds

about the church? One thing—watching the church at work in the world. But what is its work? And how does it operate? To answer these questions we must take a good look at the offices and functions, or tasks, of the church.

As you recall, all Christians have an office. We are clothed with the office of believer—the office of prophet, priest, and king. This is the firm foundation of all church life. But in the church there are also three special offices that come to expression in the work of elders, deacons, and ministers. These are special functions that grow out of the prophetic, priestly, and kingly office of all believers.

Christians who are called to fill these special offices receive their authority from Christ, the head of the church. They are responsible to Him for the way they do their work. They must exercise their office as servants of Christ in the service of His people. For these special offices were given to help the whole congregation in doing its work as good servants of Christ in the world.

That's the way it was in the life of the New Testament church. At first, besides the office of every believer, there was only the extraordinary office of the apostles. As personal witnesses to Jesus' life, death, and resurrection (Acts 1:21, 22), they were living links between Christ and His church. Theirs was a kind of three-in-one office, for the apostles served as ministers, elders, and deacons all at the same time. This apostolic office died with the apostles.

Yet the work of the apostles lived on in the church. As the church grew, this concentrated work was too much for the apostles to handle alone. So gradually they divided their work and turned it over to specially appointed men who served as elders, deacons, and ministers in these young but growing congregations.

Look at the record. In the Jerusalem church *deacons* were chosen, men like Stephen and Philip (Acts 6:2-6). Paul reminds Titus to "appoint *elders* in every city, as I gave you charge" (Titus 1:5). To fill the ranks of the *ministers* Paul gives this advice to Timothy: "The things which you have heard from me among many witnesses, the same commit to faithful men, who shall be able to teach others also" (II Tim. 2:2). Thus the Lord of the church calls leaders to guide His people in their worship, witness, and work in the world. "He gave some to be apostles, and some prophets, and some evangelists, and some pastors and teachers, for the perfecting of the saints, unto the building up of the body of Christ" (Eph. 4:11, 12).

There you have it, the basic structure, offices, and functions of church life. So far it is only a skeleton. We will have to add the nerves and muscles, the flesh and blood, when we turn to the distinguishing marks of the church: preaching the Word, administering the sacraments, and exercising church discipline.

65. OUR MISSIONARY TASK

Do you ever feel that your life is stuck at dead center? That everything's a big bore? That there's no place to go? That there's nothing worthwhile to do? Well, maybe this is a way out. Have you ever given a second thought to missions?

Being a missionary—how far away would that take you? To Nigeria? or Mexico? or Japan? The truth of the matter is, missions are a lot closer than you think. At present our churches are investing more people and money in mission work within our own country than in foreign missions. Our country is getting to be a vast mission field stretching out all around us in every direction and moving in upon us to the very doorsteps of the church. About sixty percent of our fellow citizens never see the inside of a church, and on an average Sunday less than ten percent show up in church. There are places in the world where the mission field has moved right inside the church.

Well, that throws the whole missionary challenge squarely into our laps. Ever thought of it that way? We can't escape it. The church *is* missions— or else it is nothing. And all Christians *are* missionaries, that is, disciples and witnesses of Christ, or else they are traitors.

Missions is like a two-way street. The church calls men *into* its fellowship in order to send them *out* into the world, all over creation. It sends us out to call others in. Come in to go out, and go out to bring in—this is the missionary cycle that goes on and on and on.

In the Old Testament the accent fell on the centripetal force (acting in a direction toward a center or axis) of the gospel, drawing outsiders into Israel without displaying very much of the outgoing power of God's Word. Remember the blindspot that plagued that fugitive prophet, Jonah? Sur-

prisingly enough, even Christ limited His labors almost exclusively to the "lost sheep of the house of Israel" (Matt. 10:6, 15:24). Yet all the while He trained His disciples for "greater works" to come (John 14:12). In the Great Commission (Matt. 28:19) Christ threw the doors wide open to world missions. He injected into the gospel a centrifugal force (acting in a direction away from a center or axis), an outgoing power, thrusting the church out into the mainstream of human life, at the crossroads of world affairs, at work and at play, on Wall Street as well as in the Athenian marketplace, there to call men to Christian discipleship. The Spirit of Pentecost turned the church inside out.

We twentieth-century Christians find it a little disappointing that the Catechism says next to nothing about the church as a missionary arm of the kingdom of God. It turns its eyes inward upon the inner life of the church. Its aim is to lead young members of the church from baptism to the Lord's Supper. You see, in Germany during Reformation times, the mission outreach of the church was largely under the control of the ruler or prince.

But today it's a different story. The whole relationship of church and state has undergone a radical change. So we need the Compendium to fill in the gaps in the Catechism in defining the missionary task of the church. After all, the Catechism is not the final word. Only the Bible is. And the Bible makes it abundantly clear that Christ not only calls His people out of the world, but also sends them back into the world as His disciples, witnesses, and missionaries. This calling comes to some Christians in a special way, to those whose names may be listed as missionaries and evangelists on the front cover of your church bulletin. But never forget, we too are involved, in a hundred and one down-to-earth ways, in the give-and-take of everyday Christian living.

66. FORGIVEN!

On a little plot of ground in the state of New York there is a grave marker, and on it, besides the man's name, there is this one word: "Forgiven." When you think of it, that is really the richest blessing that can come to anyone in this life—to experience the joyous relief of forgiveness for sin.

Have you ever pulled something pretty awful—something really downright sinful? Somehow it happened. And then the haunting memories! Your conscience bothered you no end. At first you thought you had gotten away with it. But those knowing looks on the faces of your parents! You began to suspect that they had seen through it all. After a while it started getting you down. You thought for sure you would blow your mind.

At last you opened up to your parents. What a load off your mind! They said they had known something was wrong. They could feel it. They asked whether you had talked it over with God. But the best part came when they said, "Let's forgive and forget." Man, what a relief! Forgiven!

But the best news is this: that's the way God is—and even more so. Nothing pleases Him more than to hold out to us the hand of forgiveness. In fact, He is more willing and eager to forgive our sins than we are to confess them. Listen: "If we confess our sins, he is faithful and just to forgive us our sins, and to cleanse us from all unrighteousness" (I John 1:9). He forgives and then forgets. Do you know what that means? It means that God no longer holds our sins against us. We are free! There is therefore now no condemnation resting upon those who are in Christ Jesus (Rom. 8:1). So we can live again with clear consciences.

But why does the Apostles' Creed and the Catechism come back to talk about our *sin* after having already called us *saints?* Well, did you think that being a Christian means that you're perfect? Forgiveness is a reality only within the bounds of the Christian life. For Christians know better than any other people in all the world just how much they really need forgiveness, day after day after day.

That's what the church is—the society of sinners, of forgiven sinners. Look at some examples. The church at Corinth was split wide open by sinful divisions and a party spirit. Paul and Barnabas parted ways as the result of a heated argument over John Mark. Peter proved to be a compromiser in playing Jews and Gentiles off against each other. The church is always made up of people like that. But the church is the fellowship of forgiveness—God's forgiveness, and our forgiveness. Like home, the church is the place where, when you come back, they have to take you in—again and again and again. Seven times? No, seventy times seven! (Matt. 18:21, 22).

Man, that's real comfort! It's good to know that there's always at least one place in the world where a man can hang his hat, and wear his heart on his sleeve, and be honest about himself, and tell the truth in love, and come clean—the church, the place where there is always grace abounding, even to the chief of sinners.

You mean I don't have to cover up for myself anymore? Right! God covers up for us in Christ. Do you know of any better news?

67. RESURRECTION DAY

Dateline: Resurrection City, Washington, D.C., 1968. Remember that? Thousands of poverty-ridden blacks and whites pitched their tents and built their shacks on the mall facing the national Capitol. Thousands more got stalled along the way on this poor people's march on Washington. In a matter of days, however, the dream was shattered by widespread indifference and resistance, and washed out by the rain and the mud. Yet behind it all there was a great vision: the vision of a new life of hope emerging out of the ruins of an old life of hopelessness.

Some day the dream of Resurrection City will come true. Only on a far grander scale. God will see to that. Out of the ruins of our sin-infested, strife-ridden world will arise a new earth under a new heaven—the New Jerusalem.

I believe in the resurrection of the world; and, along with it, I believe in the resurrection of the body (Rom. 8:18-25). God's final act in the drama of salvation will be both cosmic and personal. It will usher in a renewed world, and in it a renewed people of God—you and me and countless others.

Not that our view of the future is crystal clear. Just as the closer we get to the beginnings of human history the more we face great mysteries, so also the further we look forward toward eternity the more we face great mysteries. Yet on the pages of the Bible the main lines are visible. And this we know, the future is our friend. For it's in good hands, under God's control.

You want to know what the resurrection of the body is like? Well, then look at Jesus Christ. On Good Friday He died, as we die. He entrusted His real human soul to the care of His Father, and His real human body was laid in a grave. That's the way things stood over Friday night and Saturday, until Sunday morning broke like lightning and thunder in that garden cemetery just outside Jerusalem. Just as Christ arose by the power of God, so we too shall arise. Not with brand-new bodies, but in "this my flesh." Just try pinching your arm. Well, these arms of ours, these legs, these ears will rise again from the grave. In the resurrection day we shall be ourselves, body and soul, the whole man in perfect unity with God and ourselves and the world. What God joined together in creation, what death tears apart, that God will bring together again in a final and everlasting reunion. The seed sown in the earth will rise again to a new life (I Cor. 15:36-38). We will hold the same ID (identification) cards then as now, only we shall be wonderfully transformed.

This truth is most clearly revealed in Christ. He is the ground of our glorious hope. The same Christ who was crucified and buried, rose again. The disciples recognized Him. They saw the scars in His hands. He ate with them. This same Lord Jesus confronted Paul on the Damascus Road (Acts 22:8). He spoke to John on Patmos (Rev. 1:18). In the same way He will come again (Acts 1:11).

But with the resurrection of Christ there also came a tremendous change, a difference we can hardly imagine. His resurrection body was the same body He had had on this earth, yet it was wondrously transformed and glorified. Space was no obstacle (Luke 24:51). Doors were no barrier (John 20:26). It was something like a fifth-dimension mode of existence, or like living on a new frequency wave.

123

For us, too, the resurrection day will dawn as our final Easter victory. Our bodies, too, will be fashioned like the resurrection body of our Lord, for when we see Jesus Christ, we shall be like Him, for we shall see Him as He is (I John 3:2). Therefore with Paul "we wait for a Savior, the Lord Jesus Christ, who shall fashion anew the body of our humiliation, that it may be conformed to the body of his glory, according to the working whereby he is able even to subject *all things* unto himself (Phil. 3:20, 21). What a day of unimaginable joy that will be! So look beyond the horizon and catch a glimpse of the new Resurrection City. "Behold, I tell you a mystery. We all shall not sleep, but we shall all be changed, in a moment, in the twinkling of an eye, at the last trump: for the trumpet shall sound, and the dead shall be raised incorruptible, and we shall be changed" (I Cor. 15:51, 52). Talk about Glory Day!

You see, Christians have everything to live for, and when the time comes, everything to die for. So come what may, this is our unfailing comfort: "Whether we live therefore, or die, we are the Lord's" (Rom. 14:8).

68. GOD'S GRAND NEW WORLD

In Genesis, world history begins in a *garden;* in Revelation, world history ends in a *city,* the New Jerusalem. God planted that garden alone. It was His great creation. But the city, as God's grand finale, gathers up into it all the worthwhile products of man's cultural activities.

Now you see why we must get on with the business of Christian living, working and witnessing in the calm assurance that God will make something good come of it all. If what we are doing is worth doing at all, it's worth doing with all our heart. For Christian service counts heavily, both here and hereafter. The kingdom, which will one day break through in all its fullness, is already here. And we have a part in its program.

We can learn a lesson in this from Martin Luther. One day as he was planting peach trees in his backyard, a member of his congregation came by and stopped to talk with him. Thinking that ministers could better spend their time on "spiritual matters," he needled his pastor with this question: "Dr. Luther, what would you do today if you knew Jesus were coming back tomorrow?" Luther replied that he would first finish planting these peach trees, for then they would become part of the new earth under a new heaven.

Or take the story of the elderly retired Christian, an enthusiastic gardener, who was bothered by his lack of great longing for heaven. Was he feeling too much at home with God among his flowers? He shared these thoughts with his minister, who suggested that he should think of it this way: perhaps in the new Paradise there will be room for gardeners, just as there was in the original Paradise.

The point is clear: life in this world carries over into the life of the world to come. For heaven is the end product of the choices we make in this life. This is still "our Father's world." And in the end, God is not going to start from scratch. The number of man in this life is 666—always short of 7, the number of perfection. But on the last day God is not going

124

to start counting all over again from number one. He will take our sixes, and fives, and fours, and threes, and turn them into sevens. He will take our B's and C's and D's and turn them into A's. When that great day finally comes around, God will renew His whole creation, not by rescuing a handful of people out of a perishing world, nor by destroying everything, but by cleansing it in the fires of judgment and thus transforming it for His grand New Order. In the fire of God's refining process, the waste matter will be consumed and the gold purified.

Men who fail to take the Bible into account have long cherished the dream that man, given a little more time and a fair chance, would create his own heaven on earth. But now that dream has turned into an awful nightmare. The fear runs high that the nuclear power at our command may

one day reduce this world to a radioactive shambles. Yet the Bible leads us to believe that only the almighty hand of God breaking into history can really push us across the threshold into the final age.

But keep this in mind, our future is not something "out of this world," so foreign to our present experience that we would hardly even want it. God's new world is this world renewed and glorified, with a "fifth dimension" added. That picture certainly fits the language of the Bible. It speaks of a city that has streets and trees and a river. So, looking ahead, perhaps we should think of Toronto, Pennsylvania Avenue, the Rhine River, and maple trees. All things renewed! (Rev. 21:5).

The change to that new world will be so unimaginably wonderful that those who once were blind will see sights that no seeing person has ever seen before, and those who once were deaf will hear sounds that no hearing person has ever heard before. Heaven is the place of eternal joy and radiant activity. It is the very opposite of hell, the place of inexpressible loneliness and eternal unemployment. But in the new world we shall always be in good company. It's the place for living a full life, at Christ's marriage feast (Rev. 19:7). There every tear shall be wiped away, the world will echo with songs of joy and holy laughter, there will be opportunities unlimited to go places and do things. As a Christian chemistry teacher once said: For me one of the exciting things about the world to come is the thought of having an eternity to run new experiments under ideal conditions, and thus to keep on discovering new secrets about God's wonderful world.

The New Jerusalem! For early Christians who knew the earthly Jerusalem—with its muddy streets when it rained, and its dusty streets when the burning sun beat down upon them—the thought of those golden streets lined with ever-fruitful trees, refreshed with nearby living waters, must have kept their hopes alive. To our modern city-dwellers, living in their asphalt jungles, with little security in this life and no comfort for the life to come, we still have to talk in terms of grassy parks and shady campgrounds. Yet even then, the half has not been told.

No wonder a Christian father, seated comfortably with his family around the Sunday dinner, exclaimed: "All this, and heaven too!"

69. JUSTIFICATION BY FAITH

Accent on comfort—that's the central theme running through the whole Catechism. The *word* comfort won't come up again. But the *idea* of it is never really absent in the Catechism, from start to finish. This very practical note comes ringing through clearly as the Catechism opens the door to the truth about justification by faith alone. Listen: What does it profit you that you believe all this? What's the good of it all? What difference does it make?

Christian faith finds its focus in history, in the redeeming acts of God in Jesus Christ. It finds its focus in God's *words,* yes—but in words that cast their light upon God's *works.* In the world-shaking events recorded in the Apostles' Creed we feel the pulsebeat of His decision in favor of the world. And now His decision calls forth ours.

How can a man get right with God and thus get right with himself and the world? That question takes top place—especially today, when men are strangers to God, strangers to each other, and strangers in a vastly expanding world. How do we justify our right to life, and what is the reason for our existence?

Many people nowadays have given up on these questions. But the Bible still presses them upon us. And it points out the answers. It tells us that because of our sin, the punishment of death is all that we can rightfully claim. However, Jesus Christ sets us straight with God, ourselves, our fellowmen, and the world. In Him we discover anew our human rights. He grants us a new and rightful lease on life (John 10:10).

This discovery was the great turning-point in Paul's life. As a Pharisee he had felt that in persecuting the church he was "blameless" before God. But then in that dramatic encounter on the Damascus Road, God blinded his eyes so that he might see that all his vaunted personal gain was only loss until he had gained Christ (Phil. 3:6-9). That was his moment of justification. That moment turned his life around. In his thoughts he comes back to it time and time again. The justifying grace of God became the backbone of his new life, a driving power in his work, a central theme in his writings. Just think of the book of Romans.

Paul learned the hard way that every attempt at self-justification is a dead-end street. Yet repeatedly through history, Christians have fallen into the same kind of do-it-yourself, works-righteousness religion. Little won-

THE PACE OF MY LIFE IS KILLING....

AS A CHRISTIAN I SHOULD BE ABLE TO SLOW DOWN..

BUT I JUST DON'T LIKE GIVING UP ANYTHING

der, then, that the book of Romans was called upon to play a leading role in almost every reformation in the life of the church!

Look at Luther, for example. His problem was an agonizing replay of Paul's. The question "How can I get right with God?" tormented him. He tried to keep all the rules in the book. Yet his conscience found no peace. Then one day, while he was reading the book of Romans, the truth of justification by faith alone gripped him. Justification, he saw, comes not by a righteousness that God *demands* of us (which we could never produce), but by a righteousness that God freely *gives* us for Christ's sake. Calvin was gripped by the same conviction. He calls justification "the main hinge on which the Christian religion turns." You see, basically Luther and Calvin stand or fall together. As Calvinists, therefore, we have no problem in joining with Lutherans in commemorating October 31 as (Luther's) Reformation Day.

In many ways justification suggests a courtroom scene. Our conscience, like the devil's lawyer, echoes God's law and testifies against us. But then faith speaks, and overrules the accusations of that "still small voice" within us. Sure, we're guilty. But Christ is our righteousness. He pleads our case. And God the Judge declares us innocent. This is not a game God plays with men. It's based on justice and mercy. For the Great Exchange has taken place. Christ became a curse, that He might fill us with His blessing (Gal. 3:13, 14). Christ became what He is not—sin—in order to make us what we by nature are not—righteous (II Cor. 5:21). What an exchange— the righteous for the unrighteous, to bring us back to God. Christ clothes

Himself with our filthy rags in order to clothe us with His royal robes. And because of this we can rise to hear the Judge's verdict: "Not guilty!"

So you see, there are two key biblical truths that support our justification. The first is Christ's *substitutionary atonement,* by which He takes our place before the bar of God's justice. The second is God's act of *imputation,* by which the Father declares us righteous in His sight and reckons to our account the full merits of Christ's finished work. And the Holy Spirit drives it home in our daily experience. What more solid foundation could you seek for living a Christian life!

70. DO-IT-YOURSELF RELIGION

He was a four-star general, second in command only to the king. But you wouldn't trade places with him. His name was Naaman, a leper. Pursuing a hot bit of information, he arrived in Israel, looking for the prophet Elisha. He wanted a cure. But even more, he was eager for a sensational display of "faith healing" with publicity and fanfare. Instead, he got a very simple prescription: take a dip in the Jordan seven times. What an insult to a man of his stature! Were not the Abanah and Pharpar, rivers of Damascus, better than all the muddy waters of the Jordan? Humiliated, enraged, ready to return to Syria uncured, Naaman kept his cool only because his servant brought him to his senses. Sir, the servant said, if the prophet were to make you do something very hard, you would certainly do it, wouldn't you? Then why not do this simple act of obedience (II Kings 5:8-14)?

You know how the story ended.

But the spirit of Naaman is still alive today. By nature we all want to choose our own cleansing process, so that through it all we can preserve our pretended sense of personal dignity.

Two men went to church to pray. The one, an internal revenue officer, turned his prayer into a plea for pardon. The other, a religious leader, didn't even pray. All he did was to air his feeling of superiority and parade his piety. He gave himself a straight A in every subject. But Christ grades things differently. The tax collector went home, his life set straight with God. Not the Pharisee. For do-it-yourself religion doesn't count with God (Luke 18:9-14).

Justification by faith means trusting in Christ, not in ourselves. For we cannot be saved by our own works. Even within the Christian life, faith banishes every thought of having "arrived" at perfection (Phil. 3:12, 13). For even the best of saints has a long, long way to go on the road of sanctification, or holiness, and no one knows it better than he.

The story is told of a certain man who, upon reflection, came to the conclusion that he had done nothing wrong all year. To celebrate this achievement he decided to throw a New Year's Eve party. His minister, when notified, felt there was nothing he could do but congratulate him: "Man, that's a real first!"—and hope the man would feel the sharp edge of his biting sarcasm.

There is no room in the Christian life for showing off our spiritual accomplishments. After all, in whom did true righteousness come through? In those filthy-rich peacocks who made their handsome contributions to the temple treasury with a grand display of public pride? Or in the poor widow who quietly dropped her two pennies into the treasury? Jesus gives a clear and forceful answer (Mark 12:41-44).

Justification! It's ours only by a sovereign act of God's grace to undeserving sinners. It's ours only by a faith that casts itself upon the mercy of Christ. The only worthiness it requires is a sense of our unworthiness.

MAYBE TOGETHER WE CAN FIND SOME MEANING TO IT ALL

Yet we are always trying to save some honor for ourselves. The Catechism sees through our self-righteous counter-moves and stops us in three different ways.

First, the biblical view of justification by faith alone shuts the door on all our feelings of personal pride. For our righteousness is a gift of God, not something we have earned.

Second, the Catechism throws out every notion of perfection, for even our best works, in themselves, are still infected with sin.

Third, the Catechism checks every desire for reckless and careless living. Does justification by faith mean that works don't count for much? The libertine style of life says: since we are justified by faith, not by works, what does it matter how we live? Does being right with God mean we can do as we please? That's simply impossible. Does ragweed grow on fruit trees? Do men pluck thistles from raspberry bushes? Of course not.

Moralists, on the other hand, pay lip service to justification by faith, but then proceed to act as if their good works are the rungs in the ladder by which they must climb up into heaven. What feverish worship of "do's" and "don'ts," turning Christians into Pharisees and medieval monks!

But the most prideful distortion of Christian faith is the blind arrogance of perfectionists. They want a pure church made up of "first-class" Christians. Their thinking is reflected in the man who claimed he had not sinned in nine years! What absolutely complete self-deception!

Among us perhaps the greatest danger is that of passive Christianity. We often cover up our do-nothing lives with the argument that since Christ has done it all, let's be satisfied with this and not try to add anything to it. What pious-sounding remarks! Yes, salvation is by faith alone, but faith never stands alone. It *works!* Inactive Christianity is faith without works, and you know how dead that is (Jas. 2:26).

71. REWARDS

A guest speaker once addressed a high-school audience with these words: "A students, B students, C students—and my friends!" A chorus of chuckles arose from the crowd. Upon reflection, however, this introduction serves to pose the question: Why study? What keeps you going at school? Do you work just for grades? Would the incentive to stick with it be just as strong without this system of rewards? What if only pass and fail grades were handed out?

TALK ABOUT PRESSURE TO MAKE GRADES 🤯

You probably feel a lot of pressure on you to "make the grade." And perhaps your parents are even more "grade happy" than you are.

But really, what does a good grade mean? Simply this, that we've made good use of the time and talents God has given us. After we've really cracked the books and come out with a top grade, we must still respond with the servant in our Lord's parable: We deserve no special credit, for we've only done our duty (Luke 17:10). The very best we ever get is still at bottom a gift of God's grace. So an A is no excuse for patting ourselves on the back.

And that's the way it is with all good works in our Christian life. They are not show-case trophies. Nor are they conversation pieces to impress people with our piety or devotion. They are simply obedient responses to God's good gifts to us in Christ.

130

But God is generous. He not only gives, but also rewards our use of His gifts. He is far from indifferent about the way we put our faith to work. In fact, in keeping His law there is a great reward (Ps. 19:11). God is a rewarder of all who diligently seek Him (Heb. 11:6). One day He will answer the good works of each of His children with a "Well done, good and faithful servant!" (Matt. 25:21). For we are products of His work in us, created anew in Christ Jesus for good works, which God planned in advance for us to do (Eph. 2:10). The words of Christ are clear: Believe Me, anyone who gives a cup of cold water to a little one as My disciple shall surely not lose his reward (Matt. 10:42).

But let's keep the record straight. A life of good works is important. We are indeed saved to serve, and our service of good works will be honored by God. But no person lives up to the name Christian who seeks to serve in the spirit of "What's in it for me?" or "What do I get out of it?" The right question is this, "What can I give in return?"

Your parents may offer you some reward to get you to do some chores around the house. But that's like putting the cart before the horse. Somehow we must learn simply to do our duty—if not thankfully or gladly, then at least willingly. Then, if a reward follows, it comes as a bonus. The fact that questionable devices are needed to urge us to do what we should do anyway shows how hard it is for us to keep first things first in our lives. We should view rewards not as conditions for obedience, but as surprise endings upon our spontaneous or free-willing obedience.

If on a particular afternoon you mow the lawn around your home and your neighbor asks you to mow his too, you may receive a dollar for each job. The dollar you receive from your father is a gift (reward of grace)— you owed him that work. The dollar you got from your neighbor was earned (reward of merit)—because you were under no particular obligation to him. When we are rewarded by our Lord, it can't be a reward of merit. We *owed* it to Him.

131

That's the point of the Catechism. The Reformers felt compelled to break with a church that had set up a complicated network of rewards based on a system of personal merits. Giving alms, buying indulgences (supposed release from the punishment of sin), honoring holy relics, and praying the rosary were held up before the people as ways of earning eternal rewards. The men of Heidelberg responded with a resounding, No! Salvation is not a personal achievement, but a gift of God. We may not claim anything for ourselves that robs God of His glory.

Their criticism of the old church was not that it rejected the rewarding work of Christ, but that it cancelled it out by claiming that we can earn part of the reward ourselves.

Yes, God rewards our good works—a reward of grace. But this promise of reward must remain for us a kind of afterthought. We are simply called to do our duty as God gives us to see it—in a self-denying, self-forgetting way. There's no room here for spiritual bookkeeping. No need to keep records of the rewards we have coming. That's the wrong attitude.

When Christ returns to reward the good and the evil, He will call to His side those who have spent their lives in His service and say to them: Receive your inheritance! Then, amazed, we shall only be able to stammer: "When . . . how . . . where . . . , Lord?" We'll be at a loss to recall our good works (Matt. 25:34-40).

When all is said and done, rewards come our way as surprise endings, happy endings. God remembers. And that's enough.

72. THE MEANS OF GRACE

It's no secret that the church is suffering from a dropout problem. Many church leaders talk about the "lost years" between fifteen and fifty-five. Generally the trend in church membership is downhill and attendance is falling off. Some churches are closing their doors. All this is a bad sign. For if the church shuts down, then the preaching of God's Word will be silenced, the administration of the sacraments will grind to a halt, and eventually Christianity will fade out. For the Holy Spirit works through the church. The Word and sacraments are means of grace used by the Spirit to instill and to strengthen Christian faith for active living (Rom. 10:14-17).

I DON'T SEE ANY HOPE IN THIS LIFE...

I TRIED GOING TO CHURCH, BUT THERE WERE SO FEW PEOPLE

I DECIDED THAT WHAT THEY HAD TO OFFER MUST NOT BE TOO POPULAR

Up to this point in your life you have probably heard hundreds of sermons. You also carry on your forehead the sign and seal of the first sacrament, baptism. So far you've been only a witness to the second sacrament, the Lord's Supper. But you're getting nearer to the time when you yourself will become a participant. In the worship service, sermons and sacraments are two aids (the one audio and the other visual) in the preaching and teaching ministry of the church by which the Holy Spirit carries out His work in the life of the Christian community (Eph. 1:13; I Cor. 11:23-26).

The church is under orders to sow the seed of God's Word throughout the world, to everyone within our reach, to outsiders as well as insiders. We are called to proclaim the gospel everywhere—on street corners, in TV studios, on radio networks, on mission fields, on skid-row, in shopping plazas, in recreation areas.

But the sacraments are for Christians only. They belong up front in church, in the circle of believers, whether in a cathedral or on a battlefront, whether in a red brick church or in a jungle hut or in a chapel (Luke 22:19).

The Spirit of God never works in a vacuum. The open Bible in our hands and on our pulpits, the sprinkling of water, the breaking of bread and the pouring of wine—these are His means of grace. In this way the Holy Spirit personalizes His presence among us. The sermon is His voice, the sacraments His sign language. He always points the way to Christ. Without His penetrating power, the Word and sacraments would simply be like sunshine upon blind eyes and music upon deaf ears.

At the time that the Heidelberg Catechism was written, the Roman Catholic Church stressed the sacraments at the expense of the Word.

Preaching was viewed at best as a preparation for receiving the grace of the sacrament, paving the way for the Mass. Facing this situation, the Reformers set out to recover the centrality of gospel-preaching in the worship service. They believed that the Word is *primary,* the sacraments *secondary.* God's Word can stand alone, but not the sacraments. The sacraments depend on the Word for their meaning. When the Word is forgotten the sacraments become either empty symbols or magical rites.

Both Word and sacraments are ours *by* faith and *for* faith, as instruments in the loving and powerful hand of the Holy Spirit to hammer our lives into shape by reflecting the image of Christ.

73. SACRAMENTS

Christ expects us to go the "second mile" in helping people find the way of life. And why not, for God goes all the way with us. In His Word God walks with us the "first mile." But He doesn't stop at that. In the sacraments He walks hand-in-hand with us the "second mile."

But do we really need that "second mile"? Isn't the "first mile" good enough? These are questions that often cross our minds.

To get off on the right foot, let's keep the record straight. There's nothing wrong with the "first" means of grace, God's Word, that makes the sacraments, as the "second" means of grace, necessary. The Bible meets all our needs. It's more than enough. Nothing necessary is lacking. Not even the sacraments can add anything to the message of the gospel. The sacraments tell the same story as the Word.

Well then, why does God add the sacraments? The answer is: Not because of the weakness of His Word, but to help us understand the Truth better. Often we are slow to take hold of His promises. At times we end up criticizing God's Word. We say it's too hard to understand. Or it's too good to be true. To put an end to all contradiction, to show once for all that His salvation is for real, God turns to sign language in the sacraments. He confirms His truth to us not only by word experience, but by sense

I NEED ALL THE SIGNS I CAN GET!

experience as well. In the sacraments God offers us a clear-cut program of instruction to drive home to us in unmistakable terms His will for our lives.

When the road gets steep and slippery, we often feel the need for visible evidence of God's love—evidence that we can see and touch. So God meets our need. He walks with us the "second mile." In effect He says, "You can count on me." By the symbols of water, bread, and wine He underscores the "good news" in terms that we can see and touch, and thus He steadies our hearts, our heads, our hands.

The sacraments, then, are signs and seals of God's love for us. You know what signs are for—they point things out and call our attention to them. Just think of billboard advertising. But such signs are often frustrating, holding forth promises that cannot immediately be realized—like a desert sign advertising a swimming resort a thousand miles away. But in the biblical view of things, a sacrament is a sign that carries in itself something of the reality to which it points. It's like a check in your hand that has on-the-spot value. Sacraments signify the living presence of Christ in His church.

The sacraments are also seals. In Bible times, rings and emblems were royal seals of authority, used by rulers to place their official stamp of approval on letters or to seal contracts or ratify legal documents. In the sacraments God places His seal of approval on everything Christ has done for us, and says, "This is for real."

The sacraments make clear that we have a full share in Christ's saving work. As surely as we feel the water of baptism on our foreheads, so surely may we believe that Christ cleanses us from all our sins. As surely as we see, handle, and taste the bread and wine, so surely may we believe that we belong to Christ.

Among the people of Israel life was enriched by two sacraments, that of circumcision and the Passover. In both there was bloodletting which served as a preview of Calvary. Through the finished work of Christ these old sacraments became new, not by the throwing out of the old, but by the absorbing of the old into the new. The upper room marks the transition from the Passover to the Lord's Supper (Mark 12:15, 22-25), and in the Great Commission (Matt. 28:19) circumcision makes way for baptism. Yet, in the old sacraments by way of expectation and in the new sacraments by way of fulfillment, the focus falls on Jesus Christ who is the bridge between the Old Testament church and contemporary Christianity.

74. THE COVENANT OF GRACE

Let's say you're a young man just starting out in business. You need five thousand dollars to set up shop. A friend agrees to back you up with a loan in the full amount, to be repaid over five years. A lawyer draws up the papers, and so together you sign the contract. After a year, however, you find yourself in the red. Poor investment. Mismanagement. Anyway, you can't keep your end of the bargain. The contract is broken. And now you're at the mercy of your lender. But friendship is stronger than legal rights. So your friend generously agrees to refinance your bankrupt business, to renew your credit and redraft the contract, in order to put you back on your feet.

Sounds almost unbelievable? Actually, that's the way God dealt with us. After we had broken the first contract in Adam, the Covenant of Works, God our Creditor and Friend drew up a new contract with us in Christ, the Covenant of Grace.

When we by our sins fell out of the first covenant, God in His grace caught us up into a new covenant. You see, all of God's dealings with men are in the form of agreements, or covenants. The new Covenant of Grace reaches all the way back to Paradise (Gen. 3:15), and from there it moves forward in history through Noah (Gen. 9:8), Abraham (Gen.

17:7), Moses (Gal. 3:17), and David (Ps. 25:10, 14), on the way to its fulfillment in Christ (Luke 1:72). At each new stage we see a fuller development of what was already present at the outset. Then, as a climax to this covenant story, Christ wrote a final chapter at the last supper when He said, "This cup is the new covenant in my blood" (I Cor. 11:25).

At Pentecost the Covenant of Grace came of age. During the old era it seldom broke out beyond the boundaries of Israel's national life. But now in the new era it reaches out to all kinds of people. In his Pentecost sermon Peter speaks in a kind of international language of the Holy Spirit to the international crowd gathered at Jerusalem. This is what he said: "For to you is the promise, and to your children, and to all that are afar off, even as many as the Lord our God shall call unto him" (Acts 2:39). And so we too, standing at the end of a long line of twenty centuries of Christian history, are heirs of God's covenant promise, and the call to faith and obedience comes to us all.

The heart of the Covenant of Grace is God's promise ("I will be your God") and the response He requires of us ("You shall be my children"). God *asks* us to trust and obey. But He only asks what He first *gives* in Christ Jesus. Christ is head of the covenant community throughout the world. He is the one who guarantees our contract with God. He paid off our bad debts. God no longer sues us for damages. Our account is settled. This is the "good news" of God's Word, the message of the covenant. God even goes so far with us as to signify and seal this new contract in the water and bread and wine of the sacraments.

YOU MEAN THERE'S HOPE, BUT I STILL HAVE TO MAKE A CHOICE?

This means that we have only one choice in life—we can be either covenant-keepers or we can be covenant-breakers. Either we choose to live for Christ, and thus to receive all the blessings of the Covenant of Grace; or we stand in Adam's shoes, and thus obligate ourselves to keep perfectly all the terms and conditions of agreement in the old broken contract, the Covenant of Works. But that's out of the question. So please don't try the impossible. There's no future in it. Besides, God has now provided a far better way in Jesus Christ.

One more thing. We are often guilty of thinking too small. The covenant comes to our minds when we think of covenant children—child-birth, infant baptism, spiritual nurture, Christian education. But this is only a small part of the total picture. The covenant is as big as life itself. It provides the setting for our whole Christian way of life—on the job, off the job, here and there and everywhere. The covenant means living fellowship with God, in Jesus Christ, wherever we are, whatever we do. "Whether therefore you eat, or drink, or whatsoever you do, do all to the glory of God" (II Cor. 10:31).

75. BAPTISM

Growing up is a search for self-identity. Sometimes you poke around in your past. Before your mind's eye you let your life pass in review. And always you wonder about the "real me." Here's a clue. One of the most important documents in your personal file is your baptismal record. It's worth a careful reading. It's your Christian ID card.

Even if you were born in the poorest of families, baptism makes you fabulously rich. Not because you were sprinkled with holy or costly water. Nor because the minister had some magic power. Nor because the congregation showered you with expensive gifts. Rather, in baptism God made visible and tangible and audible for you "the grace of our Lord Jesus Christ, who, though he was rich, yet for your sakes he became poor, that you through his poverty might become rich" (II Cor. 8:9).

The sacrament of baptism is deeply rooted in the entire Bible. Baptism grew up, in fact, out of the Old Testament sacrament of circumcision. Many ancient peoples practiced circumcision. But for Abraham and his descendants God set aside this eighth-day ritual as a sign to seal His covenant with His people. Not that this was an automatic guarantee of salvation. For "they are not all Israel, that are of Israel" (Rom. 9:6). As signs and seals of God's covenant promises, sacraments are always a call to faith in these promises, which in the Old Testament pointed forward to the fulfillment of circumcision in Christian baptism (Col. 2:11-13).

When Christ replaced the sacrament of circumcision with that of baptism, He was not introducing a previously unheard-of practice. Among many Jews it was customary to baptize Gentiles who wished to accept the Jewish religion and become part of the Jewish community. These converts were called "God-fearers" (Acts 13:16; Luke 7:2-5).

From the recently discovered Dead Sea Scrolls we find that daily baptisms were an important part of the life of the Qumran community, a sect living along the shoreline of the Dead Sea near Jerusalem.

Some people argue that John the Baptist borrowed his "baptism of repentance" from these Qumran separatists. Actually, these two are worlds apart. John helped to forge a redemptive link, not between the Dead Sea Scrolls and the New Testament, but between the Old and New Testaments. John's water-baptism laid the groundwork for the coming Spirit-baptism (Matt. 3:11; Mark 1:8; Luke 3:16). But there was still a "not yet" dimension in it (Acts 19:1-7), so that it fell short of the moment of full reality, which broke when Jesus was baptized in the Jordan. There water-baptism and Spirit-baptism flowed together, as the Spirit descended upon the water-baptized Son and the Father voiced His approval from heaven.

After Christ's blood-bath at Calvary, to which the water-bath of baptism points, the risen Lord sent out His apostles to lay the foundation of the church with this command: "Go therefore and make disciples of all nations, baptizing them into the name of the Father and of the Son and of the Holy Spirit" (Matt. 28:19). So we now administer baptism in obedience to these marching orders. The symbol of water and the words expressing the authority of the triune God—"I baptize you into the name of the

Father and of the Son and of the Holy Spirit"— are the abiding test of a truly Christian baptism. As we use water from the faucet to wash our bodies, so we use the same kind of water in baptism to represent our spiritual cleansing from sin and our renewal in Christ.

Baptism therefore stands as the sacrament of initiation, or entry, into the church and into the kingdom of God. It's the doorway to a new life. It's a sign and seal of our cleansing from sin through Christ, once for all, for all of life, and for all time (Titus 3:5). But then that cleansing has to show up too! For baptism means that we are different from the world— that is, we are Christian. And being Christian means that we will do our best to help others come to Christ too.

Baptism is not a christening ceremony (Liberalism). And it's not just a token of remembrance (Zwinglianism). Nor is it the actual mysterious cause of regeneration (Roman Catholicism). It's the sacramental representation of our sharing in Good Friday and Easter (John 3:5; Rom. 6:3, 4). It's a means of grace in the hand of God by which He officially adopts us into His family.

Now that we have an idea of who we are—whose children we are and to whom we belong—our search for identity is off to a good start. Our baptismal record is our membership card in the Christian community. It's a constant reminder to us of the salvation our Father has given, of Christ's victory over sin, of the tremendous riches that are ours in Him, and of our urgent call to Christian service.

76. FOR CHILDREN TOO!

"Apartment for rent. No children." That's how many landlords advertise. But with God it's different. He has a heart for children. His welcome mat is always out for children—*especially* for children! (Matt. 18:2-4; 19:14; Mark 9:36).

SO YOU WANT TO ARGUE ABOUT BAPTISM, EH?

If you have Baptist friends, you've probably been put on the spot with the question, "Where do you find infant baptism in the Bible?" It's true, of course, that there is no direct command in the New Testament that says, "Thou shalt baptize children." But to give your Baptist friends something to think about, the New Testament also says nothing about baptizing children of believing parents when they reach the age of maturity. In view of the many differences on this point, we might wish the Bible had left us some clear "proof-texts." But taking the Bible as it is, we had better be careful how we use such arguments from silence. They certainly do not make a case against infant baptism. In fact, rightly understood, this silence is a strong argument in favor of it.

Look at it this way. Through the sacrament of circumcision, children in the Old Testament were included in the Covenant of Grace along with their parents. This practice, dating from the lifetime of Abraham was commanded by God (Gen. 17:9-14). Now baptism has taken the place of circumcision (Col. 2:11, 12). If the New Testament meant to leave children out, we would rightly expect not silence, but a clear-cut command. As a matter of fact, however, there is not the slightest hint in the New Testament that children must now wait longer to receive the sign and seal of God's forgiveness than children in the Old Testament. Since the "new covenant" (I Cor. 11:25) comes to full expression in the saving work of Christ, it is unthinkable that the early church would suddenly rob its own children of a privilege that children of earlier believers had always enjoyed. Therefore the burden of proof rests upon those who say that baptism is reserved for adult believers only.

In New Testament times the Jewish community welcomed even Gentiles with their children into the circle of the covenant. Well, what happened to these Gentile children who became Jews? They were baptized! Just as Jewish children were circumcised, so Gentile children were baptized. This was common practice in New Testament times. Some sacramental sign and seal was bestowed upon all covenant children. They all belonged to the "household" (Acts 16:15, 33; 18:8; I Cor. 1:16).

Looking back we may say that the God who embraced children in His covenant before Christ is the same God today. His loving concern for the younger generation is no less in the New Testament church than it was in the church of Old Testament times. In the light of the unity of the whole Bible we see that God works redeemingly within the framework of families and congregations (Gen. 12:3; Acts 2:39). He saves us not as isolated individuals, but as mothers, fathers, and children together (I Cor. 7:14). For together we are heirs of His covenant, members of His church, and citizens of His kingdom. Infant baptism is God's way of rolling out the red carpet and letting children in. This means that the church, too, must take its children seriously. Because they belong to Christ, they also belong to the church.

You see now where you stand as a young Christian? You're a child of the covenant, a member of the church, a citizen of the kingdom. So never think of yourself as an outsider or as a second-class citizen. You're a full member of the Christian community. Every gospel promise is for you to have and to hold. Through them Christ is calling you to stand up and be counted as His disciple. The door to public profession of faith stands open before you. And there is a seat at the Lord's Table with your name on it, reserved, and waiting.

77. THE LORD'S SUPPER

The road of Christian living lies open before you. Christ is the way, the Bible your road map, the Holy Spirit your guide. Catechism is like a highway planning program, planting signposts that mark the route to a public profession of faith, the gateway to holy communion.

The Lord's Supper stands at the crossroads of the Christian life. That's the way Christ planned it. The long road of redemption history coming up out of the Old Testament reached a decisive turning-point in the upper room. There, within the shadow of the cross and within shouting distance of the empty tomb, Christ the host reclined at the table and served the disciples as His guests a menu of bread and wine. He gave this meal as a lasting legacy to the church of all ages, adding this command: As often as you celebrate this feast, do it in remembrance of Me, until I come again.

We have inherited five records of the Lord's Supper in the writings of Matthew, Mark, Luke, John, and Paul. Each of these Bible authors casts his own light upon this second sacrament. Together their united witness gives us a clear picture of the meaning of the Lord's Supper.

That sacred banquet was both a *review* of the past and a *preview* of the future. Looking in from a distance, we see a sacrament in change, a Christ-centered updating of the centuries-old Passover. For two meals were crowded into that one banquet—both the Passover and the Lord's Supper. It was the *last* Israelite meal and the *first* Christian feast, all in one.

The annual Passover feast in Israel had a definite *backward* look about it, recalling God's mighty act of deliverance in the exodus. The Israelites celebrated it as their "independence day," their charter of liberation from Egyptian bondage. On their calendar they counted off the years from the time of that crucial event which marked their birth as a nation, and from there Israel's history marched forward, gathering momentum on its way to the fullness of time in Christ. So the Passover also had built into it a *forward* look (Exod. 12:13; I Cor. 5:7). In remembering what had once already happened, there was a promise and expectation of greater things yet to come. The Passover lamb and the unleavened bread predicted the Christ who would come in the fullness of time. Israel's celebration of that first "night to remember" was at the same time a celebration seeking fulfillment in the *future*.

Similarly, the Lord's Supper is also an interim or "between" feast for the Christian church. It moves along with the march of time from the *first* to the *second* coming of our Lord. Remembrance of God's *past* deeds and expectations of His *future* deeds meet together at the table. As we break the bread and pour the wine, we cast our glances back to the saving acts of God that happened nearly two thousand years ago and half a world away—

acts in which we too were involved (Rom. 6:3-6). When Christ cried out, "It is finished!" right then and there the Messianic dreams of the faithful in Israel came true.

But at this meal we also take a forward look to the kingdom yet to come in all its perfection. We come to the table to enjoy a salvation *already* accomplished, but *not yet* perfected. You see, the Christian religion is a two-directional life. It's like driving a car: you have to keep an eye on the rear-view mirror, and at the same time keep an eye on the road ahead.

The Lord's Supper, then, is open-ended toward the future. Above it there's a window opening out upon Christ's return. With expectation we scan the skies to catch a glimpse of the day when this supper will make way for the marriage feast of the Lamb (Rev. 19:7). In that day we will experience the reality of Christ's words, "I shall not drink again of this fruit of the vine until that day when I drink it new with you in my Father's kingdom" (Matt. 26:29 RSV).

78. COMMUNION WITH CHRIST

From where you are now, looking forward to holy communion, and in the meantime watching and waiting, what do you see? Just a minister reading a form, breaking bread, and pouring wine? Just elders serving at the table? Just older people eating and drinking together? Just some ordinary store bread and ordinary grape wine?

Well, as you realize, there's more to it than meets the eye. These are indeed the outward forms and elements. But there is a deeper spiritual meaning to it all. Nothing magic of course. But something wonderful that you can't see with the physical eye. That invisible something is fellowship with Christ. He is there with us as host at the head of His table. By His Spirit He calls us to join Him as His honored guests and share in His sacrament of sacrifice and victory. As He supplies the bread and wine, He imprints upon our minds His unforgettable words, "This is my body," "This is my blood." This is our food and drink to life eternal. The bread is our staff of life. The wine is beverage for thirsty people. Both are meant for real honest-to-God hungry and thirsty people—hungry and thirsty for the food and drink of life eternal—people who wear work clothes as well as Sunday suits, whose hands that take the bread and wine are calloused and still a little stained and dirty from their daily work. You see, we must guard against pushing the communion table off into some holy, but forgotten corner of our lives. It's not for some "beautiful isle of somewhere." Holy communion is the place for head-in-the-clouds, but feet-on-the-ground fellowship—a place where forgiven sinners meet with their crucified and risen Lord.

It's tragic that this wonderful sacrament of Christian communion has touched off so much heated controversy. Already in the days of the Reformation the men of Heidelberg found themselves caught in the crossfire of conflicting points of view on the meaning of the Lord's Supper. You see now why they devoted so much space to this doctrine? In their confession of faith they wanted to capture the truth of the Bible as clearly as possible.

The central question was how to understand the *real presence* of Christ in the sacrament. This issue is still alive today. We are confronted with a whole variety of viewpoints, from far right to far left. At one extreme are the Spiritualists, who have very little appreciation for the sacraments, thinking of them as too materialistic for spiritually-minded Christians.

AND I SAY THIS IS THE TRUE MEANING ··...

The Roman Catholic Church, on the other hand, teaches the doctrine of transubstantiation. According to this view, the so-called accidental features of the bread and wine—such as sight, touch, and taste—remain unchanged in the sacrament. But the real inner essence is actually changed into the body and blood of Christ when the priest speaks the words of consecration. Thus the Mass becomes a repetition of Calvary, though in a non-bloody form. But look, you can't have it both ways. Either Christ finished His saving work once for all, and then there is no place for repetition. Or His work must be repeated, which means that it was not finished once for all.

Lutherans, reacting to both of these positions, defend the view that Christ's body and blood are actually present in, under, and with the bread and the wine, though the bread and wine remain the same. Finally there were the Zwinglians, who proved to be the forerunners of many modern liberals, who view the Lord's Supper merely as a memorial that we erect in honor of Christ.

Amid this Babel of conflicting voices the men of Heidelberg, following Calvin's lead, confessed the real spiritual presence of Christ in the Lord's Supper. By the living and powerful inner working of His Spirit, Christ is really with us at His table. All the blessings of the cross and empty tomb become ours in a sacramental way, in symbol and in reality. As we fellowship with the Giver we receive His gifts.

By partaking of the one bread of life (John 6:49-51), may we all as Christians become knit together more closely into the one body of Christ (I Cor. 10:16, 17). Greater Christian unity, richer communion, genuine ecumenicity—these are hopes that spring eternal in the hearts of Christians. This is the clue: the closer we get to Christ, the closer we will get to each other.

79. WORTHY PARTAKERS

The call to communion comes to all confessing Christians. It's a friendly invitation, but with an "RSVP" (please respond) attached. Even stronger, it's a command from Christ Himself, "Do this . . . ." But remember, it's not an empty call. For Christ promises that as surely as we eat and drink in faith, so surely we may go our way in the confidence that He has purchased our salvation for us once for all and that He now daily strengthens our life. If we come to His table with the prayer, "Lord, I believe, help thou my unbelief" (Mark 9:24), then we may rest assured of our eternal security, as certainly as the bread is broken before our eyes and the cup is given to us and we eat and drink in remembrance of Him.

As we wait at His table, Christ stands ready to fill our lives to overflowing with His blessing. But how long shall we keep Him waiting? When shall we be ready? How shall we come? What does it take to be a worthy partaker?

Well, this much is clear: there is no room at His table for hypocrites. No room for people who think they do not need the food and drink of life. No room for those who think they are spiritually healthy and do not need the Great Physician. No room for the spiritually sick who want no healing.

OH, MY MUSICAL, I MEAN MY
SPIRITUAL LIFE IS FINE, MAN

But now let's accent the positive. At communion there is an open-door policy for all prodigal sons and daughters who, sitting among the swine, finally make up their minds: "I will arise and go to my father" (Luke 15:18). But then something has got to give. You can't just stay there with the swine— the "old gang"—and watch them trample pearls underfoot (Matt. 7:6). And you had better not wait until the swine-stalls—your "old life"—are hospital clean, because then you'll never make it. "Just as I am"—that's the password.

No Christian ever has a good excuse for absenting himself from the Lord's Supper and thus turning down Christ's standing offer. For holy communion speaks to all of us in all our needs and in every situation in life. You say you're not good enough to come? Who ever said you had to be perfect! You say you're not worthy? The only worthiness Christ expects is an honest sense of our unworthiness! You say you don't need it? Well, then you really do, and badly, in order to come face to face with your real self! You say that you're in trouble with a fellow Christian or neighbor or friend? But we may never let trouble keep us away, but rather in hearing the call to communion we must also hear Christ's call to clear up our troubles.

143

Some Christians seem to view the Lord's Supper as an almost unapproachable "holy of holies." They say that we should celebrate it sparingly, lest it become commonplace. Others seem to view it as an annoying interruption in their regular church-going routine, and therefore just go through the motions of eating and drinking. Their hands and mouths may move in unison with the congregation, but they go home just as empty as they came. Still others seem to think of it as an oasis in the desert of life, a mountaintop experience that lifts them up above the barren wilderness of daily humdrum living. So the more of such spiritual retreats the better.

None of these views of communion will do. It's not the reasons men give, but the reasons God gives that settle the question of worthy participation. It is Christ Himself who calls us to take our places at His table. When He calls, we must answer. Then communion becomes not only a confession of our need for renewal, but at the same time a confession before the church and the world of our faith in Christ. For these reasons we must always see to it that the table of our Lord stands squarely in the middle of the mainstream of Christian living. That's where Christ placed it. Then we can look to the fellowship of Christ's table for strength and courage—to hear His voice and to feel His presence in our everyday lives.

80. THE KEYS OF THE KINGDOM — PREACHING

It's a great day when you can say, "Dad, may I have the keys?" There's something unique about a set of keys. They're more than status symbols. Keys give you a feeling of belonging somewhere. They are signs of rightful possession, something that is really yours to use and enjoy. For example, when a dignitary comes to town, the mayor hands him a key to the city, thus publicly opening to him the doors of the community.

On the other hand, when your father takes away your keys, you know you're grounded. Or when a bank teller leaves her job, she must turn in the keys to the till and the vault.

Keys are symbols of entrance and exit, of being in or out, of locking and unlocking. The Bible often uses the symbol of the key to get its message across to us. In appointing a new leader in Israel, God said, "And the key of the house of David will I lay upon his shoulder"—they had pretty large keys in those days!—"he shall open, and none shall shut; and he shall shut, and none shall open" (Isa. 22:22). Jesus accused the scribes of His day of taking away "the key of knowledge" (Luke 11:52). On Patmos Island the glorified Christ reminds John, "I have the keys of Death and of Hades" (Rev. 1:18). The authority to open and close the doors to heaven and hell belongs to our Lord.

But now Christ has assigned to His church the authority to exercise this power in carrying out His work in the world. Twice while talking with His apostles, who formed the core of the New Testament church, Christ entrusted to them the keys of the kingdom. Once, speaking directly to Peter, Christ said, "I will give unto you the keys of the kingdom of heaven: and whatever you shall bind on earth shall be bound in heaven; and whatever you shall loose on earth shall be loosed in heaven" (Matt. 16:19). Later He conferred the same power upon all His apostles (Matt. 18:18).

The Catechism speaks of two keys—that of the preaching of the Word and that of the exercise of Christian discipline.

OH, OUR PREACHER IS ALRIGHT I GUESS...

BUT I CAN'T JUDGE...

I'M A POOR LISTENER IN CHURCH

Gospel proclamation is a power of God for salvation to all who believe (Rom. 1:16). But it also falls in judgment upon those who refuse to take its message to heart (John 3:18). There is a disciplining power in God's Word. It cuts both ways like a two-edged sword (Heb. 4:12). When we hear it we can never just shake it off as though nothing had happened. For whenever we hear the gospel, the door to kingdom life goes a little further open or a little further shut. The key turns in both directions. It either locks us in or locks us out—and faith makes all the difference.

> What will you do with Jesus?
> Neutral you cannot be;
> Some day your soul will be asking,
> What will He do with me?

81. THE KEYS OF THE KINGDOM — DISCIPLINE

The second key on the key-ring given by Christ to His church is that of Christian discipline. We all tend to shy away from the idea of discipline. Yet down deep in our hearts we all know we need it. To be a Christian *disciple* means to place our lives under the *discipline* of our Master, who firmly and lovingly molds our lives into shape through the ministry of the church.

It is by the exercise of Christian discipline that Christ reinforces His Word and sacraments in the lives of His people. The history of the church is filled with pointed reminders of how important and necessary this discipline is. Many churches have dropped it, only to discover that the Word soon loses its hold on men's lives and the sacraments become mere for-

I GET ALL SHOOK-UP WHEN I THINK ABOUT DISCIPLINE

malities. For pastoral care is the church's way of personalizing the means of grace to fit our varied needs.

In making public profession of faith we answer Yes to this question: "Do you promise to submit to the government of the church and also, if you should become delinquent either in doctrine or in life, to submit to its admonition and discipline?"

Christian discipline is not only the work of ministers and elders. It is every Christian's business. For we are not merely our brother's keeper. We are his brother, and sister, and guardian, and friend. How easily we forget! When a fellow Christian leaves the track, we often try to cover up for him. Or when he falls off the deep end, we often talk behind his back. These are undisciplined reactions on our part. In the Christian community, as nowhere else in the world, we must speak the truth to each other in love (Eph. 4:15). We must look up the possible dropouts and try to win them back (Matt. 18:15-17). In doing so, don't underestimate the Bible, for it is intended for our reproof and correction and instruction (II Tim. 3:16).

As Christians, you see, we are bound together as members of the body of Christ, as eye to ear and hand to foot (I Cor. 12:12-21). If one member suffers, we all suffer. If one rebels, we all feel it. If one is in trouble, we must all help him along. For we must bear each other's burdens, and thus fulfill the law of love. In a frank but friendly way we must stand ready to give a helping hand by mutual encouragement and warning and forgiveness. How often? Seven times? Seventy times seven! (Matt. 18:21, 22).

There are two goals we must keep in mind in Christian discipline. First we must do our best to help stumbling Christians find a firm footing and to bring those who are breaking away back into the Christian community. And second, we must demonstrate our loyalty to Christ both in principle and in practice by maintaining the truthfulness and purity of the church. The image of the church may never become so dull that the world can no longer see the image of Christ clearly reflected in the lives of His disciples. Our ministers and elders have a special task in exercising church discipline. That's why they call on people and counsel them how to fight against sin and how to live a Christian life.

Yet if at last someone should slam the door on the minister and elders and deacons and members of the church, then the church has no choice but to

SOME PEOPLE TAKE CRITICISM VERY POORLY!

apply the "shock treatment" of judgment and excommunication. For the deserter, by cutting himself off from the fellowship of Christ and His people, thereby puts himself outside the kingdom of God. In the name of Christ, the church must tell him so. But still we do it with a heavy heart.

PART THREE: SERVICE

82. GOOD WORKS AS FRUITS OF A THANKFUL LIFE

"What! Was only one man grateful enough to come back and say, Thank you? And he an alien at that! Didn't I heal ten lepers? Where are the other nine?"

This is the way Jesus reacted in that disappointing episode recorded in the gospel (Luke 17:11-19). Ninety percent ingratitude!

I wonder how much genuine thankfulness Jesus finds in our lives. You see, gratitude is the theme of the third part of the Catechism. The story of the first part is our sinfulness—which is like that sickness-unto-death called leprosy. The second part tells the amazing story of our healing by the power of Jesus Christ. But now the story moves forward. Now the accent falls on thankful Christian living.

But is that the way you think of yourself—grateful for being a Christian, ready for thankful service? Let's face it, such a spirit is not in step with our times. Many people live as though thankfulness had gone out of style. Just stand on a busy street corner sometime and watch the milling crowds.

What do you see written on their faces? Happiness, contentment, gratitude for countless undeserved blessings, a service-seeking outlook on life? Far from it! Instead, there are protest demonstrations, violence, riots. A spirit of dissent threatens to rock our society to the very foundations. And as men continue turning their backs on Christianity, this restless spirit is bound to grow. What a far cry from gratitude!

But for Christians there's a better way. For we live not by the shifting circumstances around us, but by a deeply rooted faith. That's the only way you can explain the first Thanksgiving Day among the Pilgrim Fathers.

By our standards they could count up their blessings in a hurry. Yet they experienced real gratitude. For thankfulness does not depend on things. It's anchored in the heart and life.

The Lord's Supper is meant to express such thankfulness. Another name for it is "Eucharist," which means "Thank you." Holy communion is a thanksgiving feast, reminding us that in Christ, God freely gives us all things (Rom. 8:32).

Thanksgiving and grateful living are directed to the same end: "Praise God from whom all blessings flow." Behind every good gift is the hand of the Giver. The Bible puts it this way: don't just be thankful *for something,* but thankful *to Someone.* God's blessings come to us as a call to a full Christian life of service. This holds for all Christians, for there are no age limits when it comes to sin, salvation, and service.

Christ stated the point very clearly. *Hearing* God's Word is not the end of the matter. The real test is *doing* His will (Matt. 7:21-27). The whole epistle of James makes the same point. There is no good in forever talking about our faith, unless we are also prepared to translate our faith into action. If we fail in this, people will say: Your deeds (or lack of them) speak so loudly I can't hear what you say.

Christians sometimes give the impression of saying: "Thank God, I'm saved! Amen—Period—Now I can wait around for heaven." What an awful misunderstanding! For we have been saved to serve. God's good work in Christ is meant to unlock the power of good works in our lives.

For example, as you go out for an evening, you can grab a dollar bill from your father's hand on the run, and shout back a quick "Thanks, Dad!" But words alone can be very cheap—just lip service. Words of thanksgiving must lead to deeds of thanks-living.

Actually, it's unthinkable for living Christians to fall short of a life of good works. For at the heart of the Christian life is a holy "must." God chose us to be Christians in order to declare in our lives His wonderful works

(I Pet. 2:9). He calls forth good works in our lives in obedience to His will (John 15:16; Rom. 12:1, 2). That is the goal of our salvation (Eph. 2:10). Just as we identify a tree by its fruit (Matt. 7:20), so Christians declare their identity by their new way of life. But the opposite is also true: as an unfruitful tree serves no good purpose, so an empty Christian life also defeats its purpose.

A thankful, fruitful Christian life doesn't just happen. It has to be worked at. But we never have to go it alone. Christ is always at our side. Through the power of His Spirit, we too shall overcome. For God will never let us down.

> The work Thou hast for me begun
> Shall by Thy grace be fully done.

83. GOOD WORKS AS SIGNS OF PERSONAL ASSURANCE

A life of good works stretches out in every direction. It reaches up to God as a visible expression of our thankfulness for His great salvation in Jesus Christ. It reaches out in love to our neighbors to offer them a helping hand, and so becomes a Christian witness. But a life of good works also brings with it another important by-product and effect. It reaches deep into our own hearts to reassure us that our faith is real.

So once again it's a question of self-identity. Who am I anyway? Am I really a Christian? At one time or another every Christian wrestles with this problem. Sometimes we go through periods of terrible doubt and inner conflict, just as did John the Baptist (Matt. 11:2, 3) and Peter (Luke 22:31, 32). But Christ stood by these two disciples. And that is our comfort too. We never face these searching questions alone. Christ will see us through. Believing in Him is the way to discover our real selves.

There are two ways of settling this question of self-identity—the front-door way and the back-door way. The direct, front-door approach to personal security is to face up to the biblical challenge: What do you think about Jesus Christ (Matt. 22:42)? Who is He to you? But the Catechism also enters this question by way of the back door: as we review our lives and thankfully discover there some evidences of good works, we may be assured that we stand within the circle of the Christian faith.

We gain such certainty by walking in the *way* of good works, we do not gain it on the *basis* of good works. If we think otherwise we are Pharisees, not Christians. For the road of good works is not a do-it-yourself project. It is not an independent witness, as a substitute for Christ or His Word or His Spirit (Rom. 8:16). Our personal assurance of salvation, which is strengthened by the signs of good works in our lives, is anchored by faith in Christ alone.

Recall again Christ's word-picture of the tree: when, for example, we see the branches of a tree hanging heavy with apples, we conclude immediately that it must be an apple tree—not a cottonwood or a sumac. So also we may be assured of our faith in Christ by the fruits of faith in our lives.

So now we have another answer to the question: Who am I?—I am a Christian! Christ lives in me and through me. I couldn't possibly bear good fruit on my own. That is something only Christ can do, through His Spirit —and thanks be to God, He will fill me with His Spirit so that I can bear the fruits of faith in my life.

Or look at it this way. The more we exercise our muscles, the more we strengthen them. Or again, the more money we deposit in our bank accounts, the more our interest grows. In some such way it is true that the more we exercise ourselves in good works, and the more we invest our energies in Christ-centered, action-packed living, the more the Christian faith comes to its own in our lives. When that happens, then we know with certainty whose we are and whom we want to serve.

84. GOOD WORKS AS A CHRISTIAN WITNESS

"I've long ago forgotten his name. But the passing years have not erased his memory. We served together as infantrymen in the North African campaign, during World War II. Returning one evening from a hot and dusty raid, almost too tired to eat, the whole company turned in for the night. We sprawled out on our bunks and called it a day. But not this unforgettable foot-soldier. He first took time to kneel at his bunk. It made me furious to see him pray. So I threw a dirty boot at him and then rolled over to sleep. The next morning I found that boot standing with its mate next to my bunk, cleaned and polished! That young fellow had something I lacked. I wish I could meet him again some day."

In this true story from a man who was there, one point stands out clearly: never underestimate the impact of a Christian witness. If only we are faithful in sowing the seed, God will take care of the fruit—in His own good way and in His own good time. So carry on with your life of good works. God can make something good come of it all in changing the lives of people around you.

"We've a story to tell to the nations . . . ." How true! But if we don't tell that story, who will?

But life is more than words. Sure, the world needs sermons. But even more, it needs sermons *in action.* We must practice what we preach. Our lives must be open epistles, written in large letters, spelling out the "good news" in deeds of love and justice, honesty and compassion. Our lives must be living Bibles for people who never read the Bible.

GOOD WORKS HAVE TO START SOMEWHERE!

Being a Christian witness must become a deeply ingrained habit with us—a new style of life. But like any good habit, newly adopted, it takes a lot of practice. It's something like a dope addict turning over a new leaf: he must strengthen his new pattern of good habits by seizing every opportunity to act upon them. This can be done best by showing other dope addicts—those who are still enslaved to dope— a better way of life. As Christians we also must be ready to put our faith into practice as a way of winning our neighbors to Christ. When words fail, our deeds must carry the day. In fact, good works must always go hand in hand with good words, if people are to believe what we say. Often we can say more to a person in trouble by putting our arm around his shoulder than by a ten-minute talk. And when we visit the poor, our words of comfort are empty unless we also pull out our wallet.

I'M ALWAYS ON THE LOOKOUT FOR HERETICS IN THE CHURCH

WITNESSING FOR CHRIST?

I JUST DON'T HAVE TIME FOR THAT!

Christian outreach is a fairly silent note in our Catechism. But it breaks through at this point. The door of the church stands open toward the world, and through it must flow a steady stream of good works, so that the world—our neighbors in the inner city, in suburbia, and in the country-side—may see the peace and joy and love that God has given us, and so be led to find Jesus Christ as their Lord and Savior.

But where shall we start? In a village compound in North Africa? On a volunteer program in Chicago? At a state university?

FIRST I WANTED TO BE A MISSIONARY IN AFRICA······

THEN I THOUGHT ABOUT INDIA···

THEN I LOOKED NEXT DOOR !

No, you don't have to look that far. You can get started right in your own home, in your own neighborhood, at your own school, on your own main street. And there is no time to get started like *now.*

> You are writing a gospel,
> A chapter each day,
> By deeds that you do
> And words that you say.
> Men read what you write,
> Whether faithless or true—
> Say, what is the gospel according to you?

85. CONVERSION

Sometimes we act as if covenant people don't need conversion. But where did we ever pick up that idea? Certainly not from the Bible, nor from the Catechism. Both of these books tell us clearly that at some decisive crossroad in his life, everyone who grows up within the church comes face to face with Christ. Then we must make the choice of our lives.

We call such turning-points *conversion.* You see, no one ever just drifts into the kingdom of God. Sooner or later we must stand up and be counted for something—for Someone! Conversion means deciding for Christ. God somehow creates a situation in our lives, and in it we hear His call to come and join His family. That choice, more than anything else in the world, charts the course of our future lives.

Recall what happened to Paul. As a veteran apostle, looking back over his stormy career, he gradually became aware that God had been busy hammering his life into shape for missionary service from the very day of his birth. But you would never have guessed it, judging by his fierce hatred of Christians during his late teens and twenties. Then, one day, Christ arrested him as he was speeding in pursuit of the Christians in Damascus

152

(Acts 9:1-6). Paul's misdirected life was brought to a halt, and turned around. Christ converted this enemy into a friend.

Then there was Matthew, the customs officer, associated with the black market dealings of the Roman-Jewish internal revenue department. But when Christ came by and called "Follow me!" Matthew turned his back on his former colleagues and started a new chapter in his life (Matt. 9:9-13).

And don't forget Timothy. He was brought up in a pious Jewish home. But God-fearing Jews need conversion too. The Holy Spirit used Paul's preaching to do it, leading Timothy to a new way of life (Acts 16:1-5).

You can add to the list. Just think of Peter and the other disciples. Think of Augustine, Luther, Calvin, Charles Spurgeon, David Livingstone, Abraham Kuyper, Billy Graham, and . . . you?

We often think of conversion as a spectacular change that takes place in the lives of notorious sinners. But really, whether dramatically or quietly, conversion is a transformation that Christ looks for in the lives of each one of us. God leads us to it in many different ways, making His grace personal to meet our individual needs. Yet for every Christian, conversion is a holy "must."

True conversion is a fruit of faith in Christ. Our heart must be in it. A phony conversion—putting on a pious front—is like a sports car with a gleaming hood, but a blown motor underneath. You can't fix it up by applying decals to the side panels. There's just one way to make it run— a complete overhaul. So conversion calls for an inner transformation of our lives. Like the prodigal son, we must come to our senses before we can travel the road home (Luke 15:17-19).

Conversion covers a lifetime. Christians of all ages—children, young people, adults, middle-aged, and senior citizens—travel together along the road of sanctification with its ups and downs. With Christ's help, wonderful achievements in Christian living are possible. But without Him we are bound to lose ground. This is the clue to a converted life: "growing up into Christ" (Eph. 4:15).

The life of the converted Christian is like a coin with two sides—a negative side and a positive one. We call the negative side "mortification," which implies sincere repentance for our sins and the desire to stamp sin out of our lives. Just think of Peter the turncoat, weeping bitter tears in the darkness of the courtyard (Luke 22:60-62). Mortification is a godly sorrow that works repentance unto salvation (II Cor. 7:10, 11). It is that long and hard task of uprooting and killing the weeds of greed and hatred in our lives. It means detesting sin, breaking with it, and resolving anew to quit playing around with fire.

But conversion means not only turning our backs on our sinful past. It also means making a full turn around toward Jesus Christ. We call this positive side of conversion "living the new life." For the road of the Christian does not stop at the cross. Rather, that is where it begins. From there it goes on past the empty tomb of Easter to a life that is filled with the presence of our risen and living Lord. Christ now makes His home in our hearts and lives (Gal. 2:20). The Spirit of truth, whom Christ promised, guides us into all truth, and helps us to live the Spirit-filled Christian life (John 16:13, 14; II Tim. 1:7).

Have you come to that turning point and found a new life in Him?

86.   GOOD WORKS IN THREE DIMENSIONS

The Christian life is like a house—the "house of good works." The welcome mat is out, the doors are standing wide open, and there is room for action-packed Christian living inside. We have already opened three doors to this "house of good works": the door of thankfulness, the door of personal assurance, and the door of Christian witness. So make yourself at home. The whole house is yours, with opportunities unlimited for a life of good works.

Looking over this house more carefully, we discover that it is built in three dimensions: it is as deep as faith in God, as wide as the law of God, and as high as the glory of God. You see, God is at the center of it all. He is the Landlord. The house is His world. Those who share this house are called to God-centered living. That is what Paul tells us: "From him and through him and to him are all things" (Rom. 11:36). This is how Jesus said it: "I chose you and appointed you that you should go and bear fruit, and that your fruit should abide" (John 15:16).

Let's take a look at these three dimensions of good works as three standards by which to test ourselves.

First, good works must spring from true faith. That we do good works is important. But even unbelievers perform acts which, to all outward appearances, are good. The Bible, however, takes an in-depth look at our good works and asks *why* we do them. What is our motivation? Are these works born of faith? Certainly, faith without works is dead. But it is also true that works without faith are a pretense. Just think of the Pharisees, for example. Good works that are not rooted in true faith are like cut flowers. They soon wither and die in your hand because their connection with the life-giving root is broken. The same is true of good works: they must be rooted in a living faith.

Second, the value of good works must be measured by the standard of God's law of love—loving God above all and our neighbors as ourselves. Unbelievers may perform acts that pass the test of man-made laws. But the Christian must pass the test of God's law. Do our works spring from true love for God, first of all, and then also for our neighbor? Or are our motives mixed with selfish interests—greed or pride or selfish pleasure? God's law of love is not a list of do's and don'ts that hems us in and pours our life into a straitjacket. Rather, it's a law that expands our horizons and leads us along the pathway to true freedom.

It's pretty clear that we need a higher standard than public opinion if we are to make proper judgments about what is right and wrong, good and bad. So often we think that being free means doing as we please. We rationalize our behavior, trying to make wrong appear right when personal advantage or safety is at stake. We devise clever ways of covering up our sinful practices. We appeal to human traditions and the "everybody is

doing it" line to justify our actions. If we truly want to know right from wrong, then our conscience must be attuned to God's will, just as the class-room clocks are synchronized with the master clock in the office. Other-wise we will be tempted to live like revolutionaries rather than reformers. Then we will be an easy prey for the so-called "new morality" and "situa-tional ethics," instead of living a life of good works in keeping with God's law.

Third, our good works must be directed to the glory of God. How true it is that by nature we want to set ourselves in the limelight! It's hard for us to keep ourselves in the background, so that God may take the fore-ground. Yet that is the point of doing good works: that others may see God at work in us. Our lives must be mirrors, reflecting God's glory.

155

These, then, are the three dimensions of a Christian life. Measured by this triple standard, we all fall far short. Even our best works are infected by sin. But this is no excuse for quitting. It's a call, rather, to daily conversion—a daily turning away from sin and back to the Christ, who saves us and gives us the Spirit of power.

87. GOD'S LAW OUR GUIDE FOR CHRISTIAN LIVING

If repetition is the key to learning, we should all be ready for a "Doctor of Laws" degree. Time and again we hear the law of God. Or don't we hear it anymore?

Playing possum is a dangerous game—just letting God talk, but paying no attention to what He says. When we do that we are asking for trouble. Besides, we are missing something great in life. For the law of God is the cement that holds the building blocks of life together. When men break His laws, life falls apart. Isn't that just what is happening in our world today? God's laws for human life are being trampled underfoot—in the home, the school, the church, the state. "Down with the law!" "Freedom now!"—these are slogans that make the headlines.

As Christians we don't have to turn into rebels to gain our freedom. We are already free people. For Christ has set us free from every form of earthly bondage.

God's law, you see, is not opposed to Christian freedom. It's rather a teacher that leads us to Christ by showing us our sinfulness, our need of the Savior. And Christ, in turn, leads us back to the law as a guide for thankful Christian living. The law of God is not our enemy; it's our friend. It's not the voice of some stranger; it's the voice of our Father. To live according to the law of God means to walk with Christ—and that is true freedom.

What curbs are for a car and rails for a train, what water is for a fish and air for a bird, what a shepherd dog is for a flock of sheep—that's what

God's law is for His children. It's the Father's hand in our lives. It's the key to liberty and love and truth (Ps. 119:45, 97, 142; Rom. 7:22). God holds the law out to us as a lantern to cast its light upon our path. Little wonder that His law fills the psalmist with delight and makes him leap for joy (Ps. 1:2; 19:7-9).

Keeping God's law helps us avoid pitfalls. On the one hand is the danger of *legalism*. This was the gospel of the Pharisees. They served the law instead of God. What a heavy burden of idolatry that is! Touch not, taste not, see not, handle not. Pull the shades on Sunday. Never laugh out loud. Walk the tight rope, with barbed-wire fencing on both sides for those who lose their footing.

On the other hand is the danger of *libertinism* (immoral living). You know this line: Man, nobody is going to tell me what to do! I don't care who you are—God or man—don't ever try to get in my way! I know what I want, and I want it now! Laws? They're made to be broken.

FIRST I DUG LEGALISM...

THEN I DUG LIBERTINISM....

I JUST DIG ISMS

False notions of freedom have taken hold even in some Christian circles. Christ fulfilled the law, it is said, and so He has abolished it forever. We have nothing to do with the law anymore. The law belongs to the Old Testament, and that is past.

With all these conflicting voices dinning in our ears, where shall we turn? There is just one place to go: turn to Christ. Receive the law of God from His hands as your friendly guide for Christian living. For He says, "You are my friends, if you do the things which I command you" (John 15:14).

Look at it this way. Have you ever argued a point with your parents until you wear down their resistance? Finally in despair they give in and say, "Okay, have your own way then." This is not really an answer of love, but a sign of weakness. You can't use such tactics with God. He always stands His ground. As a good and firm Father He sticks to His point: "Love Me above all and your neighbor as yourself." His law is sure, and that is good, for it is meant for our good and for His glory.

88. THE TEN COMMANDMENTS

"Well, don't expect me to believe the whole Bible—all that ancient history, those long lists of 'begats,' plus the unscientific ideas in it. The Sermon on the Mount and the Ten Commandments—that's my Bible." Likely you've heard that story before. It has hypnotized thousands. Many people act as if they can pick and choose what they wish to believe in the Bible, and let the rest go. From the New Testament they pull out the Sermon on the Mount and from the Old Testament the Ten Commandments. And so they come out with their own "bible" within the Bible.

MY THINKING IS KINDA SHALLOW ON THE TEN COMMANDMENTS!

But you can't do that with God's Word. It's all of one piece from start to finish. No part of it stands alone—not even the Ten Commandments. They are part of the total message. On the mountain in Galilee, the place of Christ's hillside sermon, we hear the distant echoes of Mount Sinai, the place where the Ten Commandments were given, and we also see the approaching shadows of Mount Calvary. All three heights are linked together in an unbroken mountain range of God's saving acts in the life of His people.

Another name for the Ten Commandments is the Decalogue, which means the Ten Words. The Bible often uses the number ten as a symbolic number, representing something full and whole. These Ten Words are therefore keys that unlock the full meaning of God's laws, covering the full range of our lives—in every place and at all times.

The language of the Ten Commandments reflects life among the Israelites long before the coming of Christ. As God's revelation moves forward across the pages of the Old Testament, it steadily updates the meaning of these Ten Words until they reach their climax in Christ. The letter of the law is important. But it is more important that we catch its life-embracing spirit.

Listening to the law, you can't help noticing that it is heavily loaded with negative words: "Thou shalt not . . ." comes through repeatedly. That's the way we often talk to youngsters when we want to make a point simply and forcefully. Well, that is what Israel was at Mount Sinai—an adolescent nation. Yet even these negative admonitions carry with them a positive meaning that we may not overlook. They are something like the road sign on a hill, "No Passing," which is really a positive warning: Stay in your own lane.

When we think of the Ten Commandments, we usually think of Moses. For he was God's right hand in giving the two tablets to Israel. But the law was not born on Mount Sinai. From Paradise on, it was woven into the very fiber of human life. The Sabbath, for example, goes back to the seventh day of creation. When Cain killed Abel, he was violating a law that was in force from the beginning. But with the passing centuries, sin dulled men's minds to the will of God. So at Sinai God called man back to His law in ten unforgettable words.

Actually, God's law spans all of history from the dawn of creation to the end of time. It finds its place in the gospel and comes to its own within the Christian life. In the New Covenant (Testament) as well as in the Old, the law is our guide for living a new life (Gal. 3:15-22). We see this already in the Old Testament where the Ten Commandments, recorded in Exodus 20, are part of a larger document—Exodus 19-24—called the Book of the Covenant. It was amid the smoke and thunder of Sinai that God made the law a living part of the Covenant of Grace—a covenant which He announced first to Adam, then renewed with Abraham, and reestablished ith His chosen people at Mount Sinai.

The parallel between the law in Old Testament and New Testament times may be seen when we view the exodus as the gospel, the story of God's mighty act of salvation. Sinai is the law, the constitution for our covenant life among God's liberated people, to keep us from falling back into slavery. To a people already redeemed, God says in the prologue to the Ten Commandments: Remember who I am, the Lord your God, the God of Abraham, Isaac, and Jacob. I am your Savior, who rescued you from bondage and made you free.

This "good news" of God's salvation is the motivation and power behind a life of obedience, both in the old covenant and in the new. With this motivation, God's people are ready to live according to His law as a way of demonstrating their thankfulness for the salvation so fully and freely given.

In the Sermon on the Mount, Christ updated the law—deepened and enriched it—for our new life in His kingdom. Taking His cue from the Old Testament (Deut. 6:5; Lev. 19:18), He gives us a summary of the Ten Words in a positive and sweeping form: Love God with all your heart, and your neighbor as yourself (Matt. 22:37-39). For love is the fulfillment of the whole law (Gal. 5:14). Love for our neighbor is rooted in love for God. In fact, we demonstrate our love for God by loving our neighbor (I John 4:20, 21). Loving God without loving our fellowmen is empty religion. And loving our fellowmen without loving God is empty humanism.

As heirs of the exodus and of Calvary we are now free people—free to live the Christian life spontaneously and gladly. Such freedom clears the way for thankful service to God and to our fellowmen.

89. GOD COMES FIRST, LAST, AND ALWAYS

In a church announcement appearing on the front page of a local newspaper the readers were told to take a look at the back page. There, in large bold print, appeared this question: "Is this where you are putting God?"

What place does God hold in your life? First place? Last place? Or somewhere in between? You see, that is the point of the First Commandment: God must come first because He *is* First. Lest we lose our sense of priorities, the law at the very outset clearly reminds us that God holds a total claim upon our lives and that we owe Him our highest loyalty.

Israel was foolish enough to try to serve two gods (Jer. 2:11). Christ's words are clear: "No man can serve two masters . . ." (Matt. 6:24). God will not tolerate released-time or shared-time programs. He must reign supreme, and He must reign alone. There is no room on His throne for any rival.

This First Commandment forbids all fire-truck religion—calling on God only in an emergency, after the fire is out of control. No, says God, give Me first place in your lives. Love Me above all. No other gods before Me! I can't stand two-timing lovers or double-faced disciples.

It just won't do to work for Mammon all week and then "piously" turn to God on Sunday. That's nothing more than lip service.

You know how it goes. There are so many things competing for your loyalty, so many little tin gods tugging at your heart strings, so many winking idols making a pitch for your love. You could actually go crazy trying to satisfy every god that comes along. No, the old Baals and Molochs and Asheroths don't bother us much anymore. But men keep on manufacturing new substitute gods—like sex and sports and money and success—that

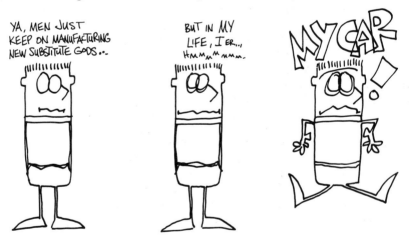

get in the way of our service of God. At the bottom of such idolatries is the nasty god of self, who is always tempted to push God off into some forgotten corner of our lives with such selfish questions as these: What's in it for me? Does it pay?

Remember, there is no comfort in man-centered religions. A wealthy businessman, his life ruined by a broken home, finally admitted, "I made work my god for twenty years—and this is all I have to show for it."

On a larger scale, too, men create gods in their own image. Six million Jews were sacrificed on the altar of Hitler's god, the German Reich. Whole nations have been overrun in the name of a Communist god, the Party. The switchblade takes its heavy toll in the service of a juvenile god called the Gang. Many decent citizens put the interests of their race, their class, their country ahead of everything else.

Every man needs a god—the true God! Every man does in fact have some god. Paul talks about people "whose god is the belly" (Phil. 3:19). To the people of Athens, crowded in among their gods, Paul says, "In all things I perceive that you are very religious" (Acts 17:22, 23).

But for Christians there are no two ways about it. There is only one God, the God who comes to us as our Father in Jesus Christ. He claims our love, our worship, our service (Deut. 6:4, 5; Mark 12:29, 30; Matt. 4:10). Angels are no substitutes (Rev. 22:8, 9). Nor may the apostles or saints take the place of God (Acts 14:11-18).

This is the cost of discipleship—following Christ, and Him alone. But what a great investment! For having Christ, we have all we could possibly ask for (Matt. 6:33). In his heart the Christian echoes the words of the psalmist: "Whom have I in heaven but thee? And there is none upon earth that I desire beside thee" (Ps. 73:25).

90. TRUE WORSHIP

The Ten Commandments are like signposts along the road of Christian living. We have passed the first marker, which answers the question: *Whom* shall we worship? "Thou shalt worship the Lord thy God, and him only shalt thou serve" (Matt. 4:10). Now the second marker comes into view, answering the question: *How* shall we worship? "God is a Spirit: and they that worship him must worship in spirit and truth" (John 4:24).

Many people serve false gods; therefore you must be sure you are serving the true God—that is the point of the First Commandment. People sometimes worship God in wrong ways; therefore you must be sure you are worshiping Him in the right way—that is the point of the Second Commandment.

Looking back into history, and reflecting on our own experience, we are struck by the fact that people often turn worship of God into pagan rituals that dishonor Him. At the very time that Moses was standing on Mount Sinai receiving the Second Commandment, the people of Israel were busy breaking it by engaging in a pagan dance around the golden calf. What a stunning contrast! Israel knew better than to worship a golden calf. They realized that this animal-like thing, which they had made with their own hands, was not divine. In the back of their minds they still believed that Jehovah was their God. But somehow they made themselves believe that they could worship God better by bowing before this image.

Similar cases of idolatry, borrowed from the surrounding pagan peoples, kept arising in Israel. For example, God used the brass serpent to arrest a deadly plague among His people. But later the Israelites turned to worshiping that symbol instead of the God who was behind it. King Hezekiah

161

told it like it was: he called the brass serpent "Nehushtan," which means "a thing of brass." To prevent further false worship he ordered its destruction (II Kings 18:4). At other times the Jewish people were guilty of worshiping the ark (I Sam. 4:3), the temple (Jer. 7:4), the law (Matt. 23:23, 24), and their father Abraham (Matt. 3:9), instead of God alone.

The strong warnings of the prophets usually fell on deaf ears. Finally it took the captivity to cure the Hebrews of idol worship. Many Jews then went to the extreme of condemning all works of art and sculpture. They even tore down the golden eagle from Herod's temple, thinking that this too was a violation of the Second Commandment. When the victorious Roman general Titus marched into the Jerusalem temple, he looked for the local idol. Finding the inner sanctuary empty, Titus came to the conclusion that Jews must be atheists, since they had nothing visible to worship.

Today false worship often parades under the title of broad-mindedness. You know the slogans: "Every man has a right to worship as he pleases," and "A man's religion is his own business." Some people call it tolerance.

Actually, it is glorified indifference. What such people are really saying is that how we worship God is not important, just so it is done sincerely. But it is possible to be sincerely wrong as well as sincerely right. You may sincerely believe that you can worship God by stealing money and then putting it in the offering plate on Sunday, but that does not make it right.

So it is possible to attempt worshiping God in many false ways, if we do not follow His law as our guide. Men can make an idol out of creeds, for instance, by worshiping them instead of the Christ to whom they witness. Or they can make an idol out of the house of God. They can also worship the bread and wine of the Lord's Supper instead of Him who said, "Do this in remembrance of me."

All such false forms of worship are idolatry. The evil of image-worship lies not in the objects, but in the person who refuses to be guided by the Second Commandment; just as murder is not the fault of the gun, but of the man who pulls the trigger. Images are crutches for people who are too weak to walk by faith alone, and thus come face to face with God.

The men who wrote the Heidelberg Catechism issued a strong protest against their mother church on this point. In giving an honored place to images, the old Roman Catholic Church tended to push God into the background. When men turn to images, what starts out as being a *means* to worship in the end becomes an *object* of worship. The purpose of the Second Commandment is to keep our worship pure. Even the figure of the cross may not become an object of worship; but only Christ. Nor may we worship the Bible itself; but only the God who there commands our loyalty and love.

Worship Him, then, in spirit (led by His Spirit) and in truth.

91. HONORING GOD'S NAME

When ninety percent of the people claim to believe in God, but only fifty percent are members of a church, and only ten percent actually worship God on Sundays—that's taking God's name in vain.

When a nation inscribes "In God We Trust" on its coins, but actually puts its trust in military power—that's an open violation of the Third Commandment.

When we bow to the pressure of atheists and secularists by cutting God out of public education and public life—that's defaming God's name.

When politicians just tip their hats to God to win a few extra votes—that's blasphemy.

When free-lance ministers engage in religious racketeering—that's an outrage against God's name.

And now coming closer to home: when we try to spice up our conversations with flippant references to God, when we pray thoughtlessly, when our talk about God is cheap and easy, when we make public profession of our faith without meaning it—all this is a dishonor to God's name.

Sometimes we think we can split our lives ten ways, with one commandment to cover each part. Actually, this Third Commandment, like every law of God, touches our life at every point. In essence, the Third Commandment comes down to this: don't a phony Christian. When you call upon God, mean what you say. Mere lip service is an abomination to Him. He wants you to put your heart in it. He wants us to be honest with Him, and sincere.

Jesus says, "Not everyone that saith unto me, Lord, Lord, shall enter into the kingdom of heaven; but he that doeth the will of my Father who is in heaven" (Matt. 7:21). So it is possible to be profane in our actions as well as in our speech. If we confess God's name in our words, but don't do anything about it in our deeds, then we have broken the Third Commandment just as surely as if we had used blasphemy.

In the Bible, names are important. There a name is never just a label or identification tag. It's the doorway to someone's personality. Thus, God's name reveals who He is and what He does. His name is His person. What we do with God's name we do to Him. Defiling God's name is character assassination. It's an insult to God's majesty and holiness. And by attempting to defile God, we actually defile ourselves. For it is not the things that enter our bodies through our mouths, but the things that flow out of our hearts through our mouths that pollute us—evil thoughts, slander, profanity (Mark 7:14-23).

In the Third Commandment God is not merely insisting that we observe rules of proper decorum and good taste. He is calling us to a covenant style of life with Him as our Father and we as His image-bearing children. Do right-minded children drag their family name through the mud? God called the children of Israel by His own name (Isa. 44:5). We as Christians are called by the very name of God's Son (Acts 11:26). And Christ's name is above every name (Phil. 2:9).

But perhaps the worst profanity of our times is refusing to use God's name at all. The Jews were guilty of a similar sin of omission. As they reflected upon the reasons for their captivity, they came to the conclusion that this judgment fell upon them because they had used God's name too freely. In reaction, they decided not to use God's name at all. What a false sense of God's holiness! Many modern people also ban the use of God's name, but for different reasons. They think God doesn't count in their daily lives. By ignoring Him and cold-shouldering Him, they are failing to honor God's name as certainly as if they were guilty of cursing and swearing.

The Third Commandment marks off the boundary between a sanctified or holy life and a profane life. It rules out all swearing, a sin common to the Jews and perhaps public sin number one today. How frequently we

hear God's name used to confirm a truth. How lightly people speak of being damned. Jesus spoke against this sin when He said, "Let what you say be simply 'Yes' or 'No'; anything more than this comes from evil" (Matt. 5:37 RSV). If we are called to testify in court, we are to take our public oaths seriously.

165

Though put in negative terms, the Third Commandment carries a positive message. Primarily it calls us to put our heart into our worship of God—in church, in family devotions, in personal meditations, and in our daily lives. It means that all our words and all our deeds in the full range of our daily lives must bear witness to the honor of God, whose children we are and whose name we bear.

92. THE LORD'S DAY

I wonder how our Sundays would look to some unexpected visitor from another planet! Could he make any sense out of this weekly day in our lives? Sunday means different things to different people—like sleeping in, overtime work, gardening, golfing, TV sports, picnics, traveling, family life, going to church, reading, and so on. For most people it's a holiday. For millions it has ceased being a holy-day. Yet that's precisely the way the Fourth Commandment states it: "Keep the sabbath day holy." Would anything of that biblical truth get through to our foreign guest?

MY THINKING ABOUT SUNDAY IS A MESS!

But more important, how do *you* feel about Sunday? Is it a boring day to you, filled with dull duties? A day hemmed in with prison bars? What thoughts cross your mind as you join the congregation in singing "Day of all the week the best," or "My heart was glad to hear the welcome sound, the call to seek Jehovah's house of prayer"?

Actually, the observance of Sunday as our Sabbath, or day of rest, is one of our greatest blessings. To a large extent Christianity stands or falls with this day. Must we lose the Sabbath day before we will stop long enough to appreciate it? Have you ever tried to imagine what life would be like without Sunday? Christians in Ceylon could tell you—by hard experience. A few years ago, anti-Christian forces succeeded in wiping out their Sunday as a day of rest. Now a work day like the other days of the week, the Sabbath can be observed by Christians in Ceylon only as they gather for worship early in the morning, before going to work, or later in the evening, after work. Such persecution cuts deeply into the biblical rhythm of work and rest, worship and service.

Our Sunday comes up out of a long journey through history. It's a day of remembrance, recalling the mighty acts of God both in creation and redemption. Originally the Sabbath was observed at the end of a six-day week of work. Now it stands as a red-letter day at the beginning of a new week.

You remember how the Sabbath began. Near the dawn of creation, after six days of creative activity, God rested the seventh day and set it aside as a day of special celebration (Gen. 2:1-3). Centuries later, as God led His people out of Egyptian slavery, He invited this nation of ex-slaves to enjoy their new freedom by walking in His footsteps—working for six days

166

and then taking a day off for physical and spiritual refreshment (Exod. 20:8-11). The Sabbath was a call to rest in the creating and saving work of God. Even servants must lay down their labors (Deut. 5:12-15). In Egypt there were no sabbaths, no holidays, no vacations. But in Canaan things would be different. There God would restore His creation order, so that His people could rest from their work, as God did, and worship Him and fellowship with Him in a special way, thus to be renewed for service in God's world.

By Jesus' day, the Pharisees had succeeded in straitjacketing the Sabbath with their hopelessly complicated system of human traditions. They had actually compiled a list of 1521 do's and don'ts, which they imposed upon their fellowmen. Jesus attacked this deadening system with all the force of His divine authority. When the Pharisees accused the disciples of harvesting on the Sabbath (Mark 2:23-28) and criticized Him for healing on the Sabbath (Matt. 12:9-14), Jesus appealed to God's law of liberty by declaring, "The sabbath was made for man, and not man for the sabbath: so that the Son of man is lord even of the sabbath" (Mark 2:27, 28). But Jesus never throws out the good with the bad. He Himself "entered, as his custom was, into the synagogue on the sabbath day" (Luke 4:16). For He came not to destroy the Sabbath, but to fulfill it. If our Master took time regularly for worship, can we His disciples get by with less?

The early church kept the Sabbath alive as a day of celebration to commemorate the creation and the exodus, but especially to commemorate the Easter victory of our Lord. The seventh day was God's day of rest from creation and therefore, in Old Testament times, the day in which man rested too; but man finds his true rest in the redeeming work of the Lord, which was climaxed by the resurrection on the first day of the week. As the full meaning of Christ's resurrection grew upon the early church, they shifted their day of worship from the old Sabbath to the new Sunday. Since this was the day on which Christ arose, it became known as the Day of the

Lord (I Cor. 16:2; Rev. 1:10), or the Lord's Day. Now every Sunday is an Easter celebration, with Christians gathering to celebrate the victory of Christ and looking forward to the eternal sabbath rest that awaits the people of God (Heb. 4:9).

How can we celebrate Sunday in a holy way? The way we work out our answers to that question will set the pace for keeping the weekdays holy too. For Sunday's worship is a preparation for Monday's work and witness in the world. As a football team goes into a huddle before a big game, so Sunday is the time, and the church is the place, for us to be coached on how to live for Christ in the week ahead. A good Sunday makes the rest of the week worth living.

93. HONORING YOUR PARENTS

We hear a lot of talk these days about the generation gap. You've probably given the phrase some thought too. Is the generation gap real? And if so, how big is the gap? Many teen-agers are saying, "You can't trust anyone *over* thirty." Meanwhile older people are asking, "Can we trust anyone *under* thirty?"

Do you feel that you and your parents live in two different worlds? But how can that be? There is just one world—our Father's world. And in every generation there is just one Savior and Lord—Jesus Christ. And there is just one guide for Christian living—the Bible. This is the one faith that binds parents and children together.

Perhaps you sometimes feel that your parents don't understand you. Tensions arise between you and your parents about what you wear, the way you groom your hair, the hours you keep, your friends, your studies. All this is part of growing up. Still, amid all these differences, the Fifth Commandment stands: "Honor your parents." For this is God's way of claiming your love within the family circle.

Respect for authority is on the decline these days. Yet the Bible speaks with command to the rising generation: "Thou *shalt* honor thy father and thy mother." God's laws, however, are not like military regulations. They are more like rules for family life, guidelines for living in covenant fellowship with God and in company with our dear ones. The home is the training center and proving ground for living under the rule of God's law of love in every part of life. But the implications of the Fifth Commandment reach out in every direction. In court the minister must submit to the authority of the judge, while in church the judge must take to heart the authoritative word of the minister. In a traffic jam the doctor must obey the authority of the policeman, while in the hospital the policeman must bow to the authority of the doctor. God has established various centers of authority in life to govern human relations. But true respect for authority starts in the home. If we disobey God there by dishonoring our parents, then we can only expect that some day our children will also rebel against our God-given authority. People who destroy home life, in the long run destroy themselves.

If you find it hard to follow your parents' leadership, remember this: Jesus was once a teen-ager too. The Bible is nearly silent on these growing years in His life. Yet it tells us that at twelve years of age He put quite a strain on His parents by going off on His own for three days in Jerusalem. When Joseph and Mary finally found Him in the temple, He was unable to get them to see things His way. Yet "he went down with them and came to Nazareth; and he was subject unto them . . . ," and He "advanced in wisdom and stature, and in favor with God and men" (Luke 2:50-52). Christ is the Bridge spanning the "generation gap." For He took our place. For us, therefore, keeping God's law means walking in Christ's footsteps.

We can trace family life back to the very dawn of human history. Under God, each newly rising generation owes its very existence, plus innumerable blessings, to the older generation. Parents therefore never outgrow their claim upon our honor, even though they often make mistakes and fail to live up to their calling.

As Paul looked around him, he saw that many homes were suffering a severe breakdown, due to the sins and delinquency of parents. Therefore he writes, "Fathers, provoke not your children to wrath" (Eph. 6:4). Parents must seek God's help in being worthy of the honor which they may rightfully expect of their children. Parental authority and youthful obedience—this is a two-way street that paves the way for sharing Christian comfort in the home.

94. LIFESAVERS AND PEACEMAKERS

Movies slay their thousands and television programs their ten thousands. Day and night, murder strikes faster than the clock. And there are three suicides for every killing—especially among the younger set. Time after time it happens that people will stand by with their hands in their pockets, muttering something about "Why should I get involved?" while within plain view some innocent victim gets a vicious going over at the hands of a hoodlum.

You can easily add to the list: gangland battles, political assassinations, racial warfare, lethal drugs, illegal abortions, airplane bombings, deathtrap cars. And don't forget the way we threaten life on a larger scale by air pollution and water pollution, mass starvations on the other side of the globe due to overpopulation and underproduction, the over-kill that comes with war, the atrocities of concentration camps, and the mushroom clouds of atom bombs over Hiroshima and Nagasaki.

Don't get the idea, however, that killing is a modern invention. Down through all the ages of human history the blood of countless Abels has cried to heaven for revenge. That same Cain spirit is still with us today: "Am I my brother's keeper?" (Gen. 4:8-12). Men will pull a trigger to settle a minor dispute. Violence is almost an accepted way of life: it stalks our streets and rocks our campuses, with guerrilla warfare in our cities lurking just around the corner. Look what sin has done to God's world! You would think men had never heard of the Sixth Commandment: "Thou shalt not kill."

The choice is clear: it's either the switchblade or the sword of the Spirit, which is the Word of God. At the foot of the cross men trampled on the blood of the Son of God Himself. Yet through that death of all deaths God opened our eyes to the meaning of life, and its worth. Life is a gift of God. It is not our own to do with as we please, for we belong to Christ. We are made in the image of God to reflect His glory. So when we lash out at the life of a fellow human being, we are striking out at God Himself.

You see how far sin goes—destroying life itself. But God goes even farther. He sent Christ into the world as "the Life" (John 14:6) in order that we "may have life, and may have it abundantly" (John 10:10). Now God calls us to be lifesavers among men. Through the Prince of Peace He appoints us as His peacemakers in the world.

I'M GLAD I'M NOT THAT WAY

Maybe all this leaves you feeling pretty pious, with the justifying thought, "I've never killed anybody." No, you've never pulled a trigger on someone. But have you ever told someone to "drop dead"? What about those angry looks that kill? And have you never stabbed someone with sharp words? Or engaged in character assassination? The Catechism gives the Sixth Commandment a broad sweep, including our thoughts, words, and gestures, as well as our deeds. This interpretation is true to the Bible, which says, "Whosoever hates his brother is a murderer" (I John 3:15).

In the Sixth Commandment Jesus teaches us to hear a loving call to thankful obedience not only in our outward acts, but also in our inner attitudes. Banish anger from your life. Live by the law of love.

So if you should be sitting in church as the offering is being taken, and then suddenly remember that things are not right between you and another person, step out quickly and settle your differences, and then return to present your offering (Matt. 5:21-24). For anger, which is the root of the urge to kill, stands in the way of our worship of God and our service of others.

The positive meaning of the Sixth Commandment is the same as for the whole second table of God's law: Love your neighbor as yourself (Matt. 22:39)—even your enemies (Matt. 5:44). Respect the life that God has given. Do all you can to promote the welfare of your neighbors.

We may not be reckless with our own lives, nor endanger the lives of others. For God has given life, and He alone has the right to take it away.

Just living on, however, is not the thing that makes life worthwhile. It's the quality that counts. What we live for, as Christians, is of greater value than mere length of years. Some people pack more real Christian living into twenty years than others do into sixty. Christ calls us simply to place our lives in His hands and then go out to look for the best ways of using our lives in His service.

95. SEX IN THE CHRISTIAN LIFE

The subject of sex is discussed more freely and openly nowadays than in times past. This is good. But it's not an unmixed blessing. For it brings with it a lot of loose and cheap "sex instruction" that is just as deceiving as the older "stork stories" and tales about "the birds and the bees." In taking a Christian look at sex, it pays to be honest—honest with ourselves and honest with God. For that's the way the Bible is.

Our comfort, which lies at the very foundation of a healthy Christian life, is this: we are not our own, but with body and soul we belong to Christ, our faithful Lord and Savior. So in learning to handle our sex life aright, we are never on our own. We have God's Word as our guide. There we hear God's law about sex, which arises out of His loving concern for purity in our relationships with those of the opposite sex. Our bodies are temples of the Holy Spirit, who dwells within us (I Cor. 6:19, 20). Then how could our conscience allow us to grieve the Spirit (Eph. 4:30) by a life of sexual immorality or perversion!

But what is the truth about sex? Let's go back to the beginning. Sexual attraction is a gift of God. He created us male and female (Gen. 1:27). So sex is not a dirty word. It should not cast a spell of embarrassing silence over our conversations. Nor should it arouse brash laughter among boys or giggles among girls. The sex impulse is God's way of leading us to courtship and marriage in the bond of Christian love.

But sin spoiled sex—as it spoiled everything else in life. Instead of purity we get pornography. Instead of doxologies for the wonderful way God made us (Ps. 139:14) we hear men punctuating their sentences with filthy four-letter words. Instead of love, ungoverned passion. Instead of true marriage, prostitution and divorce and broken homes. How evident it is that sin has ruined our life at its deepest and most intimate level!

But Christ came to renew our lives at every turn along the way—in that friendship with the boy next door, or the girl down the street, in dating, courtship, and marriage. You are not yet of an age to consider marriage. But remember, a sound Christian marriage begins long before you say "I do." It is built upon the capacity to love and the pure attitudes of heart that you are developing now already at this early age.

Sex is indeed a thing of beauty. But in our lives it needs the disciplining power of God's law of love. The Seventh Commandment points our affections in the right direction. When we walk in the way of divine law our love life is free. When we walk outside that law we become enslaved to shameful lusts. Think of the young man Timothy getting a letter from his spiritual father Paul, with this advice, "Flee youthful lusts . . ." (II Tim. 2:22). And recall Joseph, who under the pressure of great temptation, answered Potiphar's wife with these words of faith, "How then can I do this great wickedness, and sin against God?" (Gen. 39:9).

Christ reminds us that we can violate the Seventh Commandment within

the privacy of our own hearts (Matt. 5:27, 28). If we want to break the law but just don't dare because of the consequences, we are in fact guilty, just as those who have openly committed immoral acts. The love of Christ calls us away from entertaining such lawless desires. Yet even in dreams our passions sometimes get the best of us. Still we need not go through life with a guilty conscience. For Christ came to forgive and to cleanse the thoughts of our minds and the secrets of our hearts, as well as our words and deeds. He creates within us a new heart and gives us the power to do God's will.

In a day of sexy songs, gutter talk, and suggestive advertisements— with the so-called "new morality" on the march—with many movies giving the impression that the only real fun in life is transgressing the Seventh Commandment: remember, young Christians, don't betray yourselves, or your parents, or your Lord. By the power of the Spirit, learn to overcome temptation. Let the words of Christ ring true in your lives, "Blessed are the pure in heart . . ." (Matt. 5:8).

96. THE STEWARDSHIP OF GOODS

Have you ever met a kleptomaniac? He is a person with an uncontrollable desire to steal. Such a person needs the care of a psychiatrist. Not many people are kleptomaniacs, yet all of us are infected with greed. Stealing, in one form or another, is a stubborn disease in human life.

But there is "good news." The Great Physician has come into our world to cure this infection. God prescribes His law of love to free us from our grasping nature and to set a new pattern for Christian life: "Thou shalt not steal."

Yet many people reject Christ's remedy. So stealing still spreads like a contagious sickness through our society—including young people. Why should there be so many itchy fingers in our affluent age? Poor people steal as a way of getting a share of the world's goods. But how do you explain the well-to-do helping themselves to other people's possessions?

Thievery has many faces: paying starvation wages, failure to give a fair day's work for wages earned, exorbitant loan rates, hidden clauses in the fine print of a contract. In one form or another, countless numbers of people try to make their dreams come true by getting something for nothing at the expense of their fellowmen.

Christ frees us from slavery to such a coveting spirit. He leads us to the Eighth Commandment as the doorway to a new style of life. He tells us that we are not our own. Nothing we have, and nothing our neighbor has, is really ours. All that we have is a gift—a trust from God. As the psalmist says, "The earth is the Lord's, and the fulness thereof" (Ps. 24:1). Look up Exodus 19:5, 6. This grand confession, that everything belongs to God, is the heartbeat of David's prayer in I Chronicles 29:10-22 as he makes final preparations for the building of the temple.

So the truth that lies at the bottom of the Eighth Commandment is: God's primary ownership of all things. Only in a secondary sense can we speak of man's ownership. We are trustees of His goods. Our ownership of goods is a God-given right; but with it comes the warning not to squander His goods, but rather to use them as concrete ways of putting the law of love into practice (Matt. 25:14-30; Acts 4:32).

What makes stealing such a serious violation of God's will is that it robs a man of the means by which he is called to serve God. God holds all of us responsible for the goods He entrusts to our care—time, talents, money, clothes, everything. Therefore this commandment is one of the highways we must travel in the exercise of Christian stewardship.

It's a bad sign when people have to keep almost everything under lock and key—cars, bicycles, lockers at school, books at the library, candy at the store. Most often this is a protective measure against petty thievery. But just think of all the grand larceny—looting, blackmail, hijacking, shoplifting, false advertising, gambling, speculation, price-fixing, tax evasion, safe-cracking.

The Bible has its cases too. Remember how Ahab and Jezebel swindled Naboth out of his vineyard—under the pretense of "due process of law." Recall God's bitter complaint that His people were robbing not only the poor (Amos 2:6), but were also robbing Him (Mal. 3:8). Think of how Christ drove the money-changers out of the temple because of their unscrupulous business practices!

Theft is wrong, not only because it's a civil offense, but in the deepest sense because it undermines God's law of love. Honesty, respect for the God-given property rights of our neighbors, and promoting the welfare of our fellowmen are our new way of life under the rule of God in His kingdom, here and now.

There are roughly four kinds of people in the world. "What is yours is mine, and I'll take it," says the robber. "What is mine is mine, and I'll keep it," says the miser. "What is mine is yours, so I'll share it," says the humanist. "What is mine is God's, so I'll share it," says the Christian.

97. SPEAKING THE TRUTH IN LOVE

The word "witness" is a central one in the gospel. Our word "martyr" is rooted in this New Testament word. Early Christian martyrs sealed their witness with their blood when they were thrown to the lions in Roman arenas or burned to death on a fiery stake. Even though the world today is more tolerant of Christianity, Christ's command still stands, "Ye shall be my witnesses" (Acts 1:8).

Christ staked His claim to supreme authority on the fact that His life was a true witness to God's plan of salvation (John 5:30-40). In John's Gospel alone the word "witness" breaks through more than twenty times. The early disciples launched their world mission as eyewitnesses of the truth revealed in Jesus Christ. If the apostles were guilty of bearing false witness to Christ's resurrection—if there was no resurrection—then, says Paul, Christianity is a lost cause (I Cor. 15:15). But no! Paul summons a host of witnesses to demonstrate beyond doubt that the Christian faith and life is securely rooted in the facts of Christ's death and resurrection. The Christ-centered witness of the New Testament is the source of our strength in keeping the Ninth Commandment, "Thou shalt not bear false witness against thy neighbor."

Our Christian calling is clear: speak the truth in love before God and to our fellowmen. God looks for truthfulness in His kingdom citizens—not as an on-again, off-again thing, but as a steady pattern of speech and conduct that springs from hearts that are right with God. The psalmist states this law of kingdom life clearly: "Behold, thou desirest truth in the inward parts" (Ps. 51:6). But what lives on the inside must come to open expression. For our words are an index to our inner life. The psalmist therefore leads us in this prayer: "Let the words of my mouth, and the meditation of my heart, be acceptable in thy sight, O Lord, my rock and my redeemer" (Ps. 19:14).

When our modern Pilates ask, "What is truth?" what shall we say? Think of it this way: to be truthful means to live in harmony with God's will in our dealings with our fellowmen. That means in all our dealings, of course; but in this commandment the accent falls on our words. Paul sets our calling in a clear light in Ephesians 4:25: "Wherefore, putting away falsehood, speak ye truth each one with his neighbor: for we are members one of another." Bearing false witness not only betrays the truth, but also betrays the love we owe to God and to our neighbors.

Men break this law of God in many ways. Think of the kiss of Judas as he betrayed Christ in the garden; think of the straight-faced lies told by Ananias and Sapphira. And there were the Pharisees—hypocrites whose very lives were living lies—children of Satan, who is the father of all lies.

But lying lips and slandering words are as much with us today as they were in Christ's time. Sometimes they come in the form of black lies, sometimes in the form of "white" ones. Just think of perjury in court, reporters who deliberately warp the news, dealers who use high-pressure salesmanship to convince you that the car with the mileage indicator turned back shows the actual mileage, students who string a line in a test to cover up their failure to study, young people who pawn off sly lies on their parents by using selective bits of truth, prejudiced persons who peddle their opinions that all adolescents are troublemakers, neighbors who exchange juicy morsels of gossip across the backyard fence, politicians who deceive people with promises they never intend to keep, even ministers who mislead their congregations with a gospel that is not *the* gospel. All these, and many more, are examples of bearing false witness that violates the law of love.

I JUST CAN'T STAND THOSE SMARTY PROFESSORS AND MINISTERS IN OUR CHURCH...

THEY MAKE ME FEEL SMALL, MY EGO GOES DOWN, MAN...

THATS WHY I BECAME A HERETIC HUNTER !!

False testimony is like a poisonous arrow: once it leaves the bowstring, it cannot be recalled. It speeds on its way, striking its target, there to do its deadly work. Lies are destructive weapons. They sabotage the good name of our neighbor. But slander also corrodes the souls of those who indulge in it.

As long as people believe that winning a personal victory is more important than playing the game of life according to God's rules, they will resort to lies to beat their rivals—in sports, in school work, in friendships, everywhere. Whenever people think that truth is only a matter of personal opinion, they enslave themselves to a lying spirit.

But the Bible sets us straight. The Catechism takes the Ninth Commandment and pours the full meaning of God's Word into it. Truthfulness in what we say and the way we live is anchored in Christ, for He is the Truth (John 14:6). Just as the Third Commandment teaches us to honor God's name, so the Ninth Commandment teaches us to honor the good name of our neighbor. If we stand on the side of truth, we stand on God's side. We must learn to weigh the truthfulness of our words by His law of love.

98. CHRIST OR MAMMON

Try this question: How many commandments are there? That's easy, you say: there are Ten Commandments. In a way you are right. But from a more basic point of view all God's commandments, covering our whole life, come down to this one rule—love. For love is the fulfillment of the whole law (Gal. 5:14).

That's the way Jesus put it to us in His summary of the law of God: love God above all and your neighbor as yourself (Matt. 22:34-40). The Decalogue (Ten Commandments) is like a prism that takes this single ray of light—love—and spreads it into ten different beams, each with its own color and focus. Yet all ten rays or beams reflect that original single ray of light. Thus God's central law of love comes to expression in His Ten

Words to us. They serve as an index to the total will of God as revealed in Jesus Christ.

We have come now to the Tenth Commandment. Ten is an important number in the Bible—the number of fullness. Taken together, these Ten Words represent a cross-sampling of the many ways we are called to serve God and our fellowmen.

The doorway to the Decalogue is this assurance: "I am the Lord your God." As the door closes on these Ten Words, God reaches back across all Ten Commandments and down into the depths of our hearts by striking the same chord in a different key: "You shall not covet anything contrary to My will." For coveting is idolatry, and idolatry breaks the bond with God.

But we must banish the thought that God is out to destroy all desire in us. In fact, the law of God is like His hand upon our shoulder pressing us forward to seek and to pursue the rich rewards of the Christian life. Christ says, "Seek ye first his kingdom and his righteousness" (Matt. 6:33). And Paul adds, "Desire earnestly the greater gifts" (I Cor. 12:31).

The Tenth Commandment seeks to free us from wanting the wrong things: that to which we have no right, that which God has given to another, that which would hinder our fellowship of love with God and our

IT ISN'T FAIR ...   HOW CAN I LOVE MY NEIGHBOR ...   WHEN HE HAS A BIGGER, MORE EXPENSIVE CAR THAN I HAVE

neighbors. It also calls us away from desiring things in the wrong way: loving our neighbor's possessions instead of loving him, making goods our god. That's idolatry, selling our souls to Mammon. Listen to this plain talk from our Lord: "Take heed, and beware of all covetousness; for a man's life does not consist in the abundance of his possessions" (Luke 12:15 RSV).

In the positive sense, this commandment has built into it a liberating power. It creates contentment. If God has blessed us with many things, let us be thankful and seek ways of sharing with others. If we don't have much, we may expect God to provide what we need. He has promised to take care of us, so worry must be set aside (Matt. 6:31-34).

The rich young ruler asked Christ the right question: "What must I do to inherit eternal life?" But he got a different answer than he expected: "Go and sell your goods and give to the poor." And he went away sad, because he apparently couldn't stand to part with his wealth. Christ had put him to the test of the Tenth Commandment, and he had failed. For he loved himself more than he loved God. He wanted his own way more than God's way. He loved his piece of property more than God's promise of eternal life (Luke 18:18-25).

Today we stand in the same danger as did the rich young ruler. We are bombarded on all sides with advertisements designed to create dissatisfaction with what we have and a hankering after new possessions and the latest fads. Few people today covet their neighbor's ox or his donkey. But what about our neighbor's Mustang or his color TV or his rich wardrobe? The Tenth Commandment cuts through all our outward actions and exposes the secrets of our hearts, our hidden jealousies. Its goal is to write clearly upon our hearts the words of Paul, "I have learned, in whatever state I am, to be content" (Phil 4:11).

The secret of contentment is Christ: having Him, we have all we need —in fact, all we could ever wish for. "All things are yours . . . and you are Christ's; and Christ is God's" (I Cor. 3:21-23). The answer to a coveting spirit is to want Christ so much that everything else fades away in comparison.

99. HOW DO YOU MEASURE UP?

We've just finished a short course on the Ten Commandments. As we let these Ten Words pass in review before our minds, we face this question: How do we in our daily living stand up under the test of God's law?

I DON'T STAND UP TOO WELL UNDER THAT TEST

Don't be too quick with your answer. Let's explore the question a moment. Remember, the Catechism is not asking about non-Christians, who are not even interested in God's law. This question comes to us as Christians—to people who know the meaning of sin, salvation, and service, to people who seek their greatest comfort in Jesus Christ. How do our lives measure up before the standard of His law of love?

Speaking in all honesty, two things must be said. On the one hand, we have no good reason for congratulating ourselves. We will have to admit that our lives fall far short of the goal set before us.

But what about other Christians? Perhaps there are more mature believers who have reached perfection. Let's look around. Of all the people you know, whom would you rate as the best Christian? No matter whom you choose for this honor, the Catechism is still right: even the holiest person has only a small beginning of perfect obedience.

Perhaps we can find what we are looking for if we turn back to the heroes of faith in the Bible—Abraham, David, Peter, and Paul. But in their lives we find the same picture. Just read the confessions of David in Psalm 51 and of Paul in Romans 7. Even as a Christian, Paul calls himself "the chief of sinners" (I Tim. 1:15). John adds this sobering reminder: "If

we say that we have no sin, we deceive ourselves, and the truth is not in us" (I John 1:8).

Perfection is out of the question for all of us, without exception. However, this needs saying too: If we are Christians, our lives have been turned around and given a new direction. We are new people. Christ through the power of His Spirit has changed our hearts, our deepest desires, what we want most out of life. So even if we find in our lives only a *small* beginning, we must at least be thankful for that *beginning*. That is the biggest difference in the world—a beginning in godly living, or no beginning at all. For we have His promise that God, who began a good work in us, will carry it through to the day of perfection (I Pet. 5:10).

I suppose that terrible feeling has come over you too: "I try and try and try, and yet I always seem to fail!" Well, welcome to the Christian club. That is the way it goes with all of us. Paul put it into words: "So I find it to be a law that when I want to do right, evil lies close at hand. For I delight in the law of God, in my inmost self, but I see in my members another law at war with the law of my mind and making me captive to the law of sin which dwells in my members" (Rom. 7:21-23 RSV). Peter— the rash disciple with his impetuous ups and downs—went to the heart of the matter in one of his great confessions: "Lord, thou knowest all things" —all my stumbling, bungling efforts—but in it all "thou knowest that I love thee" (John 21:17).

All of us feel the dead weight of sin dragging at our heels, holding us back from becoming what we really are in Christ, and what we want to be, and what we are called to be—namely, Christians in the full sense of the word. If the demands of God's law—"Be ye perfect even as your Father in heaven is perfect" (Matt. 5:48)—were a code of rules and regulations that we had to meet perfectly in order to be saved, we would never make

179

it. But once we realize that the law calls us to a life of loving partnership with God, then there is hope. For though we often let God down, He never lets us down. So our failures must not lead us to despair. For Christ makes possible that "small beginning" in our lives, and His perfect obedience makes up the difference between what we are and what we ought to be. He is our faithful Partner. We are never on our own.

So keep moving forward, inspired by the words of Paul: "Brethren, I count not myself yet to have laid hold: but one thing I do . . . I press on toward the goal unto the prize of the high calling of God in Christ Jesus . . . . only, whereunto we have attained, by that same rule let us walk" (Phil. 3:13-16).

100. GOD'S LAW STILL STANDS

I can feel your next question coming up: If none of us even comes close to keeping God's law perfectly, why does He insist that we take it seriously? What makes it so important?

The men who wrote the Catechism also faced this question. Some Christians in Reformation times felt that once they believed the gospel, the law of God had no further claim upon them. There are Christians today who have the same idea. And there are even more radical people around, who want "freedom" without any law. So the Catechism goes out of its way to face these issues: What is the point of God's law?

Remember this: the law of God and His gospel are not at odds with each other. They are like opposite sides of the same coin. Both are the Word of God to us. The Bible tells us that Christ took our place and obeyed the law of God perfectly for us—something we could never do for ourselves. That is the gospel, the "good news." In proclaiming the gospel and living it, Christ does not turn us away from the law, but He leads us back to the law as a guide for our new way of life—a guide to thankful living.

So God upholds His law—not to make our lives hard or add to our frustrations, but to give us a new direction and help us make our lives worthwhile. The law of God is for our good.

OH, LAWS ARE FINE, AS LONG AS THEY DON'T BOTHER ME ♫

Modern society presents a quite different idea of law from what we find in God's Word. There are many civil laws on the books that are a hundred years old or more—laws that are long forgotten and that no one thinks of taking seriously today. Yet these laws have never been repealed. They are horse-and-buggy laws—completely out of date.

Or look at the way men go about changing laws. Often they are changed, not by an act of government, but simply because nobody obeys them anymore. Since everybody breaks these laws, we give up on them and they get pushed aside by default.

God's law of love never expires. Each new generation must discover how His abiding law fits the needs of its own times. The law stands—for God stands behind it. It is His will for our lives. By fixing our attention on His law, God holds our lives on a right course and leads us to Christian service.

Because we are always both sinners and saints, God's law serves a double purpose in our lives. The more we learn to recognize ourselves as sinners, the more we will grow in our appreciation of salvation, and the more we will feel a desire for Christian service. Sin, salvation, and service go hand in hand—with God's law as our guide every step of the way.

The Catechism lays out our lives in two parts: saved from sin and saved to serve. From both points of view, God's law of love plays a vital role. He sent us His Son to pay the penalty of our sin and to fulfill the law for us. And He sends us His Holy Spirit to help us live a life of thankful service. So the law is not our enemy, but our friend. It releases us from enslavement to ourselves and to our sins, and it leads us into the wide expanses of obedient service. "Away from" and "unto"—that's the two-way street of Christian living.

101. SANCTIFICATION

Another one of those "big words," you say. Well, I guess you're right. Our Catechism vocabulary does include several jawbreakers—like "revelation," "regeneration," "justification," and now "sanctification." But such words are not beyond your reach. Just think of some of the "big words" you learn to master in mathematics and science and history—words like "perpendicular," "photosynthesis," and "anti-disestablishmentarianism!" So don't let this theological term "sanctification" scare you off.

Let's think about it for a few minutes. It's a word we need in order to understand the teaching of the Bible. Paul says, "For this is the will of God, even your sanctification . . ." (I Thess. 4:3). The word "sanctification" is related to our words "saint" and "sacred" and "sanctuary." Its basic idea is holiness and purity of life. The reality of sanctification covers the full range of our Christian lives. It's more than a word. It's a task we must work at for the rest of our lives.

By faith in Christ we are justified before God, made right with God. By that same faith we are now called to walk day by day with God. This daily walk with God, by which we grow in the knowledge of His will and the grace to obey it, is called sanctification. It means working out in our everyday affairs what God has worked in us (Phil. 2:12)—a life of love and hope and service. As we walk the Christian way, faith remains our constant point of contact with Christ who says, "Lo, I am with you always, even unto the end of the world" (Matt. 28:20). The Spirit is our daily Companion to lead us into all truth (John 16:13). So in our sanctified Christian living we are never on our own. And that is real comfort. For we could never make it on our own.

A sanctified life begins with an inner transformation under the power of the Holy Spirit. Then at last we are headed in the right direction. As Christian believers born of the Holy Spirit, our aim is to follow Christ. Yet even the holiest Christian knows only too well that he still has a long, long way to go in reaching perfection—"the measure of the stature of the fulness of Christ" (Eph. 4:13).

Sanctification is the Christian life, and like all life, it grows. It strains all its energies to make progress. It fights the good fight of faith in a life-and-death struggle—putting to death the old man in us, which is enslaved to sinful practices, and working to make our real Christian self come alive by loving obedience.

There are always two sides to a sanctified Christian life: the negative shadow side, which calls for putting to death our old sinful nature; and the positive sunny side, which means practicing the law of love.

Sanctification is for saints-in-the-making, for young Christians who want to make faith come alive in both the big and the little things of everyday. It is not an evolutionary process, feeding on its own resources. It is never automatic. It must be worked at by following in the footsteps of Christ and obeying the leading of the Spirit. Learning the lessons of sanctification is an art we must cultivate, for which even a lifetime is too short.

102. PRAYER

When a man stops breathing, he is dead. So when a Christian quits praying, spiritual death sets in. For "prayer is the Christian's vital breath, the Christian's native air . . . ." It is our lifeline with God, our breath of life. For Christians to get along without prayer is just as impossible as for the human race to survive without oxygen.

Prayer is the pulsebeat of Christian living. It's the language of our daily ongoing fellowship with God. For some people it takes a major crisis to drive them to their knees—a serious accident, big trouble, a deathbed, a foxhole. Yet even then God is patient, and so it is never too late to start praying. Sometimes, while we are involved in some such crisis, the impulse to pray becomes the path by which men find their way back to God. And—wonder of wonders!—He comes to men even in such last-ditch stands. Listen to His promise: "Call upon me in the day of trouble: I will deliver thee, and thou shalt glorify me" (Ps. 50:15). For God is more eager to hear even such belated prayers than we are to press them out of our troubled hearts. He never turns a deaf ear to an earnest seeker.

But praying is more than just crying for help. Its keynote is "Thank you, God!" That's why prayer is completely at home in this third part of our Catechism, with its central theme of gratitude. In fact, it's the chief part of the thankfulness we owe God. If we would only stop once in a while to name our blessings, we would find more reasons than we could count for saying and singing "Thank you" to God. What would you think about a young lady—in love and engaged to be married—who never thanked her fiancé for his gifts, in fact, never even talked

OH, I PRAY, WHEN THINGS GET TOUGH!

with him about them? We would wonder about her love, and certainly about her gratitude. Similarly, thankfulness is the very spirit of our fellowship with God. As Paul says, "In nothing be anxious; but in everything by prayer and supplication with thanksgiving let your requests be made known unto God" (Phil. 4:6).

MAYBE I PRAY ON THE WRONG CHANNEL

A thankful Christian also dares to ask for continued blessings. For prayer is our way of laying hold on God's promises in all our needs and wants. With a "small beginning" of obedience behind us, prayer becomes the avenue along which we seek to make further progress in Christian living.

Don't ever get the idea that God can't be bothered by your worries and problems, big or small. He welcomes our running conversation, with its crescendos and its pauses. He always has time to listen. He never gets tired of our talk. Therefore, "Pray without ceasing" (I Thess. 5:17). This doesn't mean keeping our hands folded and our eyes closed all the time. It means staying in step with Christ all along the way and living in the awareness of His presence. Keep your prayer antenna up so that you can make contact at any time, wherever you are, whatever you are doing.

But does prayer really change things? Does it make a difference? Yes, God's promise is clear: "The supplication of a righteous man availeth much in its working" (Jas. 5:16). If you pray, but feel that nothing comes of it, perhaps "you ask, and receive not, because you ask amiss" (Jas. 4:3). To pray aright means that our heart must be in it. Our prayers, like our lives, must be Christ-centered. For He is the Way to the Father's heart. He gave us His word: "If you ask anything in my name, that will

I do" (John 14:14). Morever, we must pray according to God's will. Just as young people refrain from asking certain things of their parents because they sense that such things would run counter to their parents' will, so certain requests should not find their way into our prayers because we realize that they would be an insult to God.

Now is the time to make your prayer life come alive. But perhaps you freeze up at the thought of being asked to pray in the company of others.

I DO ENJOY MEETINGS AT CHURCH...

BUT I DON'T LIKE TO COME TO THE CLOSING...

I JUST MIGHT BE ASKED TO GIVE THE PRAYER

Why? Because you don't have a lot of "nice words" at your command? Don't let that hold you back. All our prayers are imperfect, just as our lives are. Our prayers, too, need God's forgiving grace. Christ's disciples felt that also. That's why they asked, "Lord, teach us to pray" (Luke 11:1). Why not make that your next prayer!

No one needed prayer so little, and yet so much, as our Lord. So much —because of the tremendous sacrifice He made for us. So little—because He Himself is the perfect Answer to our prayers. Feel free to talk with Him, for He prays for you (Luke 22:31, 32). He understands "You" as well as "Thee." Even incorrect grammar gets through to Him. For God listens for the heart behind the words, just as an understanding mother reads the mind of her lisping, stammering child.

The gateway to prayer stands wide open. And God calls us to walk in.

103. THE LORD'S PRAYER

Our best prayer guide is the Bible. Across the pages of the Old and New Testaments we meet people of God climbing the staircase of prayer. We overhear the prayers of Abraham (Gen. 18:22-33), Moses (Exod. 32:30-32), David (I Chron. 29:10-19), Solomon (I Kings 8:22-53), Hezekiah (II Kings 19:16-19), Mary (Luke 1:46-55), Simeon (Luke 1:67-79), Paul (Col. 1:3-14), and others. The Psalms resound with prayer from beginning to end.

In the Gospels we also overhear several prayers by our Lord—His prayer of thanks for humble faith (Matt. 11:25), His prayer for power at the raising of Lazarus (John 11:41, 42), His high-priestly prayer at the Last Supper (John 17), His prayer of agony in the Garden of Gethsemane (Matt. 26:39, 42), His prayer of forgiveness from the cross (Luke 23:34). The Bible is a book of prayers: there God takes the prayers of His people and of His Son and makes them His Word to us today.

Among the scores of prayers in the Bible, one stands out as the model prayer. We call it the Lord's Prayer. Ever since Christ taught it to His disciples, this has been the favorite prayer of Christians everywhere. Millions of people recite it every day. But how many really stop to think of what it means? How about you? The Lord's Prayer contains about sixty-five

words. It takes about half a minute to pray it. But I dare say that on some rushed mornings even those quick thirty seconds seem too long. Let's take the time to reflect upon the words of this prayer, lest we be guilty of taking God's name in vain in the very act of praying this perfect prayer.

The Lord's Prayer is recorded twice in the Gospels, in Matthew 6:9-13 and Luke 11:1-4. The setting is something like this. Prayer was a regular part of Christ's life. Often the disciples listened to Him as He prayed. They were deeply impressed. On at least one occasion Christ continued in prayer for a whole night (Luke 6:12). The disciples noticed how different their Master's prayers were from the empty repetitions of pagan prayers (Matt. 6:7, 8) and the showy prayers of the Pharisees (Matt. 6:5, 6). Moreover, they remembered the good example set by John the Baptist in teaching his disciples the discipline of prayer. Now as they joined Christ in prayer, they felt deeply their need of greater prayer power and richer fellowship with God. So once, when Jesus had finished praying, they came with their request, "Lord, teach us to pray." In answer, Jesus taught them the Lord's Prayer. Notice that Jesus did not teach them *about* prayer. He taught them to *pray*.

We divide the Lord's Prayer into six petitions. In the first three we pray that God's cause may increasingly become ours. In the second three petitions we pray that our needs may become God's care. Here is a simple diagram:

THE LORD'S PRAYER

The Address

The Petitions

$$
\text{"Thy" Petitions} \left\{ \begin{array}{l} \text{Thy name} \\ \text{Thy kingdom} \\ \text{Thy will} \end{array} \right.
$$

$$
\text{"Our" Petitions} \left\{ \begin{array}{l} \text{Our bread} \\ \text{Our debts} \\ \text{Our struggles} \end{array} \right.
$$

The Doxology

Amen

104. OUR FATHER

The Lord's Prayer is like a special delivery letter: it has a clearly stated address—"Our Father in heaven." At the very beginning Christ commands our loving obedience when He says, "Pray like this: Our Father who art in heaven . . . ."

It's wonderful to know that we have a heavenly Father. This knowledge gives us a sense of belonging. We are not orphans, but children, heirs of all God's riches. Our home base is in heaven. In the Apostles' Creed we confess: "I believe in God the Father . . . ." The first part of the Ten Commandments calls us to love God our Father above all. Here, in the Lord's Prayer, we learn to put this faith and obedience into practice when we pray: "Our Father who art in heaven . . . ."

It's a great privilege to have God as our Father. None of us deserves such a privilege. For like the prodigal son, we were all runaways and fugitives. But Christ brought us back home to the Father's house. He put the words of the prodigal on our lips, "Father, I have sinned . . . ." Every prayer means turning back down the road that leads to the Father who stands waiting, watching, listening for us to come home (Luke 15:11-24).

The Lord's Prayer is for Christians only. It is not, as some people say, a general prayer for all people of all religions. For Christ gave it to His disciples. It is a believer's prayer, a prayer for the Father's children (Matt. 18:3). It was never meant to keep anyone out; but it does serve notice on all men that they can enter the Father's house only by that same door through which all Christians enter—and that Door is Christ. Hear His words, "No one cometh to the Father, but by me" (John 14:6).

The name "father" was a familiar title for the head of the family in Jewish circles. Sometimes Old Testament believers addressed God as Father (Deut. 32:6; Isa. 63:16). But in Jesus' day no respectable Jew would think of addressing God by this familiar and intimate name. The prayers of the religious leaders had become stiff and formal. But Jesus always prayed as a child speaking to his father—simply and directly. And His prayers struck a happy response in the hearts of the disciples. When they asked Jesus to teach them to pray, He stood at their side as their older Brother and shared with them His loving fellowship with the Father. Such communion and conversation is the secret of true prayer.

Prayer is always a "vote of confidence" in God. We may not know just how God will answer us—whether this way or that. But one thing is sure: He will always deal with us as a Father with His children. We may expect Him to give us everything we need. But we should also expect Him to withhold from us everything that might put a barrier between Him and us. As our *Father* He is willing to answer our prayers, and as our Father *in heaven* He is always able to answer them. His high position in heaven takes nothing away from His fatherly love and care. He uses His sovereign power for the good of His people. God is not like a government official in his front office, barricaded from the common man by reams of red tape and rows of secretaries. The Door stands wide open. The Way is always clear.

PRAYER TO GOD IS THE PERFECTION OF COMMUNICATION...

NO LINES DOWN...

NO RED TAPE...

Our Father—we are never alone in coming into God's presence. None of us is an "only child" in God's family. Christ brings many brothers and sisters into His Father's home. Together we share God's blessings. But there is plenty to go around. Children from many lands are saying, "Lord, here I am. I am answering Your call. Now You have me. Give me what I need. What can I do for You?" In many languages this one prayer circles the globe and rises to heaven: "Our Father."

When we pray the Lord's Prayer we take all these other Christians with us. When we pray for bread, we pray for our brother's bread too. His needs, his joys, his tears are part of our prayers. Our Father hears—and He will answer.

187

105. HALLOWED BE THY NAME

When we set out to pray, it's important to get off on the right foot—to put first things first. The Lord's Prayer, in the first petition, sets the pace for all our prayers by fixing our faith on God from the very start.

What does "hallow" mean? You probably never use that word, except in this prayer. So we had better stop to define our terms. To hallow means to make holy or keep holy, to reverence, to glorify. For example, when God finished His work of creation He set aside a special day of rest, "and God blessed the seventh day and hallowed it" (Gen. 2:2, 3). The Fourth Commandment appeals to this act of God in calling upon us to "remember the sabbath day to keep it holy" (Exod. 20:8).

But what shall we say about God's "name"? Think back to the Third Commandment: "Thou shalt not take the name of the Lord thy God in vain." This is the point: we must honor God's name in all that we do. Now here in the first petition of the Lord's Prayer we are asking God to help us keep that commandment. This is our prayer: "May Your name be honored by us and all men." In both the Third Commandment and this first petition, God's name means His whole revelation—in His world, in His Word, and above all in Christ, who is the fullness of God's revelation.

What we are praying for in this first petition comes down to this: "Dear Father, we request the honor of Your presence in our lives—always and everywhere and in everything." These words are not a doxology. That comes at the close of the Lord's Prayer. We are not praising God here for His majesty and power. Nor is this petition a pious wish. What we are asking for here is that we and others might have open eyes to recognize God's glory all around us, a readiness to honor our Father's will in our lives, and a burning desire to demonstrate God's great salvation in the world. As Christ says, "Even so let your light shine before men; that they may see your good works, and glorify your Father who is in heaven" (Matt. 5:16).

Here is an expanded version of this petition, as an attempt to catch its full meaning: "Dear Father, take over in our lives, Take full control.

Rule us completely. Make us holy by helping us to hallow Your name, so that others through us may do so too. We pray this in Christ's name. For He led the way in honoring Your name. Amen."

Christ speaks plainly about honoring God's name: "Father . . . glorify thy Son, that the Son may glorify Thee" (John 17:1). God hallowed His name most fully in the saving work of Christ. Now we hallow it best by listening to Christ's call to obedient living.

When we forget what we are praying in this first petition, then failing to honor God's name will show up in our lives as well. How? By walking blindly past God's revelation in nature—in sun and surf, in budding blossoms and singing birds. By allowing our Bibles to collect dust on the shelf. By fearing to breathe God's name in prayer in a crowded restaurant. By hanging out a church sign, "Closed for the Summer." By deliberately silencing God's name in our schools.

But now in this petition we are asking God to help us in setting things straight. "Lord, help us to honor Your name in all creation." But let's have no illusions that we can live holy lives on our own. This was the mistake of the rich young ruler. Holy living calls for full surrender to Christ. By hallowing God's name we will find ourselves drawn into the healing process that Christ is carrying on in the world through the power of the Holy Spirit.

"Hallowed be Thy name." This prayer is a call for missions—to make the saving name of God known to all men everywhere. It's a call to worship—to join the congregation in confessing God's name. It's a call to personal Christian living—reflecting God's glory in words and deeds that honor Him. It's a call to Christian witness—to honor God's name actively in all areas of life.

106. THY KINGDOM COME

A weakness that often shows up in our prayer life is that of falling into a pattern of I-centered prayers—"I this" and "me that." Self-centered prayers reflect a narrow-minded Christian outlook. In effect we substitute our words for those Christ taught us: *"My* kingdom come."

So we must listen again and learn anew from Christ as He leads us in prayer: *"Thy* kingdom come." In the same Sermon on the Mount that contains the Lord's Prayer we find also this royal command: "Seek ye first his kingdom" (Matt. 6:33). In the second petition Christ teaches us to pray for strength to keep His royal command.

As we move along through the Bible from cover to cover we witness the unfolding of God's great kingdom drama—the creation of the world as the arena for God's kingdom program, man's sinful rebellion against God's kingly rule, the reestablishment of God's kingship through the saving work of Jesus Christ, the steady development of His kingdom plan, and one day the perfect breakthrough of God's eternal kingdom in the new heavens and the new earth. It began in a garden. It finds its fulfillment in the New Jerusalem. It sweeps all of history along in its triumphant march to victory.

The kingdom of God was the central theme in Christ's preaching. John the Baptist paved the way with his message, "Repent ye; for the kingdom of heaven is at hand" (Matt. 3:2). With this introduction, Christ then announced with growing clarity His kingly claim, "All authority has been given unto me in heaven and on earth" (Matt. 28:18). He is the indisputable Lord of all creation. Yet He came into the world as the suffering Servant of Jehovah. But now in His nail-pierced hands He holds the scepter of the universe. He gained the crown by enduring death and conquering the grave. The cross and the empty tomb stand secure as the charter of His kingdom. They are the great moments of victory by which Christ gained the right to rule the world and bring it back under His Father's sovereign control.

By the power of the gospel, Christ enlists us as citizens in His kingdom. In the Sermon on the Mount He holds before us the constitution for kingdom life. Day by day He calls us to find our place and task in the ongoing program of His coming kingdom.

If you want to be in on this grand movement, then this prayer is for you. For this is what we are asking in this second petition: "Father, make Your kingdom come in us and through us and around us." We are praying that the Sermon on the Mount may be reflected in our lives. For the kingdom of God exercises its power through the kingly rule of Jesus Christ in the hearts and lives of His loyal subjects. It means living under the rod and staff of the Good Shepherd (Ps. 23:4).

The kingdom is a present reality. As Christ says, "The kingdom of God is within you" (Luke 17:21), and "If I by the Spirit of God cast out demons, then is the kingdom of God come upon you" (Matt. 12:28). Where Christ is, there is the kingdom.

But there are still many rebels in the world who refuse to follow this King. All around us the cry goes up, "We have no king but Caesar!" People bow to the Caesars of nuclear power, space exploration, the mighty dollar, sports, Ivy League diplomas, psychedelic experiences. The conspiracy goes on—revolt against the kingship of Christ. We pray for these insurrectionists too, that they may stop fighting their losing battle. For Christ is Victor, now, and for all time.

But we ourselves also need this prayer badly. God must often have reason to say, "It is because of you that My kingdom program gets bogged down. How do you expect to pave the way for its coming when you erect all kinds of barriers and roadblocks in its path, when you set up monopolies in your life in which I have no voice?" Indeed, God's kingdom comes "from above" as a gift of God. But it is for the earth. Therefore it involves us, our decisions, our loyalties, our activities, our prayers—here and now. Christ recruits us as His disciples, to be a salt in the earth, a light in the world (Matt. 5:13-16). By offering this petition of the Lord's Prayer we are declaring our readiness to stand up and be counted as volunteers in God's army. And we call on God to back us up. For the kingdom is His. He will not let it fail.

In this prayer we also catch a vision of the church. For the church is called to play a central role in the coming of the kingdom. It must proclaim the gospel of Christ's rule in the lives of men and the affairs of nations. It must train recruits for service in every branch of the kingdom army. It must mobilize the power of the Christian community.

Dear Father, give us faith to believe in the coming of Your kingdom, even when the cause of Christianity seems to be losing out in the world. We know that the outcome is already settled. One day you will be "all in all." This is the story of Your Book of Revelation. From now until eternity, Father, use us to push forward the program of Your coming kingdom—this is our prayer.

107. THY WILL BE DONE

If only Adam had paused to breathe this prayer in the garden! Instead —if he prayed at all—this is how it must have gone: "Not thy will, but mine, be done." And this is the way we have been praying ever since, judging by our acts. True, apart from the renewing grace of God men may perform deeds that are outwardly good; but such deeds are always geared to meet this condition: they are done according to our own human wills and standards of judgment.

The coming of Christ introduced a radical change. In Him, for the first and only time in history, God's will was done perfectly on earth as it is in heaven. The words of the psalmist, "I delight to do thy will, O my God" (Ps. 40:8; Heb. 10:7), reached their fulfillment in the life of Christ. Listen as He wrestles in prayer in the Garden of Gethsemane: "Father, if thou be willing, remove this cup from me; nevertheless not my will, but thine, be done" (Luke 22:42). God's will was Christ's way. Doing His Father's will was His daily food—not just an extra treat or frosting on the cake—but His staff of life (John 4:34).

We must remember this as we turn to the third petition of the Lord's Prayer. This was no cheap and easy line that Christ taught us to pray. It was rooted in His own unique experience. He made His life our pattern as we take this prayer to heart. But what good is a pattern without the

191

power to put it into practice? Therefore, more deeply, the saving work of Christ is our source of power as we explore the meaning of this petition and look for ways to translate it into a Christian life.

We can become partners with Christ in hallowing God's name and promoting His kingdom only by praying, in word and deed: "Thy will be done." This is a prayer for disciples. Jesus made this clear to His next of kin in this stunning announcement: "Whosoever shall do the will of my Father who is in heaven, he is my brother, and sister, and mother" (Matt. 12:50). Fellowship with Christ is dependent on doing the will of God.

But what is the will of God for us? What does He want of us? Basically this: our salvation and the salvation of others. His will is clear: "As I live, saith the Lord God, I have no pleasure in the death of the wicked, but that the wicked turn from his way and live" (Ezek. 33:11), "not wishing that any should perish, but that all should come to repentance" (II Pet. 3:9). If we pray this prayer with our hearts as well as our lips, we are making a personal commitment to Christ and dedicating ourselves to Christian witness and outreach. Then we are living by the law of love in our daily lives, in the fullest sense of the word. And that is God's will for us.

"Thy will be done"—what can this mean, but a cry to God to free us from the enslaving power of human wills that are bent on their own way: clashes between brothers and sisters, parents and children, students and teachers, blacks and whites, policemen and citizens. But Christians have a different goal and perspective. Christ leads us to say, "God's will be done." And then we should bend our wills to conform to His—regardless of the cost. In this way only will we find true peace and brotherhood.

O God, take our wills captive. Help us to surrender to Your will, "which alone is good." But we cannot do this on our own. So You do it for us.

Such prayer takes courage, especially when God's way is difficult and unpleasant for us. Take the case of a young man who prayed hard for something he wanted very much. A skeptical friend asked him scornfully, "And did God answer you?" The young man replied, "Yes, He said No."

I SHOULD PRAY..

AND I KNOW
GOD WILL ANSWER...

I'M JUST AFRAID I'LL
GET A NO ANSWER

Such an answer takes faith. It calls for more than helpless submission to God's will, or a fatalistic resignation which says, "I guess that's the way it has to be." We must pray as children to our Father, not as slaves cringing before a cruel master. In this petition we ask for a willing and glad acceptance of God's leading in our lives.

Such submissive and trustful prayer makes the devil tremble. But among the angels it touches off songs of joy. For the angels know from experience the disastrous consequences of willful disobedience and the joyous rewards of obedient service. Christ therefore holds the angels up as our examples— "Thy will be done on earth *as it is in heaven.*" The Catechism reinforces this thought by calling each of us to "discharge the duties of his office and calling as willingly and faithfully as the angels in heaven."

Carrying out the will of God is the very core of a thankful Christian life— each of us fulfilling the office God has given him: as preacher or teacher, as father or mother, as son or daughter, as student or worker, as church member and citizen.

The prayer "Thy will be done" spans earth and heaven. Ultimately, we are really praying here for the new earth, under a new heaven, "wherein dwelleth righteousness" (II Pet. 3:13)—a world where everyone will respond to God's will in perfect and joyful obedience.

108. OUR DAILY BREAD

We cannot live by bread alone (Matt. 4:4). But we cannot live without bread either. It's a law of God for human life that we need bread. After the fall, though man had to work hard in the sweat of his brow, God did not withhold his daily bread (Gen. 3:17-19). Bread is our staff of life. It's not just a "natural blessing." It, too, is a gift of love from God's hand. It belongs to the "all things" that God freely gives us for Christ's sake (Rom. 8:32).

Christ opens our eyes to see our daily bread as a symbol of our new way of life. Through our daily bread He gives us strength for hallowing God's name, for advancing His kingdom, and for doing His will. So big things are at stake in this little prayer: "Give us this day our daily bread."

How do you feel about this petition? Do you consider it a long step down from the first three petitions about God's name and God's kingdom and God's will to such a down-to-earth thing as bread and butter? Or do you feel that now at last the Lord's Prayer is coming around to things that lie close to your heart and life? Actually, this petition for our daily ration of food is right at home among all the other parts of the Lord's Prayer. For our bodily needs are an important part of God's complete care for our lives. Our Father, who feeds the birds and clothes the lilies, has a special concern for the everyday needs of His children.

Our trust in His care for us ought to put an end to merely reciting this petition by heart. Rather, it must come *from* the heart. Then we are ready to pray with the veteran saint:

Give me neither poverty nor riches;
Feed me with the food that is needful for me:
Lest I be full, and deny thee, and say, Who is Jehovah?
Or lest I be poor, and steal,
And use profanely the name of my God.

Prov. 30:8

Has it ever struck you that Christ allows us to pray for our daily bread even before we pray for the forgiveness of our sins? That is the way Jesus is—so completely practical. He is our perfect Savior—embracing in His saving work the needs of the whole man, both body and soul. Christianity never downgrades our physical needs. Along with preaching the gospel and healing the sick, Christ went out of His way to feed the hungry crowds. He even changed water into wine and took vacations with His disciples. He was concerned about empty stomachs as well as hungering souls. He realizes, you see, that we cannot very well seek forgiveness and fight temptation while suffering from that famished feeling. Therefore, "Give us this day our daily bread."

Like the first disciples, we often have trouble learning this lesson. We sometimes give the impression that bread-and-butter questions are below Christ's dignity. Not so at all, for the Christian faith touches life at every point. In our mission outreach, therefore, we might sometimes do well to send the deacons to visit a poor family, even before the minister and elders knock at the door. In world missions we must send food and medicine along with the gospel.

Our bread—this is not a prayer for selfish people. The Father has many children in His family—in the inner city, in Appalachia, in India. Many of them are in dire need. Half the world goes to bed hungry every night. Thousands of children die of starvation every day. These needs must also find a place in our hearts and in our prayers. The poor of the world need more than just a few crumbs that fall from our overloaded tables. They need our helping hand in the form of food, shelter, clothes, money, work, training, medicine. All this in the name of Christ—Christlike prayers must be translated into the language of Christlike deeds of love and mercy.

So Father, as we pray, use us to share the bread You have given us with those who look to us for help. The closer we get to Christ, the closer we will get to people in need.

God knows what kind of "bread" each of us needs. The teen-ager needs more than the man on pension. The construction worker needs more food than the teacher. The teacher needs more clothes than the construction worker. But God will fulfill our daily needs—to each his own—so that we may all serve Him in the work to which He has called us.

But do we really take this petition of the Lord's Prayer seriously? Most of us have never missed a meal in our lives. Our warehouses bulge with surplus goods. We count luxuries as necessities. Science and technology promise us every gadget we could possibly wish for. God may care for the birds and the flowers, but we can take care of ourselves—that is the spirit of our times. Meanwhile, we are so overfed that we can't appreciate our daily bread. And still we want more and more.

Clearly this is not the spirit of Christ's model prayer. We must learn again and again, like the Israelites in the wilderness, to live from daily manna. And this includes rich people as well as poor. For prosperity, without God's blessing, is a curse. If we try to snatch riches from God's hand, without taking hold of His hand, we doom ourselves to terrible poverty of the Spirit, and loneliness.

So Father, give us whatever we need to serve You aright. But what if the answer to that prayer might be hunger? Still, a crust of bread, with Christ, is enough.

O Father, take care of us—give us our daily bread, our daily health, our daily work—so that above all, we may never lose You!

109. GOD'S FORGIVENESS, AND OURS

As Christians we know that we never get beyond the need for pardon. Christ knows this even better than we do. Therefore, near the heart of this model prayer, He places in our hearts and on our lips this plea for forgiveness.

The plea for forgiveness runs in two directions. There is the vertical dimension—"Father, forgive us our debts." And there is the horizontal dimension—"As we forgive our debtors." This two-way prayer is like the two sides of a single coin. God's forgiveness of our sins and our forgiveness of the sins of others go hand in hand. There is no forgiveness for the unforgiving. We can live as sons of our heavenly Father only as we are willing to be brothers to our fellowmen. Our readiness to forgive others is an inner testimony of the reality of our own forgiveness.

This petition of the Lord's Prayer opens our lives to the joyous freedom of canceled debts. By nature we are all debtors to God and to each other.

There is a heavy mortgage on our lives, which we could never possibly pay off. Rich and poor, black and white, we all have this in common: we are snowed under with bad debts. *Our* debts—therefore this prayer is more than a bit of private, personal piety. I carry the whole mountainous burden of the sins of the world before God's throne of grace. For the debt of the world is my debt blown up into gigantic size. And my debt is the debt of all God's people in miniature.

But there is "good news." This petition brings us back within the shadow of the cross. There we hear the echo of Christ's prayer, "Father, forgive them . . ." (Luke 23:34). Once this word of pardon has sounded in our lives, it must also resound through us into the lives of others.

Forgiveness is a miracle of grace. Our sins create a yawning chasm, separating us from God and from our fellowmen. But the cross of Calvary falls across this chasm like a bridge. Christ *is* the Bridge. By walking this Bridge, we find forgiveness and reconciliation.

Forgiveness means that God wipes out our debt. He no longer holds our sins against us. He assures us that nothing can separate us now from His love in Jesus Christ (Rom. 8:38, 39). For His love is greater than our sins. Forgiveness therefore paves the way for freedom, so that the road of life lies open before us as converted sinners.

IT'S TOUGH TO BE HUMBLE

We often rattle off this petition of the Lord's Prayer as if it were mere words. But prayer is no cheap and easy way to get out of debt. For praying does not stop with reciting words. True prayer moves us to put God's forgiving love into practice in our relations with our brothers and sisters, parents, friends —and even our enemies. That's when this petition begins to hurt. To say "Please, forgive me," or "I apologize"—that's the hard part. Following up God's forgiveness with our own costs us something: it takes self-denial, humility, honesty, love. But remember, it cost Christ something too! It cost Him more than we will ever realize. And unless the reality of forgiveness is shown in the lives of Christians, how can we expect to convince the world of the reality of God's forgiveness?

But how far must we go? That was Peter's question. If I forgive my brother seven times, is that enough? No, said Jesus, but seventy times seven! In other words, there is no end to the number of times we must forgive others who sincerely ask our forgiveness (Matt. 18:21, 22).

For look how generous God is in forgiving us! The offenses of others against us are mere pinpricks compared to our hammer-blows against the will of God. This is the point of one of Christ's parables on pardon (Matt. 18:23-35). He concludes by warning us that God will deal very severely with us if we fail to forgive others genuinely.

And don't overlook the way Christ applied the parable of the creditor and his two debtors to the case of a certain sinner-turned-saint (Luke 7:36-50). The point of Christ's teaching is this: love and forgiveness are forged together as links in one unbreakable chain.

This fifth petition of the Lord's Prayer is the only one to which Christ adds a footnote: "For if ye forgive men their trespasses, your heavenly Father will also forgive you. But if ye forgive not men their trespasses, neither will your Father forgive your trespasses" (Matt. 6:14, 15).

Our forgiveness is not the ground of God's forgiveness. The only ground of our forgiveness is Christ's atoning work. Nor is our forgiveness the measure of God's. If our forgiveness were the measure, we would be doomed. For how often we are stingy about forgiving—reluctant to forgive the wrongs others have done us. It is rather this way: that our forgiveness of others is an expression of our appreciation for God's forgiveness of us. If we do not truly forgive others from our heart, it's a question whether we truly know the reality of God's forgiveness in our lives.

So back to the words of Christ. "Pray thus," He says: "Forgive us our debts as we forgive our debtors." Then go out and *do* it! *Obey* the voice of the Good Shepherd. For the one way to learn the meaning of this petition is by applying it in our lives.

110. TEMPTATION AND DELIVERANCE

We often smile at the story of Martin Luther and his inkwell. Who ever heard of trying to kill the devil with flying glass! Yet this much at least must be said to Luther's credit: he took the devil seriously. And so did Jesus and His disciples. But do *we?* How many "Be gone, Satan's" have you shouted in your lifetime? When was the last time you had that feeling of crossing swords with the devil or one of his henchmen? For he has a legion of demons at his command, each one with his own bag of tricks.

In the conflict of the sixteenth century the Reformers recognized who their real enemy was, the mastermind behind the scene—the devil. But today people say the devil is dead. They think of him as a medieval bogeyman or a first-century myth. Twentieth-century scientific people, they say, have outgrown such nonsense. At best Satan belongs in the comic strips, dressed in red, with horns and tail and carrying a barbed fork. Others, as in San Francisco, turn from mockery to open blasphemy by establishing the First Church of Satan. The devil has a lot of people eating out of his hand, swallowing his sugar-coated pills of poison.

But such spiritual blindness does not mean the end of the devil. This last petition of the Lord's Prayer—"deliver us from the evil one"—is a stern reminder that the Christian life is a battleground. In our own strength we are unable to hold even one front; and yet we find ourselves under attack on three fronts—our own sinful flesh, the unbelieving world around us, and the devil. Temptations besiege us on all sides. Some are of our own

making. Others come upon us from worldly forces invading our lives. But behind every temptation is the unseen, spellbinding power of Satan, the sworn enemy of God, who specializes in plotting the downfall of Christians.

Think of Peter, who once became Satan to Christ, so that Christ had to unleash these stinging words of rebuke, "Get thee behind me, Satan!" (Matt. 16:23).

Because of our ever-present sinful nature, the "father of lies" always has a foot in the door in our lives. Moreover, the "prince of darkness" is always setting his traps in the world around us, sometimes acting like a "roaring lion," but just as often flattering us and flirting with us like an "angel of light." It's a terrible mistake to underestimate the powers of the opposition or to overestimate our own strength. But at the same time, take courage: though the devil is far stronger than man, his strength cannot be compared with that of God. Remember, "God is faithful, and he will not let you be tempted beyond your strength, but with the temptation will also provide the way of escape, that you may be able to endure it" (I Cor. 10:13 RSV).

In this last petition of the Lord's Prayer, Jesus sounds the note of deliverance. The fifth petition is a prayer for the forgiveness of our sins. This sixth petition is a prayer for power to overcome sin in our lives. Christ is the secret of our power: "For because he himself has suffered and been tempted, he is able to help those who are tempted" (Heb. 2:18 RSV).

The sinful world has a way of bringing us under its seductive influences —first leading us to walk along in the counsel of the wicked, then standing together in the way of sinners, and finally feeling right at home while sitting in the seat of scoffers (Ps. 1:1). Christ's prayer is our only way of escape: "I pray not that thou shouldest take them from the world, but that thou shouldest keep them from the evil one" (John 17:15). Faith is the victory that overcomes the world (I John 5:4).

All kinds of innocent-looking things can become temptations to us— interesting friends, a recommended film, a best-seller book. Especially success—for when we succeed we are tempted to stop asking in whose

198

Name we are getting ahead, and at what price. Television and radio pop-programs are dangerous intruders too, because they take up so much of our time that we don't give ourselves a chance to ask the right questions

anymore or to look for the right answers. But the worst part of any temptation is the danger of losing contact with our Father.

We have our hands more than full with ourselves too—our hot temper boiling over into bitter words, and then slamming the door behind us. We become traitors to the Christian life, collaborating with the enemy. Those who want to "live dangerously," "experiment with evil," and "play with fire" are making a mockery of God's word and selling their birthright for a mess of pottage. Satan knows how to personalize his temptations to fit each case. In our own strength we are no match for him: what good are our toy guns against his heavy artillery?

There is only one way to win: "Resist the devil, and he will flee from you" (Jas. 4:7), "neither give place to the devil" (Eph. 4:27). In other words, don't sit at Satan's table. Keep away from his hangouts. For the Catechism is right: "we are weak in ourselves." Remember David (I Chron. 21:1) and Judas (Luke 22:3) and Ananias and Sapphira (Acts 5:3). Therefore, "Watch and pray, that ye enter not into temptation" (Matt. 26:41). We can never have too little trust in ourselves, or too much trust in Christ.

The devil is a clever schemer. He never says, "Come, let me lead you into sin." He is not that stupid. He prefers working secretly, as if he is not there, or like a wolf in sheep's clothing. He is an expert in quoting Scripture. He is a crafty general at the head of a vast army with officers and soldiers.

SOMEHOW I DON'T THINK I'LL ESCAPE FROM THE DEVIL BY MYSELF

199

He has class and style, as is evident from his temptations of Christ in the wilderness (Matt. 4:1-11).

But Christ showed us the way to overcome by turning the power of God's Word against our enemy. That was the beginning of His victory. Later Christ saw Satan cast out of heaven (Luke 10:18). Christ then bound this "strong man" hand and foot (Matt. 12:29). Easter was the final victory. The decisive battle has been fought and won. The issue of salvation is settled. The outcome is sure. Christ is Victor. Our struggles against temptation are now rearguard actions and mopping-up campaigns. Prayer is the way to gain the strength we need to be conquerors with Christ.

Satan tempts us—not God. God sometimes tests our faith. And Satan tries to turn these tests into temptations. But Father, deliver us from the evil one!

There's a very interesting book on temptation that you might like to read sometime. It's called *Screwtape Letters*, written by an Englishman named C. S. Lewis. It should prove an eye-opener, especially if you read it in connection with Ephesians 6:10-18. Until you've read it, you've likely never guessed how active the demons are in the lives of each one of us.

111. THE DOXOLOGY

Put yourself in a musical mood and listen quietly for a moment—you can almost hear the swelling notes of Malotte's stirring anthem, "The Lord's Prayer," rising to a crescendo on these words: "For thine is the kingdom, and the power, and the glory, forever. Amen."

Take a little time and let these words sink in. They reach back over all six petitions of the Lord's Prayer and gather them all up into one grand finale—the doxology. Here are notes of victory over temptation, gratitude for pardoned sins, and praise for our daily bread.

Let's not rush past that little word "for" at the head of this hymn of praise. All the preceding stanzas of the Lord's Prayer depend on the power and kingship and glory of God. So don't call a halt to this prayer until you reach the very end.

I'LL NEED MORE HELP THAN THIS TO MAKE MY PRAYERS HEARD

In every Christian's life there comes a time to stop asking and start singing, to stop praying and start praising. In the Lord's Prayer that time is now.

The message of the doxology is this: God is the Winner! He has conquered the devil. Satan is mighty, but God is all-mighty. And God's victory is ours. He will make all things turn out for our good. All God's ways lead to glory.

This means that our prayers never go astray. God is able and willing to take all our weak, beggarly, lackluster prayers and make them powerful, kingly, and glorious.

The story is told of a man who, during World War II, sat trembling in his bomb shelter while an air raid was in progress. He prayed desperately, feverishly, madly. But suddenly he changed his tune. He stopped begging that his life be spared and started praising instead—singing doxologies. It was like a replay of Paul and Silas singing songs at midnight, while locked in the inner dungeon of the Philippian jail. Then according to his own testimony, this frightened man found in his praises a wonderful peace. God answered his prayers—through praise.

The men of Heidelberg also experienced the thrill of singing doxologies. For to a large extent the Reformation sang its way into the hearts and lives of the people of that time.

"Thine," O God—Father, Son, and Holy Spirit—it's all thine! "Thine is the kingdom and the power and the glory forever." The kingdom is not a prize of either the East or the West. The power is not in the hands of either black power or white power. The glory is not even for the church. It's all for You, our God. And we are Yours. Make us Yours completely and forever. Help us to conclude our prayers—and then go upon our way —in the firm conviction that our prayers are in good hands. For we believe that You are both able and willing to answer our prayers abundantly by giving what is best for us.

112. AMEN

Maybe you always thought of the doxology as just a good way to round out the Lord's Prayer. But as we have seen, there is more to it than that. The doxology is not a tapering off point in the Lord's Prayer, but a climax.

So also with the Amen. Perhaps you always thought of the Amen as being like a period at the end of this series of prayer sentences. We sometimes give the impression that the Amen is not very important and does not have much real meaning. That could be the reason why we often say our prayers without really praying, and then wind up just mumbling "Amen" at the end.

But the Amen is more than just a stop signal. It goes back to the biblical word "verily." Recall how often Jesus spoke with emphasis by using these words: "Verily, verily, I say unto you . . ." which means the same as "Amen, amen, I say unto you . . . ." When we say "Amen" we are actually saying, "So be it," or "In truth it is so." It's a confession of faith, undergirding our prayers, and meaning: "It shall truly and surely be." The word "Amen" is an expression of certainty and assurance that God will hear and answer our prayers beyond the shadow of any doubt. It means that we can count on God to take our prayers to heart even more eagerly than we present them to Him.

This certainty is rooted in Christ, who is the Truth. The Bible actually calls Him "the Amen, the faithful and true witness" (Rev. 3:14). Closing our prayers with Amen means closing them with Christ, just as we also begin our prayers in His name. Without Him, it is impossible even to end our prayers in the right way.

In Bible times it was the custom of the whole congregation to respond to God's Word and the prayers of their leaders with a hearty and united Amen (I Chron. 16:36; Neh. 8:6; I Cor. 14:16; Rev. 1:7; 22:20). Even the saints in heaven, worshiping God, respond to doxologies with an Amen in unison (Rev. 5:14).

So let the Amens ring out in our prayers and in our worship services. For saying Amen is like writing a personal signature to endorse a check. It's a vocal way of taking a public prayer and making it our own personal conversation with God. It might even be appropriate to say "Amen" after each petition in the Lord's Prayer.

Say it, then, with all your heart as you come to the end of that perfect prayer which the Lord Himself has taught us—Amen, and Amen!